COME TO THE FEAST

ALL-AGE SERVICES FOR COMMON WORSHIP

STUART THOMAS

First published in 2002 by
KEVIN MAYHEW LTD
Buxhall, Stowmarket, Suffolk, IP14 3BW
E-mail: info@kevinmayhewltd.com

9 8 7 6 5 4 3 2 1 0

ISBN 1 84003 975 2
Catalogue No 1500542

Typesetting by Elisabeth Bates
Printed and bound in Great Britain

CONTENTS

FOREWORD

For those who enjoy a little light redaction criticism, the origins of *Come to the Feast* go back to 1992, and the publication of a small volume entitled *Christian Services for Schools*. Intended for ministers who have to lead worship in a school situation, it provided some simple liturgical resources for that purpose. It sold well enough for another book to appear the following year, directed specifically at all-age worship in the church and suitably called *Keep it in the Family*. Steady sales led to decreasing stocks, which were noticed at the same time as the Church of England was introducing its new three-year lectionary. The opportunity was thus taken to completely revise these two smaller books and produce a resource for each Sunday in the Church's calendar. *Come to the Feast* (Book 1) appeared at the same time as the new lectionary (in reality the Revised Common Lectionary with a few Anglican modifications), and covered the Penitential and Festival seasons, from Advent to Epiphany, and from Ash Wednesday to Trinity Sunday, with all the Principal Feasts. In addition other Principal Feasts and Festivals were included, together with Harvest Festival and three extra Christmas services. Book 2 appeared the following year, covering all the other Sundays, four in Epiphanytide, five before Lent, and the period 'after Trinity' up to All Saints' Day, plus the three Sundays before Christ the King.

Four years have now passed, and Common Worship has arrived on the scene. Dwindling stocks again have presented an opportunity for a thorough revision, and an integration of the material into chronological sequence in one volume. Much of it has been updated, some completely renewed, and all of it has been roadtested. As before, for each Sunday there is a brief introduction; suggested hymns, a chant and a children's song taken from *Complete Anglican Hymns Old and New*; the readings for that Sunday's Principal Service; a Confession and Absolution; a form of responsive Prayer; and up to three suggested all-age address outlines. Please use the material with sensitivity to context and circumstances and adapt any of the items to suit your local situation – they were not produced as a straitjacket and many have been altered over time in the light of experience.

I wrote in Book 1 that the contents of the book weren't the feast themselves, more like the list of ingredients or a menu. The intention is that acts of all-age worship are put together to provide a feast of good, lively, thoughtful worship. Like all liturgical resources, this one exists only as a means to an end, that worshippers should be enabled to engage more fully in worship, and enter into a deeper relationship with Jesus Christ. This book is offered as part of that process, so that our worship remains vibrant and dynamic, engaging and involving every member of the church community, and also with those who visit occasionally or with whom we have contact – not to mention those we never see and know nothing about. Every Sunday then becomes a celebration of our faith in our crucified and risen Lord, worship which can then be taken out into the business of everyday living. As we learn more of Christ week by week, month by month, we are fed and nourished in our spiritual life and continue to grow in him, and our faith is strengthened as we live for him and serve him in our daily lives. The feast of worship is a foretaste of the feast which we will one day enjoy in heaven – the good news we have to share is that all are invited, by the host himself. It's up to us to make sure that they hear about it, and come to taste and experience it for themselves.

STUART THOMAS

INTRODUCTION

It's more than a decade since I first introduced readers to the neighbouring parishes of St Grump's and St Hilarius the Great. That was back in 1992, when the Internet was in its infancy, the ASB was in its heyday, and most trains ran vaguely to time. But some things never change, especially (if by no means exclusively) the Church of England. Like many other parishes these two were debating how to tackle the challenges of declining membership (particularly among the young), dwindling resources and increasing marginalisation in society. All-age worship seemed to provide one answer – inclusive of all, contemporary, exciting, and meeting everyone's needs. Unfortunately, as they discovered, there isn't one simple formula or approach which will solve all the Church's problems at one fell swoop.

You can read the full story in the introductions to *Keep it in the Family* and *Come to the Feast* (Book 1). Enough for now to say that St Grump's took a stance which the media like to label as 'traditionalist', while St Hilarius adopted a more progressive approach of the sort described as 'liberal' or 'charismatic' by those who feel uncomfortable with it. Both had valuable insights, but there was little hope in those days that they might get round to learning more and developing in ministry by sharing these. Tradition and innovation, formality and spontaneity, were seen as mutually exclusive rather than rich resources to be integrated and used for the benefit of all. As a result, St Grump's became well stuck in the mire of preserving the past, both metaphorical feet so rooted to the spot that no forward movement was possible, while St Hilarius' never seemed to touch ground at all, so busy were they being spontaneous and 'relevant'. To be fair, both were at least making some effort to respond to the ever-changing world around, a world in which since then the rate of change has become ever more rapid.

By the time *Come to the Feast* appeared in 1997, both churches had put a great deal of

effort into moving forward. St Grump's had instituted a 'worship planning group', which didn't always agree on whether ancient was preferable to modern, but did agree a service outline for each monthly service, so that everyone was committed to the plan, and supported the vicar in realising it. Meanwhile St Hilarius' had formed a 'mission taskforce' to make sure that their worship was attractive to, and meeting the needs of, the community around. They'd also discovered musical riches beyond Songs of Fellowship, surprising themselves by enjoying Taizé chants as much as their neighbours at St Grump's, and exploring the Celtic tradition as well as the possibilities of 'alternative worship' for teens and twenty-somethings in a more contemporary style.

But in the years since then the process and sheer pace of change has forced the Christian communities of both St Grump's and St Hilarius', with their very different traditions, to keep reviewing and updating their practice. For a start, they've had to take on board the introduction of Common Worship and work out how to make best use of the variety and flexibility it offers. They've also been influenced by members of their congregations visiting Taizé and Iona, or encountering these approaches to worship elsewhere, as well as the musical styles that accompany them. Then there's the whole question of technology: CD-ROMs are now part of the furniture at St Hilarius', which as you might imagine has created its own website; however, St Grump's are still reliant on the vicar's ageing PC, which despite having a modem attached to it is no more reliable than the train service at the station down the road. Underlying these immediately visible differences lies the much more intractable problem of actually getting people into church. Neither church has declined in numbers, but achieving growth is a major concern, not because their communities are opposed to the Christian faith, nor even by and large to the church as an institution, but because social changes mean patterns of attending worship have shifted dramatically. Mobility, working commitments and family pressures have all led to people worshipping less regularly. There's still a tendency for the St Grump's PCC, and even its worship planning group, to wring their hands in despair at this trend, while one or two hardliners at St Hilarius' have been heard to pronounce judgement on such 'ungodliness' (though not too loudly in these politically correct days).

Change for the better?

The Church of England is hardly unique in being resistant to change. It's just a lot better at resisting it! Its structures may seem increasingly out of touch with the twenty-first century but they're still remarkably effective at keeping things as they always were, are now, and ever shall be. Even so, despite well-publicised wrangles at local and national level, invariably portrayed as between 'traditionalists' and 'liberals', there have been considerable shifts in fundamental attitudes and perspectives. To take a couple of examples, the ordination of women to the priesthood, a real hot potato during the 1980s and early '90s, raises few eyebrows now; similarly, a recent survey indicated that a great majority of churchgoers were in favour of divorcees being allowed to be married in church. Neither of these would have been thinkable twenty or thirty years ago.

The Church certainly isn't in the business of accepting the popular ethos and culture without question, but like Christ himself it has to accept people where and how they are, while at the same time exercising its prophetic ministry, upholding the values of God's Kingdom and challenging places where secularism and evil hold sway. Worship is at the heart of the Church's life, and for many it will be the place where they become aware of another outlook, a fundamentally different attitude to the one they encounter in the secular media and culture. Liturgy has changed for many reasons: we use language differently; the world situation has changed dramatically; worshippers are probably far better informed and aware than ever before; and most significantly, they come to church (if they come at all) with entirely different expectations and needs. Aspects such as choice, flexibility and accessibility have all increased hugely in importance, yet on their own they'll soon start to pall. Worship needs to reflect something beyond us and greater than us if it is to have any real impact beyond 'lovely service, vicar'. Most important, it has to be more than innovative or traditional if worshippers are to encounter the living Christ and be transformed in both mindset and lifestyle.

All-age worship is a particularly demanding form of liturgy to put together and deliver. It started off with the 'Family Service' movement in the '60s and '70s, a first reaction to the need to provide something attractive and spiritually nourishing for families with younger children, who were already starting to become conspicuous by their absence. This also made sense of the Church's view of the family as God's gift to humankind. But since then the image of the happy nuclear family of Mum, Dad, one-point-eight kids and golden retriever smiling at each other over their healthy breakfast cereal with gleaming white fluoride-enhanced teeth, going to work and school with a cheery wave, or enjoying a stress- and conflict-free holiday on a sunny Mediterranean beach, has taken a bit of a battering. Few would disagree that it was never more than an image, but it's been swept away by the reality of the rising tide of divorce, and the advent of both single and 'reconstructed' or 'alternative' families. The word 'family' can have negative connotations for many: children, who spend alternate weekends with separated parents; older folk living on their own, whether through choice, circumstances or bereavement; parents of young children who have been left struggling to bring them up alone; those whose experience of family life has been altogether more damaging and abusive. Even those of us who claim to enjoy a happy family life are all too aware of the potential for peace and security to be replaced by conflict and anxiety. So 'all-age worship' has gradually become the more generally accepted term for a style of worship that acknowledges the presence of children and young people, without putting the needs of older members of the congregation on the back burner. In many places it will also need to recognise and involve those who come from a different ethnic background or culture, those with learning or emotional difficulties, and those who have little previous experience of church. All-age worship is no soft option!

Importantly, the Bible tends to refer to 'a household' rather than a family, written as it was in a culture where the extended family was the norm – not just grannies and uncles but second cousins, great-nieces and slaves and servants too, who were considered to be part of the whole unit. While it wouldn't be possible, or even desirable, to return to this sort of pattern in the context of western society today, we shouldn't jump to the conclusion that the small nuclear family is God's norm. Of course married couples and parents with children need space and privacy to develop the necessary intimacy, but that shouldn't preclude awareness of and care for the wider circle of family, friends and community – many are isolated from the support networks they need as a result of the fragmentation of family life, with all the attendant problems of loneliness, depression and social difficulties. In many ways the Church mirrors an extended family in its network of relationships and complex interactions. The New Testament writers often see the relationships between Christians in terms of the family, or household, particularly as brothers and sisters. Just as a child is born into its human family, so a new Christian is born again into the family of God's church; as a child grows up in a family learning to relate to its environment and its fellow human beings, so a new Christian grows spiritually in God's family, learning to relate this new faith to the world around and belonging to the fellowship of believers; as in an earthly family, there will be the sharing of joys and sorrows, the handling and resolving of conflict, the mutual support at times of crisis and difficulty, all of which enable us to grow. And just as any worthwhile family activity needs to allow for the aspirations of all its members, young or old, male or female, single or married, so all-age worship needs to encompass and embrace all who are present. Realistic in this day and age? Probably not all the time, and there will be proper occasions when smaller interest groups meet together, but if God's people are called to reflect his reconciling love to the world, there must be some visible unity of purpose and love.

Suffer the little children . . .

Unfortunately far too many churches have read this as 'make the little children suffer'! The Victorian dictum that 'children should be seen and not heard' no doubt contributed to quiet and orderly mealtimes in a large family, but it also served at times to justify a repressive approach to education and development which damaged many sensitive souls. The days of sending children out to do some quiet colouring or gluing so that adults can worship in peace are mercifully now past, but many churches find themselves challenged to know how best to integrate children into worship. It's still sometimes said that our children's work is important 'because they're the church of tomorrow' – the problem, of course, is that they're the church of today. They make a unique contribution to worship and church life, and without them there won't be a 'church of tomorrow'. As adults we can learn as much from them as they do from us.

But an all-age service isn't a children's service, at least not exclusively. If the whole liturgy is taken up with songs suitable for under-7s and a sermon designed for the pre-school contingent, the rest of the congregation (i.e. those aged 12 and over) will feel patronised and excluded – and not without good reason! Children have every right to enjoy their own worship and fun, but just as in the family they learn to take meals with the whole family and adjust their behaviour accordingly, so part of their spiritual development is learning to worship with the rest of the church family. That said, those who passed that stage a few years, or even decades earlier, will have to allow for the presence of young people. A sermon packed out with theological jargon will soar over their heads (and over most other heads too) while dreary tunes with matching words will bore them to tears (and may well have the same impact on adults, even if they are less likely to admit to it). All-age worship draws in all members of the congregation in a way which will be simple, but not simplistic or shallow; accessible, but not superficial; enjoyable, but not trivial. Pitching it at the right level is a skill which takes time and practice to develop – those who seem to do it with the least effort are those who work hardest at it.

Active service

If children are to be present during an act of worship they clearly have to feel they're part of it. In an Anglican context a choice has to be made between eucharistic and non-eucharistic worship, though other traditions may not give this the same weight. Some will argue that the sacraments are for the whole church family, and should therefore be an integral part of all-age worship, enabling children to grow up familiar with them and willing to accept them; others would respond that those less accustomed to them might be put off by a ritual they feel excluded from. Both views deserve consideration, and the growing number of ecumenical partnerships and shared churches means they are fairly evenly represented, although the former has gained considerably with the increasing trend to allow children to receive Communion before Confirmation, after a suitable period of preparation. On a practical level, including the Eucharist will obviously change the shape of the service a bit, and probably mean it lasts slightly longer.

Putting it into shape

The arrival of Common Worship has given us the Service of the Word (on page 24 of the 'Sunday book'). At last the Church of England has an authorised non-eucharistic liturgy which isn't the daily office! It doesn't reinvent the wheel, but brings together in a structured form what many churches had been doing for some years. There is also a brief introduction on how to make use of it (pages 21-23), which contains no surprises, but offers helpful guidance. The advantage of this Service of the Word is that alongside the great flexibility it offers there is a consistency of shape and content, which provides useful landmarks for those not so used to structured liturgy and helps to retain an Anglican 'feel'. Ecumenically it also has the advantage of being very comparable to what happens in many non-conformist churches. There are no set texts, simply an order to follow, which divides into four sections: Preparation; The Liturgy of the Word; Prayers; and Conclusion. Some authorised resource material is supplied, in the form of Confessions and Absolutions, and Affirmations of Faith (pages 123-152), and this will be supplemented by the 'seasonal material' when it appears, essentially a reworking of Lent, Holy Week and Easter, The Promise of his Glory, and Patterns for Worship. An increasing number of churches are now valuing some of the creative alternatives now available, especially those originating from the Iona and Taizé communities, though the Franciscan Office book, *Celebrating Common Prayer* also contains good liturgical material for wider use, as do the Prayer Books from other parts of the Anglican Communion. Not the least significant aspect of the Service of the Word is the possibility of adding to it a celebration of Holy Communion (page 25), (though you should note that the Confession, Affirmation of Faith and Eucharistic Prayer must be chosen from the authorised alternatives). This enables a much smoother transition into the Eucharist for those unfamiliar with it, while retaining a recognisable look to the first part of the service.

A well-planned framework will certainly be more user-friendly, but like all worship, it must never be allowed to draw attention to its own beauty or correctness. A liturgy which does so is as self-defeating as one at the opposite end of the spectrum where the desire for freedom and spontaneity becomes anarchic in its effect. God alone is the object of our worship. The use of particular patterns or materials is simply to assist those who worship to draw closer to him, grow in faith and love, and be better equipped to serve his kingdom. The best shaped liturgies are those which worshippers don't notice for themselves, as through them they are drawn deeper into the love of God through encountering it in Jesus Christ.

Policy for inclusion

Every act of worship should contain the reading of Scripture, and prayers of confession, thanksgiving and intercession. To this might be added the singing of hymns and psalms (which are said even in a spoken daily office), and in most major services a time for explaining the Bible readings and encouraging the faithful who are gathered (politely known as the 'sermon slot'). A Creed or Affirmation of Faith might be said, words of praise spoken, and where possible drama, dance or a time of testimony. Many churches will try to include Baptisms into all-age worship, too, though this is less straightforward if there's also a Eucharist. Both change the shape of the liturgy somewhat, and provide a different focal point. With the exception of the sacraments, however, it's important not to let any one element or person dominate the proceedings, or take up a disproportionate amount of time.

The truth of the Christian faith is too broad to be included all in one service (though it's amazing how many churches attempt to!), so when suitable material has been chosen for the various sections, review it critically against the overall theme and objectives and be ruthless in discarding any extraneous material – there are few more embarrassing spectacles in church than a congregation fidgeting and looking anxiously at their watches while the service meanders on with little sense of direction. Far from being virtues, length and verbosity invariably function as major obstacles to good worship and spiritual growth.

The food of love . . .

. . . or the fuel for conflict? If any one thing is guaranteed to arouse the passions of almost any churchgoer after a service, then the music has no competition! Is it possible to choose four or five hymns without irritating someone in the congregation? 'Why did he choose that dreadful dirge?' is a commonly heard complaint in most churches, as is 'Why can't we sing things we all know?' and 'We'll have guitars in this church over my dead body!' Unfortunately it's very difficult to agree on the definition of a 'dreadful dirge' and quite impossible to decide on what's well known to everybody (apart from Christmas carols and 'All things bright and beautiful'!). In fact we've lost much of our heritage of community singing and music-making, with the result that many younger people are growing up with little experience or common material to draw on.

Every church has its own musical tradition, be it high church formality, cathedral choir or instrumental worship group, and for this rich variety we should be thankful to God. But whether you're an *English Hymnal* addict or *Songs of Fellowship* fanatic, hymns must be well accompanied and inspiring to sing. There's no wetter blanket to throw over a service than music that's poorly played and drearily sung. All-age worship aims to encourage the whole congregation to be involved in the liturgy and participate with enthusiasm. Out-of-tune instruments, a sour-sounding organ, or a choir that's seen better days have quite the opposite effect. So does a very formal service with magnificent music, as it soars into the vaulting far above most people's comprehension levels. (Those who choose this type of service do so because they enjoy sitting and listening – it's perfectly acceptable as worship, but hardly suitable for all ages.)

One school of thought about music for all-age worship is that every hymn should be well-known. This isn't unreasonable in principle, as people will sing with more confidence if they know the tune. Sadly, only a small handful of hymns can be described as 'well known to everyone', and even *Songs of Praise* seems to have little impact on the younger generation. In reality each congregation establishes for itself what's familiar, depending on its tradition, the hymn book in use, and the musical resources available. Provided that the musicians are confident and competent, most congregations learn a new hymn or song without difficulty and it soon becomes part of their repertoire, although as a general rule it's preferable only to introduce one new item in a service.

Some churches deliberately aim to appeal to younger folk, filling the service with more contemporary hymns and songs. This may well have the benefit of using material known to them from school, and will be in a style they enjoy, but has the potential to alienate older members of the congregation and make them feel excluded. It also needs a capable group of musicians to provide effective and singable accompaniments. It would also be sad if they grew up not learning some of the great hymns of the past, and we shouldn't assume they'll enjoy them any less (though they may associate them with negative and rigid attitudes). The value of music isn't dependent on the date when it was written, and while we accept young people's taste for the latest pop idols, we wouldn't want them to reject Bach or Beethoven. Young people will come to appreciate both without difficulty if the way is opened up to them.

The all-age worship ideal is a blend of old and new (see Jesus' words about 'bringing out of the store treasures old and new' in Matthew 13:52), an approach the Church has adopted throughout its history. In musical terms this leads our own church to start with a familiar, usually traditional item, and to finish with something rousing and easy to sing. In between there's usually a mixture of older hymns, newer songs, Taizé chants and Iona songs moving from vibrant and upbeat to gentle and reflective. One new song is plenty for most services, and this needs to be reinforced until it achieves the status of 'one we all know'. It's quite acceptable, even desirable, to use organ, music group and choir in the same service, or even in the same hymn (though make sure tuning has been checked beforehand!). This prevents any one style or group being regarded as preferable (or worse, superior!).

The choice of music should reflect and develop the theme of the service, as well as the particular season. It shouldn't become an end in itself but like the rest of the liturgy be directed at enabling worshippers to draw closer to God and grow in faith. Hymns and songs might pick up or meditate on words from one of the Bible readings, lead people quietly and meditatively into prayer, or inspire renewed commitment and service. Music prepared as thoroughly and prayerfully as the sermon or intercessions is unlikely to provoke many complaints, but if it's all thrown together half an hour before the service and no one's had time to practise, it will almost certainly draw unintended attention to itself.

Read, mark and learn . . .

In 1997 the Church of England adopted the Revised Common Lectionary (having made further revisions of its own!) which brings it into line with most other mainstream traditions. Apart from the major festivals the emphasis is less on a Sunday theme and much more on the consecutive reading of the Bible each week. The public reading of Scripture has always been a key part of Christian worship, and the choice of two or three readings, drawn from the Old and New testaments and the Gospels, enables those at worship to recognise the con-nections and links between its different parts. The Common Worship Lectionary, like any other, is an effective way of making sure that the whole range of the Bible is used, not just the bits that seem easier or more attractive. On the other hand, a church may have a particular teaching programme from time to time, which necessitates the use of readings specific to its theme. In either case the Bible must be heard by those listening as God's word to us, and read with understanding.

It can also be read with some imagination. Many readings, particularly passages from the Gospels where there is dialogue, lend themselves to being read by more than one voice, as do parts of the Old Testament. Readers can be chosen for reasons other than being on the rota that day – perhaps a mother and child on Mothering Sunday, or someone with a disability reading about the gifts of the Holy Spirit. This is also an excellent way for people to become more involved with the church's ministry. Some passages in the Common Worship Lectionary are rather long, and you may feel it better to abbreviate them, though this isn't always easy in narratives. If you opt for brevity make sure that any cuts made don't lose the fundamental sense of the message.

It's fruitless arguing over which translation of the Bible to use, as there are almost as many opinions as there are versions. The Lectionary books available all use the New Revised Standard Version, which has considerable academic support, but the New International and Good News Versions are both still very popular, as is the Revised English Version. Many churches have a preferred version, and if everyone's familiar with it, or there are copies in the pews, there's no need to use anything else.

The go-between prayer

In some ways the prayers of intercession are the most difficult part of any service to integrate into the whole. As with reading the Bible there is a great opportunity to involve more members of the congregation, but whoever leads them has both to be sensitive to the atmosphere at that point of the service, and express succinctly what everyone else is thinking and praying. No easy task! In a fast-moving world there's always the possibility of a major international event preoccupying many thoughts, there may be sensitive local issues to tackle, and in any event few people would be comfortable with the idea of praying extempore in public. Experience suggests most are happier with something written down, even if they do it themselves – and beware those who don't think they need to! A congregational response at suitable points is also helpful to worshippers, not only to keep them awake, but also to feel the prayers are their own – just make sure they know what the response is in advance!

Those who read from the Bible, and those who lead intercessions, need some instruction and training in their ministry. It's vital to keep a sense of balance, so that from within the church community Mr Jones in hospital and the recently widowed Mrs Smith are not lost beneath last week's headlines, but equally so that Miss Brown's heavy cold doesn't overtake worrying international events. Another facet of this is ensuring that the intercessions don't become an opportunity for those with high ideals but lower sensitivity to air their own opinions without fear of contradiction, or bang a personal drum loudly and annoy many of the congregation. Simple, short prayers or biddings are best, and children are often able in a couple of sentences to touch depths which adult wordiness misses completely. Perfectly formed prayers in beautiful flowing English may impress the congregation greatly, but God isn't looking for a linguistic masterclass, nor does he need informing or reminding of what's going on in the world. And though some might be surprised at the idea, he doesn't value our prayers according to their length, complexity, or wealth of knowledge about what's happening. The late David Watson, when he was Rector of St Michael le Belfry in York, once pointed to the reredos on which had been painted centuries earlier the words of the Lord's Prayer. The artist must have had problems with spacing so that the first line read: 'Our Father, who art in heaven, hallo-'. As he observed, the heart of praying is contained in those few words.

Almost all major services (and all eucharists) also include prayers of penitence, when the congregation together acknowledge their sins and failings and need of God's forgiveness in the words of a Confession. Indeed it's only through the death and resurrection of Christ that we can stand in God's presence at all. However, the emphasis in any Confession is not on our wrongdoing, but on God's mercy and grace. These are normally spoken by the priest or authorised minister presiding at the service, but on occasion it would be quite in order for a member of the congregation to do this, though the Absolution in its 'you' form should always be pronounced by a priest.

A word in season

A wise preacher was once asked how long he would take to prepare a sermon. He replied, 'If you want me to preach for an hour, I'd take about an hour to prepare. If you want me to preach for half an hour I'd need about half a day. But if you want me to preach for five minutes, then I'd probably need a week!' The sermon or address is often the focal point of an all-age service, because it draws together the various elements and strands of the theme and seeks to explain them. The two greatest dangers are aiming solely at adults, and pitching solely at children. An academic, non-visual, dry style of preaching will switch off all youngsters within seconds, but a style aimed exclusively at 7-year-olds, will make all those of 8 and over feel it's beneath them. Visual aids, however simple, are a great asset – you don't need to afford the latest PowerPoint technology to make a real impact. However, they shouldn't take over and obliterate the message. A group of children rushed excitedly home after one all-age service to inform their parents that the preacher had eaten a daffodil as part of his address. It was obviously very memorable, but regrettably no one could remember what the sermon was about!

It's very easy to become discouraged about preparing and delivering all-age addresses when confronted with someone who finds it easy. But don't despair! Those who have such natural facility always run the risk of turning the sermon slot into a liturgical cabaret act, and too much patter can easily double its length. In reality, however 'off-the-cuff' someone's delivery may seem, that's the result of putting a great deal of preparation and practice into it. And even though the sermon will often end up as the central point, it shouldn't overwhelm the other components but lead naturally from them and into them.

The Holy Mysteries

Although there are certain elements which must be included in the first part of a eucharistic service, i.e. a Confession and Absolution, the Collect and the Gospel, these can be included into a Service of the Word without disrupting it. The Liturgy of the Sacrament then starts with the Peace and continues with the Eucharistic or Thanksgiving Prayer, leading up to the Breaking of Bread and Giving of Communion, which will inevitably form the climax of the worship. The whole service will be directed towards it and look forward to it. An all-age Eucharist is a powerful symbol of the unifying love of Jesus, who draws all humankind to him, whatever their age-group, gender, ethnic origin, social background or education. In him, through his death and resurrection, we are made one, reconciled both to our heavenly Father and to one another. Humanly erected barriers are completely demolished as we join together to experience his risen presence by sharing the bread and wine. Jesus is with us throughout our journey of faith, and though we know his gift of forgiveness and new life isn't restricted to a particular act of worship, there's something uniquely compelling about participating in it together.

Every church has its own sacramental traditions and emphases, and it would be invidious to single out any one approach as superior. However, mystery and approachability aren't mutually exclusive – God our Father is both transcendent and immanent. The major festivals can be particularly good occasions for an all-age Eucharist, and even if there are visitors they can be encouraged to come to the altar-rail too, either to receive Communion, or a blessing, if they prefer. Those who don't feel able to share in the bread and wine often like to come to the altar rail for a blessing rather than remain in their seats, often enabling whole families to come up together. Some folk find the presence of children at this point of the liturgy rather distracting, but provided

there are other services they can attend, it's better to encourage the children not to see the altar as somewhere for adults only and out of bounds, but a place where they can join with the rest of their Christian family, to meet with their heavenly Father through his Son, and enjoy his blessings. They also learn very soon that it's a place to be reverent and quiet.

Extra blessings

You may want to incorporate a Creed (a title properly given only to the Nicene, Apostles' and Athanasian Creeds) or an Affirmation of Faith appropriate to the season or theme. Spoken words of praise can form a good starting point, and there are plenty of options available for prayers to start or conclude the service, many of which can be said corporately or as responses. Psalms can be spoken or sung in a variety of forms, and even if Anglican pointed chanting doesn't seem to fit easily into an all-age liturgy, that's no excuse for omitting psalmody. To give an example that needs few resources, Psalm 103 can be said using the Taizé chant 'Bless the Lord, my Soul' as a refrain. Common Worship provides alternative seasonal words to introduce the Confession, the Gospel and the Peace, as well as the Blessing, and there's a wide range of other resource material available. In fact there's no reason why any service should be dull, dreary or stuck in a rut! Dance and drama can also make a powerful contribution to any act of worship if they're carefully integrated into it, and there are plenty of books on the market containing lively sketches and short dramas. Adequate rehearsal is vital, however, as anything substandard will be compared unfavourably with the professional standards now expected.

One in the eye

The technology for visual aids has moved on apace even since *Keep it in the Family* first appeared. But the basic principle remains the same – they are aids, not control panels. Used well, visual aids can reinforce and emphasise the message very effectively, and help people understand it more clearly. But however apparently simple they may seem, if they're not supporting the rest of the service, they'll soon take it over. Overhead projectors (OHPs) are still very popular, as much for carrying the words of the hymns and the liturgy as for illustrating addresses, and most owners of a computer will be able to create artwork on screen and print it directly on to an acetate designed specifically for an inkjet or laser printer. There are now many CD-ROMs available with a variety of wonderful clip-art graphics which can be utilised to great effect, and some websites also allow you to download suitable images. The age of the home computer means that professional-looking OHP transparencies can be produced without either great technological know-how or artistic ability. There's also the possibility of using PowerPoint technology which is undeniably effective when properly prepared but can run the risk of seeming a bit too slick. However, the laptop and projector required will stretch the budget of many churches – a good opportunity for local ecumenical co-operation!

Having sung its praises, all this state-of-the-art technology could easily blind us to the effectiveness of the simplest visual aids, to be found or created at home – the rest of the book suggests many ideas for this. People are also excellent visual aids (usually if briefed beforehand!), though again there's a risk of obliterating the valid point being made. I heard of a Free Church minister, also an excellent gymnast, who performed a handstand on the pulpit, much to the delight of the children and consternation of the adults – unfortunately they were so absorbed in this unlikely physical feat (and its attendant risks) that no one could remember what point it was meant to illustrate!

Service sheets

'Not a prerequisite' in 1997, service sheets have become virtually *de rigueur* with the near universal availability of computers and copying facilities. Larger churches will probably have both in the parish office, but a basic laser printer would serve a smaller congregation admirably with well-presented and attractive orders of service. It could be argued that Common Worship is almost tailor-made for this – the multiplicity of choices doesn't make a book particularly user-friendly. Large or bulky service books are also expensive in large numbers and not easy to store, though regular production of one-off service sheets also causes concern about paper usage and costs. Our church tries to encourage worshippers to take them home and look at them through the week rather than leave them on a seat to be gathered in and sent to the recycling bin. Common Worship is entirely contained on Visual Liturgy, in format, which means that a service sheet can be constructed with a minimum of effort, once decisions have been made about its contents. It also contains the words of a large number of suggested hymns, but do remember to acknowledge copyright, and if necessary write to obtain permission for use of material – many holders are happy to allow one-off non-commercial use of material provided their authorship and ownership are acknowledged. Other material, verbal and visual, can be added to make a neat and presentable service sheet which aims not to impress those at worship with technological prowess, but to ensure that the worship is of the highest standard possible, bringing glory to God and drawing all those present closer to him. By the same token, there's no excuse for anything that looks amateurish or slipshod, or is full of errors – if the order of service isn't up to the mark, it's unlikely the worship itself will be much of an improvement. A well-prepared one, however, will ensure the liturgy itself has been well-prepared.

Traps for the unwary

Technology can never eliminate the human factor, and all the pitfalls highlighted in previous editions are still there, ready to undermine all the good work. Unlike film and TV awards these are in no particular order:

1) Accusations of 'designer liturgy' have been increasing recently, as a result of the much greater choice of material now available. This may be unfair in many ways, but it's still easy to get carried away by the sheer range of options, and forget that the main aim of worship hasn't changed at all – to enable those present to be drawn by the Holy Spirit into a living and ever closer relationship with their heavenly Father through his Son Jesus Christ.

2) Church attendance is probably not quite as bad as the merchants of doom and sections of the media would have us believe, but it's still declining, especially among younger people. Against this backdrop it's very tempting to allow a proper desire to appeal to the relatively unchurched to descend into an attempt simply to entertain or be popular. Even if the end product is both entertaining and popular, that doesn't necessarily mean it's good worship.

3) There's no reason to assume that if it's traditional most people won't like it – or that if it's contemporary they will! There's little evidence to suggest that they'll embrace one and reject the other. On the other hand there is a lot of evidence to suggest that people are searching for a meaning and purpose (often summed up in that much-used term 'spirituality'), and that they value a degree of quiet and meditation. And no one would argue that worship prepared and presented with integrity and conviction has far greater impact than a slick but superficial 'liturgical cabaret'.

4) With so many youngsters wanting to become TV presenters, the dangers of adopting the 'compere' style of presidency are great. Not only can this come across as superficial, it also undermines a good liturgy. Effective liturgy will speak for itself, and those who insist on trying to enlighten the congregation about everything may well end up leaving them in the dark.

5) Children take in an enormous amount with little or no explanation from adults, even when quite small. This entirely natural phenomenon is, however, a source of amazement and disbelief among some, who seem determined to squeeze every last drop of educational juice from whatever is done. From a child's point of view this simply makes it an extension of school, which is not the aim at all. Increasing knowledge and understanding of the Christian faith is a worthy aim, provided it remains subsidiary to enabling everyone, even the children, to praise God and enjoy his presence.

6) Spontaneity should never be equated with sloppiness. Flexibility is almost an essential for all-age worship, and there may be occasions when the Holy Spirit leads towards a change of direction – a different hymn, maybe (if the musicians are happy with the idea) or a period of quiet reflection. It might even be right to allow the congregation to contribute prayer items or biddings, though some find this rather uncomfortable. However, this should be the exception rather than the rule, and the Holy Spirit never leads to inadequate planning or careless leading of worship. A vicar climbed into the pulpit for the sermon at a church and realised to his horror that his notes were still lying on his desk. 'I'm afraid I've left my notes at home,' he confessed to the congregation, 'so you'll have to listen to what the Spirit gives me. But don't worry, it'll be back to the usual standard next Sunday!' Some speakers have a natural gift of sounding spontaneous, but they can do so because they've prayed and prepared adequately, a quite different matter from 'busking it'. Similarly, if there's a clear pattern to the worship, an occasional departure from it will end up fitting in well. But if no one knows what's going to happen next or who's responsible for it, the congregation will get fidgety and start clock-watching, tempers may get frayed, and time will be wasted. And it won't be honouring to God.

. . . AND ON TO THE REST OF THE BOOK

The days are long since gone when the local priest knew his entire parish, rarely stepped beyond its boundaries, and conducted all services from the *Book of Common Prayer*. Most ministers today are torn between a desire to breathe new life into worship and the demands made on them by other areas of ministry. Time is precious, but for all-age worship there's no option but to invest some if any benefit is to be gained, and no resource book can short-circuit this reality. What this book aims to do is to extend the range of choices available to those responsible for all-age worship so that they can create services which are both enjoyable and challenging, attractive yet profound, which deepen understanding and increase faith in those worshipping.

Hymns

Six traditional and six contemporary hymns/ songs are suggested for each Sunday, along with a chant and a children's song. All are taken from *Complete Anglican Hymns Old and New*, which has as broad and comprehensive a range of worship music as any currently available general hymn book. Defining 'contemporary' was inevitably rather arbitrary, though I did include within it recently written words set to traditional tunes, as well as modern worship songs, songs from the Iona and Celtic traditions, and more reflective items from writers such as Margaret Rizza and Francesca Leftley. I can't pretend my choices are anything like exhaustive; the aim is simply to offer a starting point and maybe a few ideas you hadn't thought of. I'm bound to have omitted some favourites, but the indexing of *Hymns Old and New* is exceptionally good, and its scriptural, thematic and liturgical lists will probably furnish you with additional choices. The Kevin Mayhew catalogue also includes a wide variety of other material – *The Source* (volumes 1 and 2) and *Kidsource* in particular are worth investigating for more recent songs. *Re:Source 2000* is specifically directed at worship for teenagers, while *The Bridge* attempts to unite some of the widely differing musical traditions found across the denominations. There are also a wide range of 'Collections', three dedicated to the work of Graham Kendrick (those for Easter and Christmas in particular offer creative alternatives to the more predictable choices); two contain the work of musical-writer Roger Jones; there are collections of African, American and Australian, as well as British worship songs to provide a more global perspective; those looking for more reflective songs will find an excellent compilation by Margaret Rizza called *Be Still and Know*; and there are a number of smaller collections of the work of other composers. Elsewhere, plenty of stimulating and singable material from the Iona Community is published by the Wild Goose Resource Group in a number of excellent publications, and the Taizé

Community also publish a much wider range of their own chants and songs than can be included in a more general collection. If your church has a CCL licence please note that not all publishers of Christian music are covered by it, and that in bigger collections some of the songs won't be covered by it. Authorship and copyright should always be acknowledged, and if there's any doubt you should gain permission before publishing.

Readings

The readings given are those for the Common Worship Lectionary. While for most weeks this is the same as the Revised Common Lectionary, the few occasions where there is a difference are noted; the assumption is that most parishes will opt for Common Worship readings. In Ordinary time there is a choice of Old Testament readings, enabling either consecutive reading or a passage thematically linked to the New Testament readings, whichever is considered preferable.

Prayers

There are now many books of prayers available. Those in this book are written specifically for that Sunday or theme, but certainly shouldn't be restricted to just one Sunday if they fit well elsewhere. Most contain gaps for local and topical issues to be included as appropriate, and should be adapted as necessary to local circumstances – they should be seen as a springboard, not a straitjacket!

All-age addresses

The outlines given are mostly based on the Gospel reading for each Sunday. All-age addresses inevitably rely heavily on the person giving them, but the suggestions have all been road-tested and found to work. Again, they should be adapted to local requirements. Most rely on visual aids that are simple to produce or find, and require no more than moderate physical preparation. They should need no more than the addition of a little 'local colour'.

ADVENT to CANDLEMAS

It's often said today that the Church is increasingly out of touch with the rest of the world. Perhaps like any institution it seems a bit of an anachronism in a society that has little or no respect for institutions, but to be fair there are many examples of churches working very hard at relating to and engaging with their communities. However, there is a point beyond which the gap between the two cannot be reduced. No doubt every Christian would express concern at the gross materialism of the twenty-first century western world's Christmas festivities (a concern understandably shared by many who wouldn't call themselves Christian), but this also translates into liturgical terms. For most non-churchgoers Christmas starts to take effect around the beginning of December, which in the Church's year is the beginning of Advent. A couple of days into Christmastide, Christmas festivities have turned into New Year celebrations. For the Church Christmastide doesn't finish until Epiphany, but this is marked only in a low-key way in the rest of society by taking down the Christmas decorations. In other words the Church starts to celebrate the birth of Christ just at the point where everyone else's celebrations reach a climax and start to wind down.

Advent is one of the richest seasons in the Church's Year, but it often now gets subsumed into the great tradition known as 'the Christmas rush', when we all try to visit as many shops as possible, panic because we can't think what to buy as a present for our nearest and dearest, and end up spending more than we can afford, leading to more panic after Christmas! The last six weeks of the year are overrun by this frantic hyperactivity, even in Church, where the pressure is on to run carol services for various interest groups, from schools that want one at least a week before they break up for the holidays, to the Thursday lunch-club for the frail elderly – my personal favourite was an annual event for guide-dogs and their owners! Some ministers resent having to sing carols at all before Christmas starts liturgically, and a few even ban them, for which they might get a couple of column inches in one of the tabloids. For most ministers, however, it's the trial of imagination and stamina which is the biggest hurdle to clear before the post-Christmas break – how on earth is it possible to give everyone the full works so they don't feel deprived, and still think of something different to do from last year? One senior cleric said when asked at a conference on 'Worship between Advent and Candlemas' that while most clergy can hold out against Christmas carols and readings till the Third Sunday in Advent, beyond that they either go with the inexorable flow or risk being overwhelmed by it. Even if Church 'regulars' wish the herald angels would give it a rest or at least stay in their realms of glory for a few more days, for those who attend church less often (and many only come to worship at Christmas) it may be their one opportunity to see the reality of the Incarnation, God with us.

Recognising that many occasional worshippers will feel short-changed if they can't sing their favourite carols, there's still great scope for picking up the themes of Advent in both regular worship and special services – penitence, kingship, Christ's promise to return in glory, light. Advent rings are familiar to most people, and many churches make this a regular feature which all can identify with and understand. There's a great deal of good all-age material which can be blended in well with more traditional elements to make up a service acceptable to all. It probably won't be possible to avoid carol services during Advent, but they too can be made thoughtful and challenging. Carols can be chosen not just for familiarity (which lays them open to being bawled out with little thought for the meaning of the words), but also because they can be combined in a liturgical setting to make everyone more aware of God's limitless love for us as we see it in the incarnate Saviour.

Just as the Advent season narrows our focus down from the Kingship of Christ and his return in glory to the humble feeding trough where he was born, so the celebration of Christmastide opens out our vision again to the Epiphany, when we concentrate on the revelation of Jesus to the Gentiles. After that we travel through Epiphanytide to Candlemas, not only the Feast of the Presentation of Christ in the Temple, but the pivotal point where we stop looking backwards to the manger and turn our focus forward to Jesus' adulthood, his life and ministry, and ultimately his Passion and Resurrection. We may well sympathise with the sighs of relief that accompany the end of the secular festivities of Christmas, but we can also direct people's attention to the Jesus who can't be put away with the decorations for another year, and help them to understand that Christmas is the central point of a much longer period of worship and reflection.

The Common Worship readings are all familiar enough for this time of year, though if seasonal colours are observed in your church you should note that in a noteworthy change from the ASB Epiphanytide is now regarded as a festival season during which white is the liturgical colour, only finishing on 2 February with the Presentation. The Baptism of Christ is also now regarded as a Festival, to be celebrated on the First Sunday of Epiphany (unless 6 January falls on a Sunday, in which case it moves to the following day). The Presentation of Christ is also now a Principal Feast day, and if 2 February falls on a Sunday it takes precedence over the Fourth Sunday of Epiphany – as we encounter Jesus being taken to the Temple as the Law demanded, we take a final look back at Jesus' early childhood before we turn with him towards Jerusalem and his death. It's good to be aware, too, that Christian Unity is celebrated from 18 to 25 January during the Week of Prayer, an ideal opportunity for ecumenical relationships to be celebrated and developed. The First Sunday of Epiphany is also a good opportunity for renewing baptismal vows, and even if this is not taken, it's still an ideal time at the beginning of a New Year for us all to renew our commitment to following the way of Jesus. Finally, the Presentation of Christ, now upgraded to a Principal Feast Day, has the importance it merits as we turn from Jesus' birth and journey with him to Jerusalem and the Cross.

ADVENT SUNDAY

Although not itself a Festival, Advent Sunday is important, partly as the start of the season of penitence and preparation leading up to the celebration of Christ's birth, but also as the start of the Christian year. It's also traditionally the day when we focus on Christ's Kingship and his promise to return one day in glory as Lord of all, just as the promise of his birth at Bethlehem was fulfilled two thousand years ago. The readings all centre on this, although other important Advent themes are brought in, of which the most important is light, symbolised in the lighting each week of the Advent ring. Two alternative outline addresses are therefore provided, one on the effects of light, and the other on 'being ready'. There is also a suggestion for the traditional 'sharing of the light'. This will clearly have greater impact if the church is darkened, but its symbolism is still very powerful and launches the Advent season most effectively.

Sharing the Light

Each member of the congregation is given a candle, preferably with a drip-shield to protect clothes and floors from melted wax. If there's sufficient space, gather the congregation to the rear of the church, except for one person who stands by a lighted candle on or near the altar. If this isn't possible, select a representative group to stand at the back of the nave or worship area while everyone else remains in their pews. To the accompaniment of quiet music, the person by the lighted candle lights their own from it and walks to the opposite end to start lighting the candles of those there. The light is then shared with the rest of the congregation, before everyone returns to their seats. A choir singing a suitable Taizé chant (e.g. 'Kindle a flame' or 'The Lord is my light') provides a most effective background, though failing this a suitable hymn or song may be played on the organ, by a flute and guitar, or even as a recording. The sight of the light increasing and spreading is a powerfully effective picture of the spread of the light of Christ

throughout the darkness of this world until the whole world is filled with his glory.

Hymns

TRADITIONAL

- *Hark! a herald voice is calling (263)*
- *Lo, he comes with clouds descending (405)*
- *Mine eyes have seen the glory (449)*
- *O come, O come, Emmanuel (480)*
- *Thou, whose almighty Word (684)*
- *Ye servants of the Lord (757)*

CONTEMPORARY

- *How lovely on the mountains (295)*
- *Lord, the light of your love (419)*
- *Make way, make way (438)*
- *Sing to God new songs of worship (603)*
- *The universe was waiting (669)*
- *You are the King of glory (762)*

CHANT

- *Kindle a flame (932)*

CHILDREN'S SONG

- *Jesus bids us shine (845)*

Readings

Year A   Isaiah 2:1-5; Romans 13:11-14; Matthew 24:36-44
Year B   Isaiah 64:1-9; 1 Corinthians 1:3-9; Mark 13:24-37
Year C   Jeremiah 33:14-16; 1 Thessalonians 3:9-13; Luke 21:25-36

Confession

Lord Jesus, you are the Light of the World;
in your presence we recognise
our own wrongdoing and failure.
We confess that we have sinned against you
through uncaring actions, unkind words
and selfish attitudes.
We are truly sorry and ask you to forgive us;
open our hearts to you
and fill them with your glorious light
that others may see you
shining through our lives. Amen.

Absolution

Almighty God,
who welcomes all who turn to him
in repentance and faith,
forgive all *your* sins,
restore *you* to the light of his presence,
and fill *you* anew with his Holy Spirit,
through Christ our Lord. Amen.

Prayer

We come before Christ our Saviour
with our prayers, saying,
Jesus, Light of the World,
shine in the darkness, we pray.

We pray for all those who suffer
through homelessness, unemployment
or poverty . . .
Help them to know that in you
they have riches, purpose and an eternal home.
Jesus, Light of the World,
shine in the darkness, we pray.

We pray for all who live with failure
and distress . . .
Help them to know the victory of your Cross.
Jesus, Light of the World,
shine in the darkness, we pray.

We pray for all who are friendless,
lonely and in despair . . .
Help them to find in you the faithful friend,
who will always stay beside them.
Jesus, Light of the World,
shine in the darkness, we pray.

We pray for all who are ill in mind or body . . .
Help them to feel your healing touch
on their lives.
Jesus, Light of the World,
shine in the darkness, we pray.

We pray for those who rule our country
and our world . . .
Help them to show your compassion
to all who are helpless and vulnerable.
Jesus, Light of the World,
shine in the darkness, we pray.

We pray for ourselves,
that we may share the light of your presence
with everyone we meet . . .
Help us to draw others to you,
the one true light.
Jesus, Light of the world,
shine in the darkness, we pray,
and reveal your glory throughout the world.
Amen.

All-age address 1

This works most effectively in a darkened church (though don't forget that some people will find total darkness a bit 'creepy'). If candles have already been lit by the congregation they should be extinguished, but you'll need to keep one or two alight. Alternatively a reasonably powerful torch will help you make the same points. The aim is to highlight Jesus' claim that he is the Light of the World, and encourage the congregation to think about the effects of light, and demonstrate how Jesus can do the same in our lives. A volunteer helper is an advantage, though the idea works satisfactorily without. This address can also be used effectively at a Christingle service.

1) *Light gets rid of darkness wherever it is.* This can be indicated very straightforwardly with a lighted candle or torch (take care that the candle doesn't blow out!). Jesus comes to take away all kinds of darkness from people's lives – illness, disability, sadness – and release them into a new kind of living. Above all he deals with sin, which brings darkness into all our lives. As we allow his light to shine in our lives he drives away the dark areas, such as fear, anger and resentment.

2) *Light shows up what needs to be done.* A small pile of 'junk' should be strategically placed before the service so that when light is directed on it, everyone can see it. In the dark we can't see the rubbish and we risk tripping over it; in any event it's a nuisance and taking up space. But only when the light shines do we realise we need to deal with it. Jesus shows us the things in our

own lives which need to be dealt with, and by confessing our sins we enable him to start removing all the clutter and debris which will burden us and cause us harm.

3) *Light shows us the way to go.* A willing volunteer can be asked to go and find something in the darkness, and if it's dark enough they'll grope around and not get very far. In the dark we feel our way around gingerly, afraid to move too quickly in case we fall over or bump into something and hurt ourselves. Even if we remain intact, we haven't got a clue where we're going. Only with a light can we walk confidently. Jesus invites us to walk with him in the light, trusting him to take us in the right direction. Just as light is always there, so is he – forgiving, helping and guiding us throughout our lives.

All-age address 2

This address aims to highlight the importance of being ready at any time for the return of Jesus, using the idea of visitors to the home. This is tailor-made for impromptu drama, though you'll need to brief some helpers beforehand. Two or three should obviously be 'at home', engaged in such useful pursuits as doing homework, reading the newspaper, or knitting. Their posture should make it obvious that they're not expecting to be disturbed. The one essential prop is a doorbell sound, though armchairs or appropriate crockery and food items can be used to heighten the effect. Three or more helpers will also be needed as 'visitors'.

1) After a short preamble to set the scene the doorbell should sound for the first time to herald the arrival of an 'official' visitor, such as a policeman, a postman or a meter-reader. Point out that many people misunderstand the purpose of Jesus' coming, as they did at his birth two thousand years ago. Some think he'll be like a policeman who's come to tell us off and punish us. Others see him more like the postman who only comes when he's got something to give us. Still others view him as someone whose only interest is in checking up on us. While we're not rude to such visitors,

we only relate to them in their official role and it's unlikely they'll make any great difference to our lives. End this cameo by emphasising that when Jesus came as a baby two thousand years ago many rejected him because he didn't seem official enough to be the promised Messiah, and didn't fulfil the roles they thought he would. When he comes again it will once again be to fulfil God's promises.

2) Before the doorbell sounds again those 'at home' should be busy getting ready, clearing up, tidying and preparing a cup of tea or some sandwiches. The next visitor is clearly a friend, someone whose visit is anticipated. When we know someone's coming to see us, we usually make sure the house is in a reasonable state and put the kettle on. For a dinner party or social occasion the preparations have to be more extensive, and we may well change our clothes. Guests would be offended if they turned up to find we'd done nothing to welcome them.

3) Before the final sounding of the doorbell those 'at home' return to their previous positions and activities. This time the visitor is completely unexpected and catches them unawares. Everything's in a muddle, there's no water in the kettle and someone's just eaten the last biscuit. Conclude by pointing out that Jesus' return will come without any warning while we're going about our everyday business. There won't be any time to get ready beforehand, so we need to make sure that whenever he comes we'll be ready to welcome him. He wants to find us following his example of how to live, in obedience to God, and with other people's interests and needs our priority. That way we know we'll be prepared for the King of kings when he returns to bring in his eternal kingdom.

SECOND SUNDAY OF ADVENT

The Second Sunday in Advent traditionally focuses on the prophets, though the Gospel readings in Common Worship focus specifically on the prophetic ministry of John the Baptist. Common Worship has transferred what used to be known as 'Bible Sunday' to the last Sunday in October, but the themes of prophecy and God's message to us still apply, and if Bible Sunday is not kept earlier you may like to use this opportunity to thank God for his written word which leads us to his Living Word. Some Christians have fallen into the trap of 'bibliolatry', almost worshipping the written word rather than the Living Word, so you may feel it helpful to steer the congregation away from fruitless discussions about literal truth, which get nowhere and distract attention from what God is saying. John the Baptist, like all God's prophets, and Scripture itself, communicates God's message to his people in warnings, encouragements and promises. As we listen for that 'still small voice' we are challenged to be doers as well as hearers of the word. You may like to begin the service with the Celtic symbol of asking three people to bring to the altar or holy table a lighted candle, a Bible and a cross, drawing attention both to the written word and the Living Word, Jesus, the Light of the World.

Hymns

TRADITIONAL

- *Christ, whose glory fills the skies (105)*
- *Hail to the Lord's anointed (259)*
- *Immortal, invisible (314)*
- *Jesus shall reign (359)*
- *On Jordan's bank (527)*
- *Thy kingdom come! (690)*

CONTEMPORARY

- *Be still and know (66)*
- *Inspired by love and anger (325)*
- *Long ago, prophets knew (406)*
- *Make me a channel of your peace (437)*

- *Purify my heart (574)*
- *Restore, O Lord (582)*

CHANT

- *Wait for the Lord (949)*

CHILDREN'S SONG

- *Never let Jesus (867)*

Readings

Year A   Isaiah 11:1-10; Romans 15:4-13; Matthew 3:1-12

Year B   Isaiah 40:1-11; 2 Peter 3:8-15a; Mark 1:1-8

Year C   Malachi 3:1-4; Philippians 1:3-11; Luke 3:1-6

Confession

Heavenly Father,
your law is perfect and your word brings life,
but we have failed to heed them.
We are sorry for following our own way instead,
and not allowing you to direct our lives.
We ask you to forgive our sin and selfishness,
and to make your word a light for our path,
so that we walk with you
in the way of righteousness,
for your name's sake. Amen.

Absolution

Almighty God,
who forgives all who return to him
in penitence and faith,
have mercy on *you*, forgive all *your* sins,
heal *your* waywardness
and restore *you* to the joy of his salvation,
through Jesus Christ our Lord. Amen.

Prayer

As we read his word,
let us pray to God for strength
to live as he has commanded us, saying,
Father in heaven,
help us to obey.

When we feel angry and resentful,
or tempted to speak in unkind and hurtful ways,
Father in heaven,
help us to obey.

When we feel anxious or afraid,
and do not trust you to keep us
in your loving care,
Father in heaven,
help us to obey.

When we feel ill or distressed,
and do not experience the joy
of your presence in our lives,
Father in heaven,
help us to obey.

When we feel weak and helpless,
and everything seems beyond our strength
or ability,
Father in heaven,
help us to obey.

When we feel tempted to do things
in our own strength,
following our own wisdom
rather than your commands,
Father in heaven,
help us to obey.
Speak to our hearts through your word,
and help us to live by what it says,
through Jesus Christ our Lord. Amen.

All-age address 1

The object is to give a simple illustration of the prophet's role, using a newspaper (ideally one published that day). You may also find it helpful to ask a volunteer to read aloud a few brief sections or headlines.

1) Start by asking members of the congregation what kind of weather they might be predicting for a week's time. Most will pessimistically predict rain and low temperatures, but explain that with the help of barometers, satellites, computers and other technology, the weathermen can forecast fairly accurately whether we'll need umbrellas or sunglasses. Get someone to read out today's weather forecast before moving on.

2) The next stop is the sports pages. Depending on what events are about to take place you could ask for opinions on the results of the next test match or a forthcoming cup tie – use whatever teams or names are most likely to get a response! While no one can be certain, it's not too hard to predict, for example (at the time of writing, at least), that Liverpool would beat Torquay United comfortably, or that England will struggle against the Australian cricket team. Most newspapers have an article anticipating the outcome of a sports event, so have one read out to finish.

3) Finally move on to political and current affairs. This is likely to be more serious in tone, and again most newspapers will have an article attempting to foretell the outcome of a situation – will the government survive the next general election; will the peace talks bring an end to the war? Ultimately no one can see into the future, and you might add that even experts find it difficult to know what might happen. It shouldn't be too hard to find a suitable article to be read out.

In parallel with all of these, show how the Old Testament prophets often spoke of what was happening or about to happen. Sometimes this was as a warning about what would happen if God's people refused to obey him; at other times it was a prophecy about future events which were as yet unclear. In all of this they were pointing people towards Christ, who was the ultimate fulfilment of the whole of the Old Testament.

All-age address 2

If you prefer to emphasise God's word there are several ways in which you can illustrate its impact. You'll need to prepare an appropriate warning sign and a familiar advertising slogan to a scale that can be seen by the whole congregation.

1) *Words convey information*, which is easily demonstrated by holding up an encyclopaedia. We find this everywhere – in

books, magazines and in the broadcast media. The Bible also gives us knowledge about certain people and situations, but it goes much further than useful historical facts. It also tells us how to apply that knowledge in our daily lives so that we can live as God means us to.

2) *Words sometimes carry a warning.* At this point display a triangular road-sign with an exclamation mark in the middle. It's fairly obvious that there's some danger or hazard ahead, but we need some words to indicate what it is – a flood, an accident or long traffic queues. God's word also contains warnings about the consequences of wrong behaviour or attitudes, and of going our own way instead of following him.

3) *Words also encourage us.* Here you could hold up a familiar advertising slogan which encourages us to buy a particular product. However, you should go on to stress that God's word isn't a sales pitch. God uses his word to encourage us to keep going with the Christian faith when we feel like giving up, to take risks for the sake of his kingdom, to open our lives to his guidance. Through it the Holy Spirit persuades us of the truth, and enables us to act on it.

THIRD SUNDAY OF ADVENT

Somehow in the twenty-first century we can accept John the Baptist as a rather strange, controversial figure without being surprised or offended. However, to his contemporaries two thousand years ago he must have cut a very odd figure indeed. His desert lifesyle was without doubt eccentric, but his message was undeniably radical, and not well received in some circles. He didn't match up at all to most people's expectations, yet Jesus was at pains to emphasise his significance. The prophetic tradition had to all intents and purposes died out four hundred years earlier, so John's arrival on the scene, preaching a baptism of repentance for the forgiveness of sins, provides the vital link between the old order and the new, to be brought in by the imminent Messiah. His importance can be gauged by the accounts of his ministry in all four Gospels prefacing those of Jesus himself. The theme of readiness for the coming of Christ is still central, here in the context of repentance and righteousness. It is also a good opportunity to remember those who have suffered and still suffer on account of their faith.

Hymns

TRADITIONAL

- *Hark, the glad sound! (265)*
- *Hills of the north, rejoice (282)*
- *People look east (557)*
- *The Lord will come (655)*
- *Ye who own the faith of Jesus (759)*
- *Thy kingdom come, O God (691)*

CONTEMPORARY

- *Be still, for the presence of the Lord (67)*
- *Change my heart, O God (92)*
- *First light (175)*
- *Heaven shall not wait (272)*
- *Rejoice in the Lord always (578)*
- *We shall stay awake (722)*

CHANT

- *In the Lord I'll be ever thankful (929)*

CHILDREN'S SONG

- *Kum ba yah (856)*

Readings

Year A   Isaiah 35:1-10; James 5:7-10; Matthew 11:2-11
Year B   Isaiah 61:1-4, 8-11; 1 Thessalonians 5:16-24; John 1:6-8, 19-28
Year C   Zephaniah 3:14-20; Philippians 4:4-7; Luke 3:7-18

Confession

Loving Father,
your servant John the Baptist prepared the way
for the coming of our Saviour Jesus,
by calling your people to repent
of their disobedience,
and to follow the paths of holiness
and truth.
We are sorry for not responding to your call,
and repent of all that we have done wrong.
Forgive our sins,
direct our hearts to obey your will,
and make us ready
for the coming of your kingdom,
through Jesus Christ our Lord. Amen.

Absolution

Almighty God,
who forgives all who truly repent
and turn to him,
have mercy on *you*,
open *your* hearts to receive his love,
and strengthen *you* to follow his calling,
through Jesus Christ our Lord. Amen.

Prayer

We bring to our heavenly Father
the needs of the world, saying:
Father, take our lives;
make us ready for your coming.

We pray for all who proclaim your good news
and declare your love
in the face of hatred or violence,
opposition or apathy . . .

May we follow their example of courage
and commitment to the Gospel.
Father, take our lives;
make us ready for your coming.

We pray for all who suffer
for the sake of your kingdom,
as they live out the Christian faith . . .
May we share their integrity and devotion.
Father, take our lives;
make us ready for your coming.

We pray for all who display your justice
and truth
in their daily work . . .
May we bring the light of Christ
to those in darkness
as we follow you day by day.
Father, take our lives;
make us ready for your coming.

We pray for all who lead the affairs of the world,
whose decisions affect the lives of millions . . .
May we act wisely and seek the good
of all humankind.
Father, take our lives;
make us ready for your coming.

We pray for all going through times
of ill health or bereavement,
anxiety or loneliness . . .
May we share their burdens,
and bring your healing touch to their pain.
Father, take our lives;
make us ready for your coming.
Fill our hearts with your love
and our lives with your Spirit,
that we may be strengthened to serve you
in all we do,
through Christ our Lord. Amen.

All-age address

John the Baptist was the one who prepared the
way for Jesus, so the theme of this address is
being ready, including the themes of repentance
and change. Three volunteers are needed to
act as visual aids. There's no need for them to
do anything other than act as a clothes horse,
but a short dialogue can be very effective, provided they've been properly briefed not to say
more than a sentence – it's easy to allow this to
become a major distraction!

1) The first 'actor' should be dressed as tattily
   as possible – gardening or decorating
   clothes are ideal, preferably with holes or
   frayed at the edges. Explain that they're on
   their way to meet Her Majesty the Queen.
   A reaction is almost guaranteed unless the
   congregation are asleep, so ask them
   what's wrong. This can be developed into
   a discussion of how we prepare ourselves
   to meet someone special. We get ready to
   meet with God not by wearing special
   clothes but by getting rid of all the things
   that make us too 'unclean' to come into his
   presence. John the Baptist taught people
   that they must repent and be baptised in
   water as a sign of being 'cleaned up'.
   When God forgives us it's as though he
   gives us a new set of clothes.

2) The second actor should be wearing a long
   dressing-gown and lounging around. This
   time announce that they're ready for school
   (or work, if appropriate), which should also
   raise a reaction. Point out that we can't go to
   school or work if we're not properly dressed,
   and then remove the dressing gown to
   reveal school uniform or smart working
   clothes. God expects us to wear suitable
   clothes too – kindness, patience, love, etc.

3) The final 'actor' should appear dressed in
   sporting gear. Cricket kit is particularly good
   as there is a variety of extra items such as
   pads and gloves. However, if football kit is
   simpler then draw attention to the boots,
   and make sure the player holds a football.
   Finish by explaining that whatever God asks
   us to do for him, his Spirit always equips
   us with the necessary gifts. But like a sports
   player we have to make use of them if
   we're to do God's will and live for him.

FOURTH SUNDAY OF ADVENT

After two weeks on John the Baptist, Mary is traditionally the focus of our attention on the Fourth Sunday in Advent. Yet in comparison with the severe and eccentric forerunner of Jesus, his mother Mary seems decidedly normal. Matthew and Luke in their infancy narratives introduce us to an unassuming young girl, maybe still in her teens, who's looking forward to her impending wedding to the village carpenter. Although he wasn't born into a wealthy home, there's little evidence that suggests Jesus' infancy and early years were spent in dire poverty. Perhaps the most remarkable feature of his first thirty years is that they were so unremarkable! However, Mary's trust and obedience are well above the ordinary since her engagement, not to mention her reputation, were at serious risk, and we could understand her declining Gabriel's kind offer. But she responded in obedience to this totally unforeseen call, even though she must have questioned the implications of this at times. Obedience is a sensitive subject with children and young people around, as they'll associate it with school or parental rules. It's crucial to emphasise that in Christian terms obedience is far more than adhering to an arbitrary code of conduct. We obey God's will because we love him and put our faith in him.

Hymns

TRADITIONAL

- *Come, thou long-expected Jesus (128)*
- *For Mary, mother of our Lord (182)*
- *I cannot tell (303)*
- *Tell out, my soul (631)*
- *The advent of our king (633)*
- *The angel Gabriel from heaven came (634)*

CONTEMPORARY

- *Jesus, name above all names (355)*
- *Like a candle flame (399)*
- *Lord Jesus Christ (411)*

- *Mary, blessed teenage mother (442)*
- *Sing we a song of high revolt (604)*
- *When our God came to earth (740)*

CHANT

- *Magnificat (935)*

CHILDREN'S SONG

- *And everyone beneath the vine (774)*

Readings

Year A   Isaiah 7:10-16; Romans 1:1-7; Matthew 1:18-25

Year B   2 Samuel 7:1-11, 16; Romans 16:25-27; Luke 1:26-38

Year C   Micah 5:2-5a; Hebrews 10:5-10; Luke 1:39-45 (46-55)

Confession

Eternal God,
you call us, as you did Mary,
to trust your promises and obey your will.
We confess our self-will and failures,
and ask you to forgive us
for going our own way rather than yours.
Increase our faith in your word,
and our confidence in your guiding,
that your will may be done in our lives.
We ask this through Christ, our Lord. Amen.

Absolution

Almighty God, whose mercy is on all
who put their trust in him,
have mercy on *you*,
forgive all *your* sins,
and increase in *you* the will to walk in his ways
through Jesus Christ our Lord, Amen.

Prayer

We pray to God,
who calls us to obedience and service,
saying: your kingdom come;
your will be done.

You sent your Son Jesus into this world,
to be one with us and to share our humanity.

We pray for all who feel friendless,
lonely or marginalised . . .
May we hear your call to share the lives of others
and in them find you. Your kingdom come;
your will be done.

You sent your Son Jesus
to teach us the ways of your kingdom.
We pray for all in leadership positions,
locally and internationally . . .
May they hear your call to act with honesty
and compassion.
Your kingdom come;
your will be done.

You sent your Son Jesus
not to be served but to serve,
and to give his life as a ransom for many.
We pray for all whose lives are spent
defending the interests of the poor . . .
May we hear your call to give generously
and serve willingly,
counting it gain to suffer loss for his sake.
Your kingdom come;
your will be done.

You raised your Son Jesus from the grip of death,
defeating the powers of sin and evil for ever.
We pray for all who are facing illness or death,
or whose lives feel like failures . . .
May we hear your call
to bring healing and peace
as we share Christ's victory
and live his risen life.
Your kingdom come;
**your will be done,
until the whole earth lives
to raise your holy name. Amen.**

All-age address

Even if the concept of obedience needs rather more 'unpacking' with young people present, it can hardly be omitted from any discussion of Mary. The aim of this address is to illustrate how Mary's obedience meant that God could use her as the central part of his purpose of saving humankind, and therefore underscore the importance of all Christians being willing to respond to his call. Although perhaps most effective with 'live' illustrations, this address is also very suitable for using suitable clip-art to create OHP transparencies.

1) *Mary listened to God.* We can't obey or respond to anyone if we don't listen first to what they say. A short game of 'Chinese Whispers' with three or four people will admirably portray the need to listen carefully, though beware this doesn't create too much of a distraction! If this isn't feasible, a transparency of an ear, or of people listening to each other will serve the same purpose. Just as children in class need to pay attention if they are to complete their work, and employees need to listen properly to their bosses' instructions, so Christians must listen to God if they are to understand and fulfil his purpose for their lives.

2) *Mary accepted what God said.* 'There are none so deaf as those who will not hear' as the old proverb says. It's one thing to listen, but if we don't like what we're hearing it's very easy to switch off and not accept it. Gabriel's message was going to make Mary's life complicated and at times difficult, and we would have understood her baulking at it. Obedience sometimes involves doing something we don't like or find difficult, which can be illustrated by asking someone to eat two dry cream crackers (or a similarly impossible feat!). Alternatively a transparency of someone struggling with a task (e.g falling off a bike) will do as well.

3) *Mary remembered what God said.* Even when we've listened we're easily distracted and forget what we've been told because our attention has wandered elsewhere. Prepare a tray with ten simple objects and cover it until this point. After revealing its contents for a few seconds ask a couple of people from the congregation to remember what was on the tray. If you prefer artwork, a picture of people playing football, or having fun at a theme park will illustrate the sort of thing that can take us away from God's will (though emphasise these are not in themselves wrong, and that leisure activities are an essential part of life!). God's word is the most important thing we can ever remember.

4) *Mary did what God asked.* In the last analysis obedience involves doing what we're asked. Instructing a member of the congregation to fetch you a glass of water would be a good example of this – they need to listen, accept the need for it, remember what's been asked for, then bring it to you. The first three aren't much use unless the fourth happens! Alternatively a picture of Mary sitting beside the manger with a cross in the background will help make the same point. It cost Mary a great deal to do what God asked, but she did so willingly and without complaining, recognising somehow that in this way God's purpose of salvation for the world would be accomplished. Conclude by stressing that while God doesn't always take us along the path of hardship and pain, he doesn't promise us an easy time either. Yet only as we follow his calling and guiding will we find true fulfilment and joy – 'whoever loses their life for my sake will find it'.

CHRISTMAS DAY

For most people Christmas is the family occasion *par excellence*, and as a result it has become overloaded with the combined weight of expectation and tradition. The Church is still a part of that, even for those who otherwise never darken its doors. For a variety of reasons the Midnight Eucharist has seen reduced attendances in many areas in recent years, but this is counterbalanced by an apparent increase in numbers attending Christmas Morning worship, often as family groups. Whether or not the service is eucharistic, there will be a huge range of expectations represented in a typical Christmas congregation – some seeing it as a 'spiritual aperitif' prior to the day's festivities, others wanting to enjoy singing the good old carols, and some no doubt wanting a way to ease the pressures imposed by Christmas Day. There will be joy and pain in equal measure, frustration to add to the celebration, and for older folk especially memories as well as anticipation. No single act of worship can hope to encompass all of this, but it has to be taken into account when planning and preparing.

Tradition is important and should not be disregarded, but worship at Christmas hasn't been taken over by 'National Heritage'! There is plenty of fresh, imaginative material available to provoke new insights and fresh perspectives in those who come to worship, and there's every reason to use the opportunity to challenge contemporary standards and attitudes – the coming of Jesus into our world was a most uncomfortable experience for those with vested interests! There are plenty of carols, some more familiar than others, which can add welcome variety to the 'old favourites' – people enjoy singing heartily at Christmas, but enthusiasm shouldn't be allowed to displace thoughtfulness. Those listed here are particularly suited to Christmas morning, but there are many options. Common Worship hasn't yet been updated with the very good resources published in *The Promise of His Glory*, but these can be used until the new package appears. A different slant can be obtained from some of the Iona Community's productions, which many have valued greatly. Many churches will have a crib scene on display, and this service is as good an occasion as the Midnight Eucharist to put the infant Jesus into the manger, so that he can take centre stage.

Experience suggests that many of those in church on Christmas morning are very open to learning more of God's love as we see it in Christ; some will even be longing for it. Perhaps the true impact of a Christmas service can best be gauged by the amount of distraction and conversation it causes later in the day!

Hymns and carols

TRADITIONAL

- *Angels from the realms of glory (36)*
- *Christians, awake! (94)*
- *Ding dong, merrily on high (148)*
- *God rest you merry, gentlemen (229)*
- *Joy to the world (370)*
- *O come, all ye faithful (479)*

CONTEMPORARY

- *The Virgin Mary had a baby boy (670)*
- *Come, come, come to the manger (112)*
- *Who would think that what was needed (750)*
- *See him lying on a bed of straw (589)*
- *Let there be love shared among us (386)*
- *Cloth for the cradle (107)*

CHANT

- *Adoramus te, Domine (921)*

CHILDREN'S SONG

- *Away in a manger (776)*

Readings

There are three sets of readings which can be used on any Christmas Day. Bear in mind that many churches will need to use at least two, one at midnight and one in the morning.

Set 1   Isaiah 9:2-7; Titus 2:11-14;
         Luke 2:1-14 (15-20)
Set 2   Isaiah 62:6-12; Titus 3:4-7;
         Luke 2:(1-7) 8-20

Set 3   Isaiah 52:7-10; Hebrews 1:1-4 (5-12);
           John 1:1-14

Confession

Lord Jesus, the angel sang the glorious news
 of your birth on Christmas night,
**but we have been too preoccupied
with our own concerns to notice.**
The shepherds heard the good news
of your birth and left their flocks to find you,
but our eyes and ears have been closed.
The magi travelled from afar to bring you gifts,
**but we have kept our time and resources
to ourselves.**
Forgive our self-interest and lack of vision,
and fill our hearts with your self-giving love;
**may we share it with all who we meet this
Christmas time, in your name. Amen.**

Absolution

May God our merciful Father forgive all *your*
sins,
draw *you* into his presence,
and open *your* eyes to see in the baby
at Bethlehem
Emmanuel, God with us. Amen.

Prayer

We come into the presence of the Christ-child,
bringing our prayers through him
to our heavenly Father, saying: Eternal Word,
be born in us today.

We pray for all Christians joining with us
to celebrate our Saviour's birth today,
remembering those in difficult or dangerous
situations . . .
With them, help us to be joyful witnesses
to your saving love. Eternal Word,
be born in us today.

We pray for all whose experience of Christmas
will be dark, sad or lonely . . .
Help us to bring them the comfort of your presence
and the joy of your unending love. Eternal Word,
be born in us today.

We pray for all whose Christmas
will be wrecked by tension, hatred or violence . . .
Help us to be peacemakers,
so that the peace your Son came to bring
may reign throughout the world. Eternal Word,
be born in us today.

We pray for all whom we love,
and who share our life in family or community ...
Help us to show your love
in all our relationships. Eternal Word,
**be born in us today,
share in our celebration,
and rule our lives for evermore. Amen.**

All-age address

The aim of this is to demonstrate how easily
we cover up the true meaning of Christmas
with superficial trivia. It's an idea I've borrowed from a friend and adapted slightly. The
impact is stunning though it can't be used too
often. It also carries a health warning – only a
few participants should know beforehand
what's going to happen, and the potential for
chaos is considerable! Be sure you can keep it
under control.

Two readers come out and start to read the
Christmas story (Luke 2 is the most familiar).
If it's been read already this will cause instant
consternation, though you could explain that
'no one was listening earlier'. Once they've
started reading, others appear with various
Christmas items – a bottle of sherry or champagne, crackers, tangerines, tinsel, decorations,
the *Radio Times*, presents, wrapping paper,
cards . . . anything which symbolises the celebratory side of Christmas. While bringing
their various offerings they should be singing
a few secular Christmas songs as raucously as
possible, drowning out the Bible reading. The
readers are then 'decorated' with the items so
that before long their words are totally lost.
The effect of this relies largely on the element
of surprise for most of the congregation. When
all the items are brought up, call for complete
silence. The point is obvious – all these other
things stop us hearing and seeing the reality of
Christmas, and, if it comes off, the illustration
is powerful enough to need little further
explanation. A one-liner to conclude? How
about, 'Don't lose sight of Jesus'?

THE CHRISTINGLE SERVICE

Although the Christingle Service is a fixture in the liturgical calendar for many churches, it isn't catered for in the Common Worship lectionary. The tradition itself seems to have originated in fourteenth-century Moravia, but in its modern form dates back to 1968, when the Children's Society revived the idea to raise funds and awareness. *The Promise of His Glory* contained a liturgy for it, and each year the Children's Society produces new material specifically for use on this occasion. Christingle services aren't tied to a particular date, so can be included anywhere between Advent and Epiphany, though some churches have found it makes less impact after Christmas Day. It work best in the late afternoon, when light is fading but before most children's bedtime.

For the uninitiated the Christingle consists of an orange, representing the world, decorated with a red ribbon to symbolise Christ's blood shed for all, and four cocktail sticks on which are stuck dried fruit and sweets, as a reminder of the fruits of the earth. On top is a lighted candle, to draw our attention to Jesus, the Light of the World. These are given to everyone present in exchange for a 'purse' or gift of money. When all the Christingles are lit, the church is darkened and carols are sung by candlelight, which is powerful enough as a visual symbol to need no further reinforcement. It isn't really possible to avoid traditional carols once the lights are out, but the overriding theme is light, and there are plenty of good Advent and other hymns which focus on this. It's important to ensure that those present see this as much more than a 'carols by candlelight' service, and with the 'ooh, aah!' factor should come elements which will stimulate and challenge the secular view of Christmas.

Hymns and carols

TRADITIONAL
- *Be thou my vision (70)*
- *Christ is the world's light (99)*
- *Christ is the world's true light (100)*
- *Christ, whose glory fills the skies (105)*
- *Jesus shall reign (359)*
- *Mine eyes have seen the glory (449)*

CONTEMPORARY
- *Light a candle for thanksgiving (396)*
- *From the sun's rising (197)*
- *How lovely on the mountains (295)*
- *Like a candle flame (399)*
- *Lord, the light of your love (419)*
- *The Spirit lives to set us free (666)*

CHANT
- *Kindle a flame (932)*

CHILDREN'S SONGS BY CANDLELIGHT
- *Away in a manger (776)*
- *Little donkey (859)*
- *O little town of Bethlehem (508)*
- *Once in royal David's city (521)*
- *Silent night (597)*

Suggested readings

Isaiah 9:2, 6, 7; Isaiah 60:1-3; Colossians 3:1-4; 1 Thessalonians 5:4-11; Revelation 1:12-16; Matthew 5:14-16; Luke 2:8-14; John 9:1-11

Confession

Lord Jesus, Light of the World,
you shine in our hearts,
showing up all that is unworthy of you.
We are truly sorry for our wrongdoing
and ask for your forgiveness.
Make us clean from our sins,
open our eyes to see your glory
and fill our lives with your glorious light,
for your holy name's sake. Amen.

Absolution

God our Father,
who welcomes all who repent
and turn back to him,
forgive all *your* sins
and grant *you* peace and the light
of his presence, now and for ever,
through Jesus Christ our Lord, Amen.

Prayer

Gracious Father, you sent your Son Jesus
to bring light to the darkness of our world.
We pray for those who live in the darkness
of war and violence, especially . . .
Jesus, Light of the World,
**shine in their darkness
and give them your peace.**

We pray for those who experience the darkness
of exploitation and fear, especially . . .
Jesus, Light of the World,
**shine in their darkness
and give them confidence in you.**

We pray for children who endure the darkness
of neglect and abuse, especially . . .
Jesus, Light of the World,
**shine in their darkness
and give them your hope.**

We pray for those who journey in the darkness
of loneliness and sadness, especially . . .
Jesus, Light of the World,
**shine in their darkness
and give them your comfort.**

We pray for those who suffer in the darkness
of illness or depression, especially . . .
Jesus, Light of the World,
**shine in their darkness
and give them your healing.**

We pray for ourselves,
that as your light shines in our lives,
so it may shine through us to others,
and help them to see your love and care.
Jesus, Light of the World,
**shine in our hearts,
and help us to bring your light to them,
for your name's sake. Amen.**

All-age address

The aim is to demonstrate briefly how the
light of Christ can shine in our darkness. It can
either follow, or be followed by, an explanation of the Christingle, since it's based on
Jesus' statement, 'I am the Light of the World'.
I find it more helpful to explain and light a
Christingle first, which I then place on a nearby
table or flat surface.

Some preparation is needed, but the basic
prop can be reused on future occasions. Take a
shoe-box, or similar sized carton, and line the
interior with black paper or card, including
the lid. On a number of small cards write various forms of 'darkness' to be found in the world.
This can be done in the first person singular –
for example, 'I'm lonely', 'I'm homeless' or 'I'm
anxious' – or less personally – 'no friends', 'no
home', 'no hope'. It's best to include both physical 'darknesses' such as poverty and less tangible 'darknesses' such as loneliness. Volunteers
can then come up, take a card from the box,
and read it out.

The light then needs to shine into this 'darkness', and the responses should be written out
beforehand on a flipchart or large pieces of
card which can be seen by everybody.
However you write the 'darkness cards', try to
use quotations direct from the Bible in
response – for example, 'I will never leave you
or forsake you'. This emphasises that it's the
light of Christ which shines into our darkness.
Before continuing with the service you may
find it helpful to mention dark situations outside our own experience – the Children's
Society can give many examples of the ways
in which children are exploited, abused or
rejected though sensitivity will be needed in
handling this. Most congregations need their
eyes opening to the reality that Christ is at
work in the wider world as well as in their
own lives, shining the light of his love into the
most desperate situations.

GIFT SERVICE

Many churches have introduced a Gift Service during the Christmas season (the secular one!) as a counter to the gross materialism which surrounds us in western capitalist society. At a time when most of us are distracted by what to spend our money on (and anxious about how much we have available to spend), we almost resent the idea of calling to mind the poverty and deprivation in which the large majority of the world's population lives. Yet this is surely the immediate and indeed only Christian response. 'Compassion fatigue' is the latest jargon to describe the long-term impact of 'over-exposure' to the needs of others, though these have certainly been well publicised by televised charity fundraising. But since all churches would endorse the idea of giving to the needy, the run-up to Christmas is a particularly good occasion to organise a way of doing so, as well as helping us to keep God's perspective on what's happening around us.

Although handled in a variety of ways, the aim of a Gift Service is to provide gifts for those who wouldn't normally receive anything at Christmas, principally young people, though not exclusively. One effective method is to get children to 'earn' money by performing a few household chores, which is then used to buy a suitable present. A local network or charity is probably the most personal way of distributing gifts, but this isn't always possible, and there are many other organisations able to help. Many churches and schools have taken to preparing shoeboxes filled with suitable gifts for distribution to young people in parts of Eastern Europe, but do note that these have to be ready for collection by early November, so a Gift Service tied in with this will necessarily take place much earlier. However it's done, the congregation will need plenty of notice in order to buy and wrap gifts, and some guidance will need to be given as to what is considered suitable. An upper limit on cost avoids embarrassment on the part of those who can afford less.

In any event this should not be seen as 'conscience money', nor should the liturgy be aimed at stirring up guilt feelings, a quite different matter from challenging them. Making people feel guilty may well provoke a one-off reaction, but it can never be the motivation for true generosity, which comes from the thankful heart of those who recognise that all they have is a gift from God. He wants us to give cheerfully, not as an irksome duty, and the central point of the worship is bringing up all the gifts to the altar or other focal point. There isn't an official liturgy for this service – the suggestions below are those found to work well.

Hymns

TRADITIONAL

- *Amazing grace (29)*
- *Angel voices ever singing (37)*
- *For the fruits of our creation (185)*
- *In the bleak midwinter (326)*
- *Praise God, from whom all blessings flow (560)*
- *Take my life (625)*

CONTEMPORARY

- *All that I am (23)*
- *Let us talents and tongues employ (391)*
- *At this time of giving (55)*
- *All that I am, all that I do (23)*
- *Brother, sister, let me serve you (88)*
- *Give me joy in my heart (201)*
- *I give you all the honour (308)*

Suggested readings

1 Chronicles 29:6-14; Malachi 3:6-12;
2 Corinthians 8:8-15, 9:6-15; James 1:12-18;
1 Peter 4:7-11; Matthew 6:19-24;
Luke 18:18-30, 21:1-4

Confession

We come before God who gives us everything
and confess our greed and selfishness,
saying,
Father, forgive us,
and put your love in our hearts.

For keeping our possessions to ourselves
and refusing to share them with those in need,
Father, forgive us,
and put your love in our hearts.

For doing what we want to,
but ignoring the claims of other people
on our time,
Father, forgive us,
and put your love in our hearts.

For losing our temper and being unkind,
instead of showing patience and sensitivity,
Father, forgive us,
and put your love in our hearts.

For trying to preserve our image,
instead of giving ourselves to serve others,
Father, forgive us,
and put your love in our hearts.
Take away our self-centredness
and replace it with your compassion
and generosity
as we see it in Jesus Christ our Saviour. Amen.

Absolution

God, our loving Father,
who gives everything good for us to enjoy,
have mercy on you,
forgive all your sins
and fill you with his Spirit of love,
through Jesus Christ our Lord. Amen.

Prayer

We bring before God the needs of our world,
saying,
loving Father,
give your peace.

We pray for your Church
throughout the world . . .
As your people serve you,
loving Father,
give your strength.

We pray for your world,
and all who govern it . . .
As they make decisions which shape our lives,
loving Father,
give your courage.

We pray for our families and friends . . .
As we live together,
loving Father,
give your love.

We pray for all who suffer or are in need . . .
As they face their problems and sadnesses,
loving Father,
give your healing.

We pray for ourselves . . .
As we worship and work together,
loving Father,
give your joy.
May we offer ourselves gladly to live for you
as you gave your life for us
in Jesus Christ our Lord. Amen.

All-age address

This reinforces the theme of gifts and giving by
focusing on various kinds of gifts and using
them to illustrate God's gifts to us and our giving to him in response. The best visual aids are
genuine gifts which either you or another
member of the congregation have received –
smaller articles are ideal as they can be hidden
somewhere discreetly and produced at the
appropriate time, though something larger
may make a stronger impression!

1) *'Earned' gifts* are really more of a reward
'for services rendered'. A thank-you present
such as a bottle of sherry fits the bill here,
or you could give a bar of chocolate to
someone present who works hard for the
local church. Explain that while it's good to
say 'thank you' in a tangible way, God
doesn't give us anything because we deserve
it. We can never earn a reward from God,
however hard we try.

2) *Unexpected gifts* are usually a sign that
someone cares about us or has thought
about us. They may be quite small but,
because they take us by surprise, they're
very special – perhaps a gift brought back
from a holiday could serve as an example.
Similarly, God's blessings often come when
we're not expecting it, and show us how
much he cares about us personally.

3) *Useful gifts* may seem a bit dull but we
couldn't do without them. A pair of socks
or a tea-towel are excellent illustrations of
gifts which don't set the adrenalin racing
but are acceptable because they can be

used. Likewise, God gives us the gifts of his Spirit so that we're better equipped to serve him both in the Church and in the world.

4) *Free gifts* sometimes come with petrol or some other consumer product – most households can usually unearth a couple of drinking glasses or something similar which were the reward for collecting a certain number of vouchers. Of course they're not really free at all, but an incentive to persuade us to buy one particular brand. God's gift of his Son isn't a sales gimmick to make us do something we don't really want to, but a demonstration of his love for the whole world.

5) Finally there are *love-gifts*. These are totally undeserved, unexpected and not given for any useful purpose. A red rose has an obvious symbolism, although an item of jewellery is also often a sign of someone's love (it could be from a parent, brother or sister as well as a spouse). Explain in conclusion that this kind of gift is a pale reflection of God's greatest gift to us, his unconditional love as we see it in Jesus.

CRIB SERVICE

Another traditional Christmas liturgy untouched by the Common Worship lectionary is the Crib Service. Many churches include this on Christmas Eve, focusing primarily on families with smaller children. The Crib is such a major visual aid, it needs no extra help and speaks for itself eloquently. A common practice is to invite the children to gather round the model crib scene for an explanation and some prayers, though St Francis, who inaugurated the idea, used real people and animals, evidently bringing tears to many eyes as he read out the Nativity Gospel. This can be done very well with a few 'actors' prepared to take part, and there's no particular need for them to speak. Our church invited a mother to play the part of Mary with her baby son as Jesus (confusingly called Joseph!), which made a great impact on the congregation. Again, everything suggested here is simply a suggestion based on what is known to work effectively.

Hymns

TRADITIONAL

- *Child in the manger (93)*
- *Infant holy, infant lowly (321)*
- *Jesus, good above all other (350)*
- *Once in royal David's city (521)*
- *Silent night (597)*
- *What child is this? (729)*

CONTEMPORARY

- *Born in the night (80)*
- *Cloth for the cradle (107)*
- *Lovely in your littleness (431)*
- *See him lying on a bed of straw (589)*
- *The King is among us (648)*
- *Who would think that what was needed (750)*

YOUNGER CHILDREN'S SONGS

- *Away in a manger (776)*
- *Little donkey (859)*
- *Little Jesus, sleep away (860)*
- *Little Jesus, sweetly sleep (861)*

Suggested readings

Isaiah 9:6-7; Titus 3:4-7; Matthew 1:18-25; Luke 2:1-7

Confession

Lord Jesus,
you came into our world
to live as one of us and die for all of us.
We are sorry for not recognising
or accepting you
and ask you to forgive us.
Please help us to trust you as Mary did,
to worship you with the shepherds,
and seek you with the wise men;
make us willing to sing your praises
with the angels,
for your name's sake. Amen.

Absolution

God our Father,
who forgives all who come to kneel before him
in repentance and faith,
have mercy on *you*,
deliver *you* from doubt and fear,
and fill *your* hearts with joy and peace,
through Jesus Christ our Saviour. Amen.

Prayer

Let us worship the Saviour.
Heavenly King,
yet born of Mary;
Jesus, Son of God,
we praise and adore you.

Eternal Word,
yet child without speech;
Jesus, Son of God,
we praise and adore you.

Robed in glory,
yet wrapped in infant clothes;
Jesus, Son of God,
we praise and adore you.

Lord of heaven and earth,
yet laid in a manger;
Jesus, Son of God,
we praise and adore you.

To you, O Jesus,
strong in your weakness,
glorious in your humility,
mighty to save,
be all praise and glory,
with the Father and the Holy Spirit,
now and for ever. Amen.

From *Worship now*

All-age address

Since the crib scene is the main visual aid, little else is really needed – if other props are to be used, it's essential that they complement the central focus, rather than distract attention from it. This idea works well so long as it's integrated into the whole service.

Display a model car or train to those present, ideally one with enough detail to look realistic. Like the real thing it can move forwards or backwards and fulfil some of the same functions. However, it has a few drawbacks too – it can't carry passengers and would take rather a long time to reach its destination on real roads or tracks (if you're using a model train, you could point out that it's much easier to run on time!). However lifelike and accurate the model, it isn't a substitute for the real thing. You could also produce a doll, again with fairly realistic features. Small children often have a real relationship with dolls and soft toys, but as they grow older they learn that this can never be a substitute for the real thing.

Finally return everyone's attention to the crib, and emphasise that while it may be beautiful and look authentic, it can't replace the real thing. Like a toy, it will be put away until it's next used, but the reality is always there. It gives us an idea of what it represents, but the real thing is far more important and rewarding. As our faith grows, we view the crib scene and thank God that through Jesus we can enjoy a real relationship with him, and experience the reality of his presence, his love and his forgiveness in a much deeper way.

FIRST SUNDAY OF CHRISTMAS

Over the past few decades the two-day Christmas break has developed into a longer holiday period, and for many folk it's the ideal opportunity to visit or entertain family and friends. There are few churches today which don't experience a significant drop in attendance over the twelve days of Christmas, while most children's clubs and Sunday Schools also take a breather. All-age worship is likely to be the most viable option in this seasonal no-man's-land, when everyone is recovering from the initial festive onslaught and regrouping for the assault on the New Year.

The readings for all three years focus in slightly different ways on the holy family, and more broadly on the institution of the family, that maligned and battered institution whose boundaries are becoming ever more flexible. Never is it more strained than over the Christmas season! Many worshippers will be feeling that strain, though for others there may be the pain of having no family to share it with, or remembering loved ones who have died. But for all the disaster areas and damage, most of us know how we'd like family life to be, and there are many positive aspects to home in on. You may want to emphasise that the Biblical 'household' encompassed far more than our 'nuclear family', and draw parallels with the church family, since for some people on their own, the church fellowship can function in that way. Most congregations are still happy with carols, and this may be a good opportunity to sing some of those which escaped the net previously. However, a few other suggestions are also included.

Hymns

TRADITIONAL
- *A great and mighty wonder (4)*
- *A man there lived in Galilee (28)*
- *New songs of celebration render (468)*
- *Of the Father's love begotten (486)*
- *Thou didst leave thy throne (683)*
- *Unto us a boy is born (700)*

CONTEMPORARY
- *Bind us together (72)*
- *Brother, sister, let me serve you (88)*
- *Come, come, come to the manger (112)*
- *Father God, I wonder (159)*
- *Let there be love (386)*
- *Jesus, Name above all names (355)*

CHANT
- *Ubi caritas (946)*

CHILDREN'S SONG
- *When Jesus was my age (911)*

Readings

Year A   Isaiah 63:7-9; Hebrews 2:10-18; Matthew 2:13-23

Year B   Isaiah 61:10-62:3; Galatians 4:4-7; Luke 2:22-40

Year C   1 Samuel 2:18-20, 26; Colossians 3:12-17; Luke 2:15-21

Confession

Loving Father,
we confess to you the times
when our lives have failed to show your love.
We have been selfish and uncaring,
insensitive and unkind,
more concerned with ourselves
than the needs or feelings of others.
We are truly sorry and ask you to forgive us.
Make us channels of your peace and love,
so that we may bring unity
where there is division,
and healing where there is pain,
for your kingdom's sake. Amen.

Absolution

Almighty God,
whose will is to make all people one in him,
forgive all *your* sins,
and strengthen *you* to witness
to his reconciling love,
through Jesus Christ our Lord. Amen.

Prayer

We bring to our loving Father the needs
and hurts of the world, saying: Lord of grace,
hear your children's prayer.

We pray for your family, the Church,
that we may be one in your love
as we worship, support and care for one another,
and serve you in our community . . .
Give us grace to overcome
the barriers of fear and distrust,
and to work together for the good of all.
Lord of love,
hear your children's prayer.

We pray for your creation,
spoiled by human greed . . .
give us wisdom to be good stewards
of all you have provided for us,
and show the leaders of the nations
how to bring an end to poverty and conflict.
Lord of peace,
hear your children's prayer.

We pray for families and friends,
your gift to us . . .
give us strength to show loyalty and respect
to all who share our journey,
and give courage to families experiencing
difficulties,
and to those who have no family.
Lord of mercy,
hear your children's prayer.

We pray for those who are unwell
in body or mind,
and those whose grief
is harder to bear at this time of the year . . .
give us love to bring them
your comfort and healing,
and give them encouragement and strength
in all their troubles.
Lord of healing,
hear your children's prayer.

We pray for those who have died in faith
and now live with you for ever . . .
give consolation to all who mourn,
and give us hope to remember
your promise of eternal life for all who love you.
Lord of life,

**hear your children's prayer,
and accept it for the sake of your Son,
Jesus Christ our Lord. Amen.**

All-age address

It's all too easy to turn the family into a sacred cow. However strongly we may believe that God put us in families for our own good and the well-being of society, we can't deny that for many the experience of family life has been neither beneficial nor wholesome. With nearly two marriages in five ending in divorce, our congregations will inevitably contain a good proportion of adults and children hurt by family breakdown, as well as those who've suffered violence or abuse, and many who are single for one reason or another. However, this address concentrates on the positive aspects of family life and draws parallels with the Christian family. Preparation isn't extensive, but a large corkboard or similar is needed to display photographs, either of yourself and your own family, or of other members of the congregation, if they're willing to co-operate – make sure you explain beforehand what you intend doing, however, and get their permission!

1) Display some photos of children at different ages, and ask one or two volunteers to come up and describe them, as most of the congregation won't be able to see. Often it's only when we see photos side by side that we realise how much children have changed, even in the space of a few years. They need a safe environment in which they can grow up and learn about life until they're old enough to take full responsibility for themselves. We feel sorry for children who have a poor experience of family life because their development will be held back or damaged, and they'll be less able to enjoy a fulfilled life as adults. Just as we all need families to provide a context to grow up and mature, so we also need our Church family to help us develop spiritually, so that we become strong enough to live as Christians in the world.

2) Next show a few photos of older members of the family (and, if possible, one or two

of members with disabilities). Perhaps Granny suffers from arthritis, or Uncle Jim has 'trouble with his inside'; maybe Cousin Joe has to get about in a wheelchair, or Auntie Flo can't see much now. As we get older we need more help and care, and, for some, disability or ill-health means they're dependent on others for much of their lives. Families provide a network of support and encouragement for all of us, so that the stronger members help those who are more vulnerable. Again, we feel sorry when we see people suffering on their own because they have no one to care for them. The Church family is also there to provide practical care and assistance for those who find it difficult to help themselves, so that they're not left vulnerable and lonely, but know they can find help and comfort when it's needed.

3) Finally, present some snapshots of whole families, preferably with three or more generations on parade. The family is made up of all sorts of people – young and old, male and female, those with clever minds, and those who are gifted in practical ways. They all belong together (even if they some-times wish they didn't!) and need one another. The young have energy and vision, the old contribute wisdom and a sense of perspective; some do the thinking, while others put it into practice; some work to earn money, and others stay at home to keep it pleasant and well cared for, or to bring up children. If one section starts to resent another, tensions develop and relationships break down. The Church family is just as varied, and we all need to value each other's contributions if we're to stay together and help one another grow. Once one group starts to assert itself or seek greater power and influence, it won't be long before div-isions appear. No one can grow spiritually in that kind of atmosphere. Just like a human family, the Church family needs to be nurtured and cared for if it's to survive and fulfil God's intentions.

Conclude by saying that families also celebrate together, and show a picture of a party or 'do' in full swing. The Church family also has a great deal to celebrate, most of all the gift of Jesus, and it should do so enthusiastically!

SECOND SUNDAY OF CHRISTMAS

More often than not, there's only one Sunday between Christmas Day and Epiphany, so an all-age service for the Second Sunday after Christmas won't be needed every year. In addition, many churches transfer their Epiphany celebration to the nearest Sunday so that more people can share in it, though you may feel that 2 or 3 January, when they fall on a Sunday, are too early for this. The Common Worship lectionary only gives one set of readings to provide for those years when they are needed. They each demonstrate that God has an overall purpose and plan for the world, and that each of us has a part in that purpose, at the heart of which is Jesus Christ, his Son – a theme particularly suited to the start of a New Year.

Hymns

TRADITIONAL

- *Come ye faithful, raise the anthem (131)*
- *Earth has many a noble city (152)*
- *Father of heaven whose love profound (165)*
- *For thy mercy and thy grace (189)*
- *God is working his purpose out (221)*
- *We have a gospel to proclaim (716)*

CONTEMPORARY

- *Father, I place into your hands (162)*
- *Jesus shall take the highest honour (360)*
- *Let us praise God together (388)*
- *Lord for the years (409)*
- *O give thanks (488)*
- *Shout for joy and sing (596)*

CHANT

- *Holy God, we place ourselves (928)*

CHILDREN'S SONG

- *Jesus put this song into my heart (851)*

Readings

Years A, B and C   Jeremiah 31:7-14

Ephesians 1:3-14
John 1:(1-9) 10-18

Confession

Eternal God,
we confess that instead of obeying
your sovereign will
we have tried to go our own way,
ignoring your purposes
and pursuing only our own desires.
Have mercy on us, we pray,
pardon our wrongdoing,
and give us a clearer vision
of what you call us to be,
for the sake of your kingdom. Amen.

Absolution

God our Father,
who receives all who come to him
in penitence and faith,
forgive all *your* sins,
restore *you* to himself
and strengthen *you* to do his will,
through our Saviour Jesus Christ. Amen.

Prayer

We approach the King of Kings
with our prayers and concerns,
confident that he will hear and accept them,
saying Lord of all,
reign in our lives.

King Jesus, your world is in confusion
and chaos,
and we weep with those whose lives
are shattered by violence and distorted by fear . . .
Give those who rule the nations
wisdom to know what is right
and courage to do it . . .
Lord of all,
reign in your world.

King Jesus, your Church is still spoiled
by division and disunity,
and we weep over futile arguments
and wasted opportunities . . .
Bless all who lead our churches,

that they may have humility to listen,
and strength to overcome the barriers
of mistrust and defensiveness.
Lord of all,
reign in your Church.

King Jesus, your creation is tarnished
with the evils of racism and poverty,
and we weep for the vulnerable, the abused
and the exploited . . .
Strengthen all who work for justice and peace,
that they may have patience for their work
and resolution to overcome obstacles.
Lord of all,
reign in our nation.

King Jesus, your people are not exempt from
illness and difficulties,
and we weep for those who are unwell,
grieving or anxious . . .
Give them courage and hope
as they face their troubles,
and give us compassion to minister to them.
Lord of all,
reign in our hearts.

King Jesus, we bring you our requests,
asking to see your hand at work in our lives,
our church and our world . . .
Give us faith to follow wherever you lead us.
Lord of all,
**reign in our lives until that day
when the whole of creation
acknowledges you as Lord of all. Amen.**

All-age address

It's important to establish a proper balance between God's sovereignty and human free will. The idea of God having an overall plan for our lives can easily become an excuse for avoiding personal responsibility. The intention of this address is to illustrate this as two sides of the same coin, using the concept of an architect and a builder. If you know an architect, he may be willing to let you borrow or have a set of plans for a building, possibly one which was never completed. These need to be displayed prominently so that you can draw attention to them as you make the following points:

1) An architect has to have an idea of what he's aiming to achieve before he produces any detailed drawings or plans. If he just scribbled things down as they came to him, the building would be full of mistakes and might not even stand up for long! So he takes care to find out what sort of ground he's building on, how many rooms are needed, and what other buildings are nearby. Then he makes the best use of the available space and designs it to look attractive in its environment. God's plans are careful too. The world we live in is beautiful and ordered in every respect – it only gets spoiled when we misuse it. His purposes for our lives are good too, and go wrong only when we try to live our own way.

2) The architect needs a builder to put his plans into practice. The builder's job is to follow those plans exactly, so that when his work is finished, it looks how the architect intended. If he tries to change it all, or include bits of other plans, the end result won't be what was meant at all, and will probably look a complete shambles! God's plans for this world need us to put them into effect, though he never forces us. Our job is to obey them and bring about what he wants.

3) Before long God realised that we weren't very good at obeying him, so he created another plan to save us from the consequences of sin, the mess we make of our lives and of the world we live in. Jesus was the central point of that plan but, although he was like us in every way, he obeyed his Father's will even to the extent of dying for us. So he was raised from death and we can share in his risen life, and know his strength, enabling us to live God's way and obey him. God's plan for us is to enjoy his love and presence here on earth and one day for ever in heaven.

THE EPIPHANY

If Advent often suffers from being surrounded by pre-Christmas tension, Epiphany has to endure post-Christmas exhaustion! Many will have gone back to school or work after the holiday period, and the temptation is to put Jesus away with the decorations until December comes round again. An infant Jesus makes few demands on us, but Epiphany opens up our perspectives on Jesus and brings to the fore the implications of his incarnation. The gifts of the Magi point us towards the cross, where Jesus was to die cruelly, just 33 years later, while their non-Jewish origin reminds us that Jesus' death was for the salvation of all people.

Despite their appearances on countless Christmas cards and in every nativity play, we know very little about the Magi, beyond their Gentile origins and journey from the East. The most likely explanation is that they were Eastern astrologers who had looked up this unprecedented star in their charts before setting out. How typical of God! The most important event in human history bypasses completely the religious leaders, government, civil service, royalty, and anyone else with power and influence. Instead, the first to hear this greatest of all news were a bunch of scruffy shepherds out in the fields, and a group of pagan intellectuals! Armed only with the theory that a king had been born, and some gifts for him, the Magi set out on their long and arduous journey. On arrival, after a detour via Herod's palace, they worshipped him despite their Gentile origins, and God clearly accepted their worship, in marked contrast to Herod himself, as well as the Scribes and Pharisees later on! A good day therefore, to look at God's work throughout the world, as well as our response to his generosity and love.

The Common Worship lectionary only gives one set of readings for Epiphany itself, and if you want to transfer it to the Sunday after Epiphany, you'll then need to transfer the Baptism of Christ, traditionally associated with the Sunday after Epiphany, to the following day.

Hymns

TRADITIONAL
- *As with gladness (49)*
- *Behold the great Creator (62)*
- *Brightest and best (85)*
- *O worship the Lord (552)*
- *The race that long in darkness pined (656)*
- *We three kings (724)*

CONTEMPORARY
- *Arise to greet the Lord of light (40)*
- *From the sun's rising (197)*
- *From the very depths of darkness (198)*
- *Go, tell it on the mountain (243)*
- *One shall tell another (526)*
- *We'll walk the land (717)*

CHANT
- *Laudate Dominum (933)*

CHILDREN'S SONG
- *All the nations (773)*

Readings

Years A, B and C   Isaiah 60:1-6
Ephesians 3:1-12
Matthew 2:1-12

Confession

King of kings,
we come into your presence
recognising our utter unworthiness
to stand before you.
We have often failed to acknowledge you
as Lord of our lives.
Father, forgive us,
and cleanse us from our sins.

We have often failed
to live up to the standards of your kingdom
or obey your commands.
Father, forgive us,
and cleanse us from our sins.

We have often failed
to put the interests and well-being of others
above our own.
Father, forgive us,
and cleanse us from our sins.

We have often failed
to give you even a small part
of what you have given us.
Father, forgive us,
and cleanse us from our sins.

We have often failed
to worship you in spirit and in truth.
Father, forgive us,
and cleanse us from our sins.
Help us to see you more clearly
and to offer you all that we have and are
for the sake of your Son Jesus Christ. Amen.

Absolution

Almighty God,
whose mercy and forgiveness have no limit,
pardon and deliver *you* from all your sins,
grant *you* a fresh vision of his glory
and strengthen *you* in his service,
for the sake of Jesus Christ our Lord. Amen.

Prayer

With the Magi we kneel in adoration
before our Saviour,
offering ourselves, and bringing our prayers,
saying:
Jesus, King of Kings,
reveal to us your glory.

As the Magi came to worship the newborn King,
so we pray that we may worship him
in spirit and truth.
Give us grace to live in unity and love
with all Christians . . .
Jesus, King of Kings,
reveal to us your glory.

As the Magi came to offer costly gifts,
so we pray that we may offer him
all of our lives.
Give us strength to work for your kingdom
and proclaim the Gospel . . .
Jesus, King of Kings,
reveal to us your glory.

As the Magi came from a distant country to
find the promised king,
so we pray for all who have not yet recognised
or owned him as Lord.
Give us boldness to bring your good news
to those around us . . .
Jesus, King of Kings,
reveal to them your glory.

As the Magi visited the infant Jesus
with his family,
so we pray for our own families
and circle of friends.
Give us sensitivity to bring his love and healing
to any who are suffering or in distress . . .
Jesus, King of Kings,
reveal to them your glory.

As the Magi heard you speak and tell them
to return home another way,
so we pray that we may hear your voice
and respond to your leading.
Jesus, King of Kings,
reveal to us your glory,
and through us to others,
so that all may be drawn to love,
worship and serve you,
the King of kings and Lord of lords. Amen.

All-age address

This address needs a certain amount of preparation, since it involves gift-wrapping a number of items. You could easily link it with a traditional Epiphany procession if your church has one, but it works just as well if this doesn't happen. First take a large cardboard box and cover it with wrapping paper – if it has a separate lid, so much the better, though this isn't essential. Then wrap up a diary for the New Year and a cheque book or building society account book, and place them in it. Finally, make sure your sidespeople/stewards/welcomers have enough strips of paper to give out to everyone, together with a few pencils for those who don't come out with a pen! To make a closer link with the procession, have ready to display an item made of gold (preferably, though not necessarily, connected with the church), a thurible containing incense and some anointing oil.

1) Gold is the most valuable of all substances and is used as a baseline for many other values. Here bring out the gold article, and speak about its worth, pointing out that gold is used for the most important people and occasions – a crown, for example, is likely to be made of gold. This gift speaks of Jesus' kingship, but it was also a most costly gift for the Magi to bring. At this point invite someone to accept a gift from your box, and give them the cheque book. As they unwrap it explain that God gives us all we have, and we can only give back to him what he's already given us. We offer him our money because it sums us up – our work, our homes, our priorities. If we value our relationship with God it'll be no hardship to offer him our money and the things we treasure.

2) Next take the thurible and say that frankincense speaks of holiness. We swing the incense over things we want to emphasise as holy. Another volunteer now comes to unwrap the diary. God wants all of our lives to be holy – every day, not just on Sundays. He doesn't necessarily want our homes or churches to be filled with incense, but he certainly wants them to be full of his love and truth. Holiness isn't the same as piety. We strive to achieve piety, but holiness is a gift of God. We become more holy as we allow God to enter our lives day by day.

3) Finally take the anointing oil and show how myrrh speaks of Jesus being set aside for a special task – to die for us on the cross. (The nearest contemporary equivalent is embalming fluid.) The point is that first we must 'die to sin', as Paul puts it, by confessing what we've done wrong and being open to receive God's forgiveness through the death of Jesus. Then we offer our whole lives to God for him to direct and use. Conclude by handing round the slips of paper and asking everyone to write down one specific thing they want to offer back to God. When completed, the slips can be collected up and brought to the altar as part of the procession.

FIRST SUNDAY OF EPIPHANY
THE BAPTISM OF CHRIST

The Church of England did not officially recognise the Baptism of Christ as a festival until the publication of *Common Worship*. Perhaps it seems odd that Jesus' Baptism has never been recognised as a festival until now, though it was set as the theme for that Sunday in the ASB. Not only was it a key point in Jesus' ministry and his own understanding of it, but it was used for a long time by the Eastern Church as the day when they remembered both Jesus' birth and his baptism – only in the fourth century was 25 December finally settled on as the date for the former, Epiphany (on 6 January) becoming for the Western Church the commemoration of Jesus' revelation to the Magi, and more widely to the Gentiles. The celebration of his baptism thus moved to the following Sunday, focusing on the inauguration of his earthly ministry, and his heavenly Father's authentication and validation of it. The beginning of a new year is an ideal point for all Christians to commit themselves afresh to their baptismal promises by renewing them, but whether or not this is the tradition in your church, opportunity can be taken to enable the whole Christian community to reaffirm its commitment to following the way of Christ.

Hymns

TRADITIONAL

- *Come, gracious Spirit (116)*
- *Come Holy Ghost, our hearts inspire (117)*
- *Eternal Ruler of the ceaseless round (154)*
- *O breath of life (476)*
- *O King enthroned on high (504)*
- *O love how deep (516)*

CONTEMPORARY

- *Come, Holy Spirit, come (119)*
- *God is our strength from days of old (220)*
- *Jesus, Jesus, holy and anointed one (353)*

- *Lord, the light of your love (419)*
- *O let the Son of God enfold you (506)*
- *The Kingdom of God (646)*

CHANT

- *Wait for the Lord (949)*

CHILDREN'S SONG

- *Father welcomes all his children (797)*

Readings

Year A   Isaiah 42:1-9; Acts 10:34-43;
         Matthew 3:13-17
Year B   Genesis 1:1-5; Acts 19:1-7; Mark 1:4-11
Year C   Isaiah 43:1-7; Acts 8:14-17;
         Luke 3:15-17, 21-22

Confession

Lord Jesus Christ, beloved Son of God,
you submitted to the waters of Baptism
and lived in complete obedience
to the will of the Father.
We confess that we have not always been
submissive to your guidance
or obedient to your commands,
preferring instead to follow our own
selfish desires.
Forgive all our sins, we ask you,
and wash us clean.
By your Spirit make us fit for your service
and ready to obey your will,
that in our lives your name may be glorified.
Amen.

Absolution

God our Father,
who forgives all who come to him
in penitence and faith,
have mercy on *you*,
wash *you* clean from all *your* sins,
strengthen *you* to walk with him,
and bring *you* the joy of eternal life,
through Christ our Lord. Amen.

Prayer

We bring our prayers and concerns
to our heavenly Father,

committing ourselves anew
to following his ways, and saying:
Lord, we ask this in your name;
hear us and answer, we pray.

We bring you the Church
in every part of the world,
praying that all Christians may be united
in vision and purpose . . .
May we heed and obey
Christ's great commission,
making disciples and baptising people
of all nations and cultures.
Lord, we ask this in your name;
hear us and answer, we pray.

We bring you the nations of the world
and their leaders,
praying that they may work together
to uphold peace and justice,
and fight evil and corruption . . .
May your wisdom direct them
in making decisions about finance and trade,
justice and care, education and development.
Lord, we ask this in your name;
hear us and answer, we pray.

We bring you the needy and suffering
of the world,
struggling with homelessness,
poverty and exploitation,
praying that they may know you
alongside them in their distress . . .
May we be aware of their needs
and alert to our responsibilities.
Lord, we ask this in your name;
hear us and answer, we pray.

We bring to you those we know who are sick
in body or mind, grieving or anxious,
praying that they may know your comfort
and healing . . .
May we be sensitive in our caring
and loyal in our support.
Lord, we ask this in your name;
hear us and answer, we pray.

We bring you those who have passed
into your eternal presence,
or are coming to the end
of their earthly pilgrimage . . .
May they know your arms of love

holding them close,
and enter into your eternal joy.
Lord, we ask this in your name;
hear us and answer we pray.

We bring you ourselves
at the beginning of this week and year;
may your unfailing love fill and inspire us,
and draw others into your kingdom of love,
for the sake of your beloved Son,
Jesus Christ our Lord. Amen.

All-age address

The Baptism of Christ and the beginning of a new year offer an ideal opportunity to think about beginnings and starting out. Sociologists often stress the significance of how things are started and finished – even a new year, let alone a new millennium! While everyone recognises it as an arbitrary point in time, we still make every effort to make sure it gets off on the right foot. We can also review the past and put it behind us as we move forward on our life's journey. Jesus' Baptism was the perfect preparation, a commissioning and act of commitment for the three years of ministry that followed, culminating in his Passion and Resurrection.

Even the most un-sporty members of the congregation will be aware of the need for any sportsman to prepare well and get off to a good start. If one of them is a serious participant in a sport, they may be willing to dress and equip themselves suitably to illustrate the points. Failing this, create some OHP slides with suitable clip-art to emphasise the same message. For simplicity's sake athletics is the example used here, but it should be clear how other sports could be fitted into the pattern.

1) No one will win a race or competition unless they're properly dressed and equipped. If you can persuade your volunteer to put on some inappropriate clothes over the top of their sporting gear, it will help reinforce the point that the correct equipment is a prerequisite to a good start. An athlete needs running shoes and starting-blocks; a racing-driver needs a car filled with petrol; a skier has to have skis waxed; a batsman

must be wearing pads and gloves ready to start the innings. Although Jesus was God's Son, it was important that the Holy Spirit descended on him to show that he was now fully prepared for his ministry over the next three years. We too need the Holy Spirit to equip us for whatever God calls us to do.

2) The right equipment is pretty useless without thorough training. At this point ask your volunteer to go through one or two fitness routines. Only with this regular training is an athlete sure to be fit enough to compete with others. Jesus maintained his spiritual fitness by keeping up his prayer life and his relationship with his heavenly Father. Our Christian life depends on us doing the same.

3) Before starting, an athlete also needs to know and obey the rules of the sport, and accept the authority of the referee. The advice of a coach or another expert is also important to listen to, so that performance is always improving. Jesus, too, lived in submission to his heavenly Father, and although he was God's Son he willingly accepted the limitations that sharing our human life imposed. Our ministry can only be exercised in Jesus' name, on his authority, and recognising our own human weakness and frailty. As we listen to his word, so we'll gradually become more like him.

4) Right at the outset, all athletes need to know what they're aiming for – the finishing line, the goal or a particular standard. Jesus was quite clear about where he was going and what he had to do. The course of his ministry certainly wasn't easy, and he knew that the pain of the cross lay ahead of him. But he also knew why he had to go through with it, and 'for the joy set before him he endured the pain of the cross' (Hebrews 12:2). We may not always be quite sure about the exact course of our journey of faith, but there's no need to doubt our ultimate destination. That will keep us going when things become difficult or tough.

Second Sunday of Epiphany

Across all three years of the Common Worship lectionary, the Gospel readings for this Sunday are taken from the first two chapters of John, covering the calling of the first disciples and the account of Jesus turning water into wine. Two different address outlines are provided, but the passages are complementary, focusing on how Jesus transforms not only the filthiest water in the house, used for footwashing, into the finest wine, but also on how his calling transforms the lives of a group of ordinary working men, who hear him and respond by leaving what they are doing to follow him.

Hymns

TRADITIONAL

- *All hail the power of Jesus' name (16)*
- *Be thou my guardian (69)*
- *Forth in thy name, O Lord, I go (188)*
- *God of grace and God of glory (225)*
- *Jesus calls us: o'er the tumult (347)*
- *O God of Bethel (491)*

CONTEMPORARY

- *Come and see the shining hope (110)*
- *James, Andrew, Peter and John (338)*
- *Jesus calls us (346)*
- *Will you come and follow me (752)*
- *You are beautiful (760)*
- *Your love's greater (765)*

CHANT

- *In the Lord is my joy (930)*

CHILDREN'S SONG

- *Life for the poor (858)*

Readings

Year A   Isaiah 49:1-7; 1 Corinthians 1:1-9; John 1:29-42

Year B   1 Samuel 3:1-10; Revelation 5:1-10; John 1:43-51

Year C   Isaiah 62:1-5; 1 Corinthians 12:1-11; John 2:1-11

Confession

As we hear the voice of Jesus calling us,
we confess the sins
which have separated us from him, saying,
Lord, have mercy on us;
forgive us and strengthen us.

Lord Jesus, you called your disciples
to follow you in faith.
We too have heard your gracious call,
yet we confess that we have
not always heeded it.
Lord, have mercy on us;
forgive us and strengthen us.

Lord Jesus, you called your disciples
to listen to your teaching and learn your ways.
We too have heard your message of love,
yet we confess that we have often not acted on it.
Lord, have mercy on us;
forgive us and strengthen us.

Lord Jesus, you called your disciples
to stay with you,
however hard the circumstances.
We too have heard your call to faithfulness,
yet we confess that we have
sometimes preferred
to take the easier path.
Lord, have mercy on us;
forgive us and strengthen us.

Lord Jesus, we are truly sorry
that we have not always followed you willingly,
listened to you carefully
or stayed with you loyally.
Strengthen us by your Spirit,
that we may be faithful disciples of you,
our Master and Friend. **Amen.**

Absolution

God our merciful Father,
who forgives all who respond to his call
to repent,
have mercy on *you*
and pardon *your* wrongdoing,

grant *you* forgiveness for all that is past,
strength to live for him now,
and in the world to come, eternal life. Amen.

Prayer

We pray to Jesus, our Saviour and Friend,
laying our concerns and needs before him,
and saying:
Lord, in the stillness of our hearts,
may we hear you speaking.

Lord Jesus, you call all Christians to live in unity
and show your love in the world.
We pray for your Church,
in war and hardship,
or in peace and prosperity . . .
Give us the will to overcome minor differences
and work together for peace and justice.
Lord, in the stillness of our hearts,
may we hear you speaking.

Lord Jesus, you call all peoples and nations
to deal fairly and justly with each other.
We pray for all who influence decisions
and actions,
most of all in places where fear and want
overshadow people's lives . . .
Show us how to bring your compassion
to the marginalised and unjustly treated.
Lord, in the stillness of our hearts,
may we hear you speaking.

Lord Jesus, you invite all who are burdened
with suffering and cares
to come to you and find rest.
We pray for those we know going through
difficult times . . .
Help us to be agents of your healing love.
Lord, in the stillness of our hearts,
may we hear you speaking.

Lord Jesus, you call us to follow you
in our daily living,
in our relationships, in activity and at leisure.
Lord, in the stillness of our hearts,
may we hear you speaking,
listen to your words,
and follow where you lead,
for the sake of your Kingdom. Amen.

All-age address 1

The idea that someone can be called by God to a particular task or ministry isn't encountered so much today. Perhaps we've become too used to shortlist interviews and IQ tests, or maybe it's now much easier to move jobs if we're not satisfied with our present employment. Somehow God's calling doesn't seem to play much part in career decisions. Unfortunately, the misunderstanding has grown that God's calling is only for those he wants in full-time ministry, that he isn't able to use human agencies to achieve his will. Jesus' calling of the disciples wasn't hampered by such misconceptions. When they heard his voice they followed at once, in part because they had little to hold them back, but most of all because he was utterly compelling.

This address makes use of the common experience of advertising slogans and campaigns, with a message aimed at persuading the consumer to part with cash. Preparation involves selecting half a dozen or so fairly large advertisements (from a magazine, colour supplement, or even the endless fliers which drop through the letter-box or fall out of magazines) and pasting them on to a suitable piece of card. As far as possible choose those with a universal appeal, rather than ones for children's book clubs or stair-lifts! The aim is to demonstrate that God's call is quite different from the blandishments of the media, not manipulative or ambiguous but direct and clear. Invite members of the congregation to give their own interpretation of each advertisement's message and whether or not they think its claims and presentation are honest.

1) Advertisements tend to appeal to our selfish instincts – a food product will illustrate this well. For example, there's nothing inherently wrong with a rather expensive brand of chocolate, but its appeal may well be more to our sense of self-indulgence than to our taste buds – we're not going to buy a product which we don't believe will fulfil our needs and make us feel good. Jesus didn't appeal to his disciples' need for personal satisfaction, and God's call is never accompanied by a guarantee of permanent happiness and fulfilment. Jesus made it quite clear that the

Christian life is often difficult and demanding; but it offers a far deeper and more lasting sense of spiritual fulfilment than a 'quick fix' which wears off in no time.

2) Advertisements sometimes give the false impression that if only we'd buy a certain item our lives will be changed for ever. Here, a slogan for a household product or appliance might help reinforce the point. An electric drill is a great asset when making holes in a wall, and a microwave oven speeds up cooking times considerably, but neither are of the slightest use for washing clothes or playing CDs! God's call never exaggerates or distorts, and it applies to every part of our lives – it can truthfully claim to be life-transforming in every way!

3) It shouldn't be too hard to find an advertisement with a misleading message – something which costs 'only £ . . .' with other costs hidden in tiny print elsewhere, for example. God never misleads us. His call may be challenging or demanding, and will certainly have a cost, but we'll never feel 'conned' or disappointed if we respond to it.

4) By definition, advertisements try to push us into buying a particular product or service, investing our money in a certain account, or taking a course of action we otherwise wouldn't have considered. They try to convince us that our lives will be improved, our social status enhanced, our time and money better used – almost any advertisement could be used to show this. When the disciples heard Jesus' call it was compelling, but there were no false promises, appeals to self, misleading information or subtle attempts to overcome possible resistance. He wants us to follow him of our own free will, in response to his love and grace, not through manipulation or coercion. Many have found that the way of Jesus is costly – there's no such thing as cheap grace – but the benefits and blessings far outweigh anything this life can offer, transforming our lives for ever.

All-age address 2

As with all of Jesus' miracles recorded by John, the changing of water into wine can be taken on a number of levels. It shows Jesus' care for the guests to enjoy the wedding party and for the host not to be embarrassed; it shows him relating to the everyday joys and sorrows of human life; it shows how he takes the dirtiest water and transforms it into the best wine ever tasted; the wine is a symbol of Jesus' life given for us on the Cross and reminds us that through his death we have eternal life.

The props for this address are very straightforward – a bottle of red wine and some black grapes (a couple of different varieties if available). Start off by talking about wine-tasting and how connoisseurs savour a mouthful of each wine. Invite some children up, apologising that their age prevents you from allowing them to taste wine and offering them a grape-testing as an alternative! As they eat one, ask whether it was sweet or sharp, juicy or fleshy – there'll probably be a range of reactions.

Now explain briefly the process of making wine. The grapes aren't harvested until they're sufficiently ripe, but when they've been gathered in they're pressed either mechanically or (more rarely now) by treading. You may like to reassure the congregation that the latter won't be attempted in church – however, if you are brave enough, make sure you have the materials on hand to avoid too much mess and clean the volunteer up! It takes a lot of grapes to make one bottle of wine, and even after the grape juice has been collected it takes a long time before it can be bottled and sold, as it may be blended first, and then left to ferment until it's reached its ideal state. Make the parallel that like the grapes we can't be used until we're ready. God wants us to 'blend' with other Christians, and the Christian life is a long process of maturing.

But it's also true that we've been spoiled by sin, as grapes might rot because of a disease. We need the transforming power of Jesus to turn us from the mess of our wrongdoing into the best we can possibly be for him. By his death he gives us a completely new life, just as the grapes have a 'new life' as wine. As we live by faith so we become gradually more mature, growing more and more like Jesus as we follow him.

THIRD SUNDAY OF EPIPHANY

Last week's Gospel readings were all taken from John's Gospel. The account of him changing water into wine reappears, this time in Year B, while the account of the calling of the disciples in Year A is taken now from Matthew's Gospel. The Year C Gospel is also about the beginning of Jesus' ministry, Luke's account of him preaching in the synagogue at Nazareth, his home town. This is an event of great significance both in our and Jesus' own understanding of his ministry over the following three years, even if it wasn't the public relations director's ideal start. It also raises questions about how we measure 'success' in the context of Christian work, and how we deal with conflict and opposition. It may be useful to note that in most years this Sunday falls in the Week of Prayer for Christian Unity.

Hymns

TRADITIONAL

- *Dear Lord and Father (144)*
- *God is working his purpose out (221)*
- *Lord of our life (417)*
- *O for a thousand tongues (485)*
- *O happy day! (498)*
- *The Church's one foundation (636)*

CONTEMPORARY

- *As the deer pants for the water (45)*
- *Cry 'Freedom!' (138)*
- *God's Spirit is in my heart (231)*
- *I Love you, Lord (313)*
- *Let the heavens declare (385)*
- *Lord, we come to ask your healing (422)*

CHANT

- *Silent, surrendered (941)*

CHILDREN'S SONG

- *As Jacob with travel (775)*

Readings

Year A   Isaiah 9:1-4; 1 Corinthians 1:10-18; Matthew 4:12-23

Year B   Genesis 14:17-20; Revelation 19:6-10; John 2:1-11

Year C   Nehemiah 8:1-3, 5-6, 8-10; 1 Corinthians 12:12-31a; Luke 4:14-21

Confession

Heavenly Father, you sent your Son
to announce good news to the poor,
declare freedom for prisoners,
and restore sight to the blind.
We are sorry for failing to follow his ways,
turning our eyes from those in need,
and remaining silent
instead of sharing the good news.
Forgive our self-concern and lack of vision,
fill our mouths with your truth,
and our hearts with your love,
for the sake of Christ our Lord. Amen.

Absolution

Almighty God, whose love extends
further than we can wander from him,
have mercy on *you*, forgive all *your* sins,
and set *your* feet on the path that leads
to eternal life,
through his Son, our Lord Jesus Christ. Amen.

Prayer

We come to our Lord Jesus with our prayers
and requests,
saying: Compassionate Lord,
hear us as we pray.

Lord Jesus, you came to bring the poor
good news of salvation and hope.
We pray for all who endure
the daily grind of hardship,
or who are impoverished in mind and spirit
by circumstances . . .
May they recognise you alongside them
in their need
and respond to your love.
Compassionate Lord,
hear us as we pray.

Lord Jesus, you came to bring the captives
freedom and joy.
We pray for prisoners and their families,
and all who are enslaved
to addictive behaviour . . .
May they experience release
and a new start to their lives.
Compassionate Lord,
hear us as we pray.

Lord Jesus, you came to bring the blind
sight to banish their darkness.
We pray for those disadvantaged
in body or mind,
and all who are blinded to the truth
by fear or apathy . . .
May they experience your transforming love
and rejoice in their restored vision.
Compassionate Lord,
hear us as we pray.

Lord Jesus, you came to bring the oppressed
relief from their distress.
We pray for all burdened by illness
and infirmity,
or by circumstances they cannot control . . .
May they know your strength in their troubles,
and be unburdened
of all that weighs them down.
Compassionate Lord,
hear us as we pray.

Lord Jesus, you come to us
and command us to proclaim your love to all.
May we faithfully proclaim your good news.
Compassionate Lord,
hear us as we pray,
and keep us true to our calling,
for your name's sake. Amen.

All-age address

Jesus certainly made an impression when he
returned to Nazareth – people couldn't believe
how the local carpenter's boy was suddenly
preaching with such authority and conviction.
He had a clear understanding that the famous
passage from Isaiah did more than shed light
on what he was about to embark on. It not
only foresaw the events now unfolding but
could only achieve its true fulfilment in him.

At his Baptism the Spirit publicly descended
on Jesus, and as a result he could claim to have
been anointed for the work he was now starting.
This isn't the easiest of passages to explain in
the context of all-age worship, but the address
takes the underlying message of God's love
and care to emphasise a vital aspect of Jesus'
ministry.

Preparation is simple, involving four large
pieces of card and a marker pen. It uses a simple
acronym for CARE, and the cards can either be
held up by children at the appropriate moment
or attached to a board so that everyone can see.
In addition, you could find a suitable symbol to
display for each word, to reinforce the message.

1) *C is for Compassion* – quite literally 'feeling
   with'. A simple symbol of this could be a
   box of tissues, which we might use if we're
   feeling upset and can share with others in
   the same state. This goes deeper than feeling
   sorry for someone or giving them a bit of a
   hand. Jesus had a particular feeling for the
   poor and the vulnerable, those unable to
   help themselves, and occasionally it got him
   into hot water with the authorities. Their
   primary concern was the preservation of
   the *status quo*, and they seem to have had
   little interest in the needy, although there
   were undoubtedly some who took this aspect
   of God's law seriously. Throughout his
   ministry Jesus took the side of the poor and
   the oppressed, sharing their feelings and
   concerns. Just as we know God is alongside
   us in our suffering and pain, so we are
   called to be alongside others, showing them
   his compassion.

2) *A is for Announcement.* A large newspaper or
   magazine headline or slogan would do for
   this. Usually news is announced. Sometimes
   it's bad news, such as the announcement of
   Princess Diana's death, but it might equally
   be good news, like the birth of a baby
   or a forthcoming marriage. Jesus came to
   announce God's good news of salvation
   and new life, and this was to be directed at
   the poor – not just those who've run out of
   money, but those for whom life is miserable
   and hopeless, and those who recognise
   their own need before God. Good news is
   only really good for those who want to hear

it. News of a hundred new jobs at a local factory may please the government, economists or local politicians, but it could be the best news ever for people in the area without a job, because they need it most. The more we recognise our own sinfulness and weakness, the more we realise how good the good news of Jesus really is.

3) *R is for Release.* A length of chain is a potent symbol of captivity, especially if you tie someone up with it (if you do, make sure in advance that it's clean and safe!). In former times prisoners were often held in chains, a very uncomfortable position, but Jesus is far more than a prison reformer. Many people are imprisoned by circumstances or bad habits. Drug addicts and alcoholics aren't able to stop themselves damaging their bodies; those who get involved in crime often can't find a way out of their way of living; poverty and homelessness always seem to be a prison with no way out. Others are unable to escape from hurtful or traumatic experiences in the past. Jesus came to release all of us from the power of sin and death, and open up a whole new life.

4) *E is for Encouragement.* For those who knew their need of God, Jesus came to bring encouragement. He proclaimed 'the year of the Lord's favour' for them, that God's blessing would be on them, that God was on their side. An important part of caring is providing encouragement for those in need, reassuring them of their value to God, giving them confidence to cope with their problems, and setting hope before them instead of despair. However bad the immediate circumstances may be, there's always our ultimate hope to hold on to. Jesus encourages us to look away from ourselves and towards God, so that we can see the problems of this life in perspective, and become more determined to bring his good news to others.

FOURTH SUNDAY OF EPIPHANY

As we approach the Presentation of Christ in the Temple the Gospel readings are still concentrating on the start of Jesus' ministry. Year A now has the account of the wedding at Cana, while Year B recounts the first of Jesus' miracles recorded by Mark (the healing in the synagogue on the Sabbath of a man with an evil spirit), and Year C takes Luke's account of the Presentation itself and Simeon's recognition of the true identity of the infant in his arms. Since it often falls close to 2 February, and to acknowledge its importance as the liturgical turning-point between Christ's Nativity and Passion, the Common Worship lectionary allows for the celebration of Candlemas to be transferred to this Sunday, to enable more people to share in observing it. An all-age address is outlined for the Year B Gospel; for Year A a suitable outline can be found at Epiphany 2; and one for Year C is included under the Presentation itself.

Hymns

TRADITIONAL

- *At even, ere the sun was set (50)*
- *At the cross her station keeping (51)*
- *Glorious things of thee are spoken (205)*
- *Gracious Spirit, Holy Ghost (245)*
- *O God, our help in ages past (494)*
- *Thy hand, O God, has guided (689)*

CONTEMPORARY

- *Faithful vigil ended (157)*
- *Great is the Lord (248)*
- *I give you all the honour (308)*
- *There is a Redeemer (658)*
- *Where true love is found (742)*
- *Where true love (743)*

CHANT

- *Ubi caritas (946)*

CHILDREN'S SONG

- *Our God is so great (872)*

Readings

Year A   1 Kings 17:8-16; 1 Corinthians 1:18-31; John 2:1-11

Year B   Deuteronomy 18:15-20; Revelation 12:1-5a; Mark 1:21-28

Year C   Ezekiel 43:27-44:4; 1 Corinthians 13:1-13; Luke 2:22-40

Confession

We cry to God our Father in weakness and sin,
Lord, have mercy;
save us and heal us.

We confess to you our pride and stubbornness,
asking you to soften our hearts.
Lord, have mercy;
save us and heal us.

We confess to you our waywardness
and self-will,
asking you to set us on the right path.
Lord, have mercy;
save us and heal us.

We confess to you our blindness
and narrow-mindedness,
asking you to open our eyes
and restore our vision.
Lord, have mercy;
save us and heal us.

We confess to you our fear and lack of trust,
asking you to strengthen our faith.
Lord, have mercy;
save us and heal us,
forgive all our wrongdoing,
and make us whole, we pray,
for the sake of your Son,
Jesus Christ our Lord. Amen.

Absolution

God, whose will is for all people to be whole,
have mercy on *you*
and grant *you* forgiveness for all *your* sins,
peace in *your* hearts and minds
and strength to live for him day by day,
through his Son Jesus Christ our Lord.
Amen.

Prayer

Committing ourselves to the way of Jesus,
we pray for strength to obey his teaching,
and follow his example
in our homes, our community,
our work and our world, saying,
Lord, help us to follow your way,
and fill us with your love.

Jesus, when you lived on earth
you made deaf people hear
and blind people see.
We ask you to be with all whose lives
are affected by physical or mental handicap,
and to give strength to those who care for them.
Help us to value everyone equally as you do,
and extend your love to them.
Lord, help us to follow your way,
and fill us with your love.

Jesus, you welcomed all
who came to you in faith,
and never turned away anyone in need.
We ask you to open our eyes to see
those in need around us –
the homeless, the vulnerable, the abused –
and to move our hearts
to put their interests above our own.
Lord, help us to follow your way,
and fill us with your love.

Jesus, you confronted the scheming
of wicked people
with your truth and goodness,
and spoke out against self-righteousness
and hypocrisy.
We ask you for courage to stand firm
against evil and wrongdoing,
and, by the way we live, to challenge
the selfishness and greed we see all around.
Lord, help us to follow your way,
and fill us with your love.

Jesus, you healed people
of all kinds of illnesses and conditions
and made them whole again.
We ask you to give comfort and healing
to all who are suffering,
whether in body or mind,
and to bring peace and joy
to those who are distressed or anxious.

We especially remember . . .
Lord, help us to follow your way,
and fill us with your love.

Jesus, you came to bring us life in all its fullness.
We ask you to heal us of all that would harm,
and make us whole by your Spirit,
that we may worship you joyfully
and serve you faithfully
in whatever we are called to do in your name.
Lord, help us to follow your way,
**and fill us with your love
so that it flows to everyone we meet
and draws them into your presence,
for the sake of your kingdom. Amen.**

All-age address

It would be possible to take the passage from Mark's Gospel as a straightforward account of a healing miracle, but Mark seems to play this aspect down. Significantly, it follows straight on from Jesus' Baptism and his calling of the disciples, the emphasis being more on the power and authority Jesus demonstrated in his ministry from the outset. Following a similar line, this address outline is essentially dramatic, focusing on the different elements of Jesus' ministry and requiring a number of volunteers. It's described here as a mime, acted out without words, but if your actors are up to it, you might prefer to construct a simple script – making sure that it won't take up too much time!

1) We see Jesus first as a teacher. If possible, dress up a volunteer as a teacher in gown and mortar-board, and provide them with a blackboard and chalk (or whiteboard and marker pen). One or two children could be pupils, who give the teacher a hard time, refusing to learn their times-tables or spellings. Before long the teacher has to stop teaching and tell them off, as they're learning nothing. Point out that Jesus' teaching was nothing like this. When he spoke, everyone listened attentively, not just because he was a great speaker and storyteller, but also because his words had power and authority. Jesus was altogether different from the teachers of the law, who

went on at great length but bored everyone to tears and carried no conviction. Even today his teaching has an impact on people far beyond any other teaching before or since. We listen to his words, not to gain more information or knowledge, but because they show us the love of our Father in heaven, and set us on the way to eternal life.

2) *Next we see him as healer.* Although this certainly wasn't unknown in those days, there's little doubt that Jesus' miracles were unprecedented, seen as evidence of his authority over diseases and the powers of evil. For this tableau a doctor is needed, with a stethoscope, white coat and any other suitable props. He also needs a patient to treat, with a leg injury perhaps, or a sore throat, who could leave with a prescription in his hand. Explain that when we visit the doctor we hope he can diagnose our problem and prescribe the necessary remedy, but we don't usually expect him to make us better on the spot. In this case Jesus healed the man there and then, and even did it on the Sabbath in the synagogue. Quite simply his compassion for the man was so great that he saw no need to delay making him whole again, even in front of a full congregation! Nor does he stop at putting right or masking a symptom, but instead goes to the root of the problem. The healing power of Jesus makes us whole as people, even if we still have to go to the surgery occasionally for treatment.

3) *Finally we see Jesus as leader.* For this a soap-box, set up in front of a microphone, will be ideal for a politician – you could even hang up a poster saying, 'Vote for Jones'. After a few shouted slogans, say that we're well used to political figures telling us what's best for us and making all kinds of promises about what they'll do, though we don't always take them very seriously! Jesus' hearers were probably just as used to that from their religious leaders, who were also the government in those times. But Jesus was quite different. No one ever accused him of being 'all talk and no action'. He kept his promises and demonstrated a kind of authority they'd never seen before –

even the forces of evil obeyed him! Yet throughout his ministry Jesus made it clear that he wasn't acting off his own bat or furthering his own reputation; his authority derived from his heavenly Father and everything he did came out of that relationship. The risen Jesus still draws people to the love of God our Father, and whatever we do in his name we also do on his authority. We may not become famous that way, but with God's strength we'll get done whatever he wants for his kingdom.

THE PRESENTATION OF CHRIST

The Common Worship lectionary follows on from *The Promise of His Glory* in regarding the whole of the period from Advent, through the Christmas and Epiphany seasons, as an integral unit, with Candlemas, or the Presentation of Christ, as its 'natural climax'. It falls forty days after Christmas Day on 2 February, though it can be transferred to the nearest Sunday – and frequently is, since this enables more worshippers to share in its celebration. With Lent on the horizon it refocuses our sights on the latter part of Jesus' life, so that as well as being an occasion of great rejoicing, when Simeon takes the infant Jesus in his arms and recognises in him the fulfilment of God's promise to his people, it also has a bittersweet quality, as his words pitch us forward suddenly and directly towards Jesus' death. Some churches leave their crib scene on display until now, to emphasise this change, and while it's much less challenging to leave Jesus in the manger, the facts don't permit us to. If we're to follow the way of Jesus our eyes also have to be open to the realities of denying ourselves and taking up our cross. The Christian faith isn't the 'soft option' many would like to think it is, but demands a willingness to confront the forces of evil and the consequent opposition and conflict.

Hymns

TRADITIONAL
- *All praise to thee (22)*
- *A man there lived in Galilee (28)*
- *Jesus, the name high over all (364)*
- *King of glory, King of peace (375)*
- *Take my life (625)*
- *Ye servants of the Lord (757)*

CONTEMPORARY
- *All I once held dear (18)*
- *Faithful vigil ended (157)*
- *I, the Lord of sea and sky (332)*
- *Meekness and majesty (448)*

- *Purify my heart (574)*
- *You give, Lord (764)*

CHANT
- *Sanctum nomen Domini (940)*

CHILDREN'S SONG
- *When Jesus was my age (911)*

Readings

Years A, B and C   Malachi 3:1-5
Hebrews 2:14-18
Luke 2:22-40

Confession

We come to God our Father,
confessing our sins and failings
and seeking his pardon as we say,
Lord have mercy,
forgive us and heal us.

For the times when we have failed
to recognise your presence in our lives,
and relied on our own strength,
Lord have mercy,
forgive us and heal us.

For the times when we have ignored
your will for our lives,
and pursued our own concerns,
Lord have mercy,
forgive us and heal us.

For the times when we have refused
to accept the cost of following you,
and backed away from conflict and opposition,
Lord have mercy,
forgive us and heal us.

For the times when we have been unwilling
to offer ourselves wholly to you,
and tried to keep control of our lives,
Lord have mercy,
forgive us and heal us.
Restore and renew us
so that one day we may be presented
faultless in your presence,
through our Lord Jesus Christ. Amen.

Absolution

Almighty God,
whose will is for all people to repent
and be forgiven,
have mercy on *you*,
pardon all *your* sins and wrongdoing
and strengthen *your* commitment
to follow his ways,
through Christ our Lord. Amen.

Prayer

We draw near to Jesus, our Saviour and Friend,
confident that he will hear us
as we bring our prayers and concerns, saying,
Lord accept our thanks,
and receive our prayers.

We thank you for your family, the Church,
and for our part in its fellowship.
We pray for Christians throughout the world,
especially those whose work is difficult
or whose lives are at risk for your sake . . .
May they know your strength and peace
day by day.
Lord accept our thanks,
and receive our prayers.

We thank you for the world you have created,
and for our pleasure in its beauty and resources.
We pray for all who are responsible for its care,
especially those seeking to repair the damage
caused by greed and selfishness . . .
May we play our part in acting as wise stewards
of what we have been given.
Lord accept our thanks,
and receive our prayers.

We thank you for our homes,
and for the comfortable lives we enjoy.
We pray for the homeless, the unemployed,
the neglected and the abused,
especially those we see
in our own community . . .
May we show your care and compassion
as we minister to them.
Lord accept our thanks,
and receive our prayers.

We thank you for our families and friends,
and for the joys of human love.
We pray for the lonely and friendless,
especially those who have been hurt
and wounded by those closest to them . . .
May we bring them the warmth and security
of your love.
Lord accept our thanks,
and receive our prayers.

We thank you for health and strength,
and for the opportunities you give us
to enjoy this life.
We pray for those who are sick in body or mind,
especially . . .
May we bring to their lives your healing touch.
Lord accept our thanks,
and receive our prayers.

We thank you for your promise
to hear us when we pray in faith.
As we see your hand at work,
may we grow in confidence that you are faithful
and rejoice in your mighty power.
Lord accept our thanks,
and receive our prayers.
for the sake of your Son, Jesus Christ our Lord.
Amen.

All-age address

The purpose of this address is to try and explain in fairly simple terms some of the implications of following Jesus' way of suffering. This is bound to be challenging because Jesus himself was clear that discipleship would never be the easy way out, but that's not the same as discouraging. The underlying message is that whatever pain or hardship we may endure in serving Christ is nothing compared with the joy of serving him and the assurance of eternal life. The particular costs described can be illustrated with easily available props which need no preparation.

1) The Christian faith demands our time. A diary or wallchart will serve admirably for this, and can be contrasted with a copy of the *Radio Times* or similar publication. We may well prefer to sit and watch our favourite programmes (make it clear there's nothing wrong with this *per se*, and Jesus

took time to relax and rest) but sometimes we have to make a choice between doing what we want to and obeying God.

2) A bank statement, bundle of bills or some other demonstration of our finances will indicate that we also have to commit our money and possessions to God. Again, that doesn't mean depriving ourselves or our loved ones of the necessities of life, nor even of an occasional treat. What matters is where our priorities lie – if we spend large amounts on CDs, clothes or expensive holidays without considering our church or other Christian causes and charities, we need to ask ourselves whether we're serious about following Jesus. The account of the rich young man brings this point out perfectly.

3) Now hold up a picture of a well-known personality, someone currently in the news who has a high level of public popularity. It's straightforward to point out how precarious a reputation can be – there are many examples of fallen celebrities who couldn't handle the fame and money. As Christians we must be prepared to risk our reputations and being regarded as a bit odd if we're to serve God effectively. For some this has involved giving up a career or a comfortable home, and working in very tough situations – Eric Liddell and Jackie Pullinger are excellent examples, though there are many more.

Conclude by saying that many Christians have even been willing to risk or give up their lives for the sake of Christ, because he's the most important part of their lives. While we probably won't have to go that far, being a disciple of Jesus will always have a cost. But the rewards are so much greater that we'll find, like all these Christians before us, that turning back isn't an option. Jesus didn't turn back, either. He saw his mission through. Can we do less?

ORDINARY TIME

'Ordinary Time' in the Common Worship lectionary refers to those periods of the Christian year which are neither in a penitential or festival season. It covers two periods: one of up to five Sundays between the Presentation of Christ and Ash Wednesday, and the other of up to 22 Sundays between Trinity Sunday and All Saintstide, excluding any major festivals. The exact length of each in any given year is determined by the date of Easter. If it falls in March, there may only be two Sundays (or very rarely just one) between 2 February and the start of Lent, but that clearly means the period 'after Trinity' will be longer. If it falls in mid- or late April, there may be four (occasionally five) Sundays before the beginning of Lent, but correspondingly less Sundays after Trinity. The two Sundays before Lent are specifically described as such, but the remaining 25 Sundays are defined as 'Propers' and identified by the dates during which they are to be used. So if there are three Sundays before Lent begins, Proper 1 will be used, but not Propers 2 or 3, which are encountered more rarely. The period 'after Trinity' will then begin with Proper 6, and each Sunday will always be described as 'after Trinity', with a specific collect for that day, which will therefore not be tied in to the lectionary. The Common Worship lectionary makes a few changes from the Revised Common Lectionary on which it's based, but the principle of reading a Gospel sequentially is retained throughout Ordinary Time, apart from the two Sundays before Lent, which have specific themes, and take precedence over the Propers. The RCL also describes these as 'Sundays after Epiphany', unlike Common Worship, which prefers to call them Sundays before Lent – in other words, the RCL's 'Epiphany 5' could be the 'First, Second, Third, Fourth or even Fifth before Lent'!

Proper 1

Sunday between 3 and 9 February inclusive
(if earlier than the Second Sunday before Lent)

As the first Sunday in Ordinary Time, this Sunday sees the start of the sequential reading of a Gospel, and the themes of each are necessarily different. In Year A we read a familiar part of Matthew's account of the Sermon on the Mount; Year B's Gospel from Mark shows us Jesus both healing many people and taking time out to pray to his heavenly Father; for Year C Luke depicts the calling of the disciples, and a miraculous catch of fish. For this latter, the all-age address outline 1 under Epiphany 2 is suitable, and outlines are given for Years A and B. The absence of specific themes means that the hymns suggested are related to the readings for the day. A few of the readings are quite lengthy, and parts of them are included in parentheses, so that they can be abbreviated.

Hymns

TRADITIONAL

- *Awake, awake (57)*
- *Awake, our souls (59)*
- *Bright the vision (86)*
- *Christ is the world's true light (100)*
- *Immortal, invisible (314)*
- *We have a gospel to proclaim (716)*

CONTEMPORARY

- *A new commandment (35)*
- *Fill your hearts (172)*
- *Give me joy in my heart (201)*
- *Here on the threshold (280)*
- *Lord, the light of your love (419)*
- *Such love (620)*

CHANT

- *Veni, lumen cordium (947)*

CHILDREN'S SONG

- *This little light of mine (901)*

Readings

Year A   Isaiah 58:1-9a (9b-12);
1 Corinthians 2:1-12 (13-16);
Matthew 5:13-20

Year B   Isaiah 40:21-31; 1 Corinthians 9:16-23;
Mark 1:29-39

Year C   Isaiah 6:1-8 (9-13);
1 Corinthians 15:1-11; Luke 5:1-11

Confession

Father God,
we confess in sorrow our failure
to keep God's commandments,
or to live in love and peace with one another.
We are sorry for our waywardness,
and repent of our self-will.
In your great mercy forgive us, we pray,
and so make your light shine through our lives,
that others may see your love
and glory revealed,
and come with us to worship you,
through Christ our Saviour. Amen.

Absolution

God our Father,
whose mercy is unending
and whose love is without limit,
grant to you pardon for all your wrongdoing,
the assurance of sins forgiven,
and peace both here on earth
and in the life to come,
through Jesus Christ our Lord. Amen.

Prayer

Lord Jesus, Light of the World,
those who follow you walk in the light of life.
Hear us as we pray for the Church
and the world, saying:
Lord, the light of your love is shining;
dispel the darkness, we pray.

The world is full of despair and misery.
Lord, we pray for the millions of street-children,
refugees displaced by civil war,
and those surrounded by violence or fear . . .
Through those who minister in your name,
may their sadness be dispelled.
Lord, the light of your love is shining;
dispel the darkness, we pray.

There is corruption and evil in high places.
Lord, we pray for those in authority,
who may be tempted to act for personal gain,
and those in the mass media,
who find it easy to distort the truth . . .
Through the light of your Spirit,
may they be guided
in the paths of righteousness and love.
Lord, the light of your love is shining;
dispel the darkness, we pray.

There is conflict in many homes
and communities.
Lord, we pray for families experiencing
breakdown,
children who are abused or neglected,
neighbourhoods in fear of crime and violence . . .
Through the warmth of your reassuring
presence,
may they find hope in their distress.
Lord, the light of your love is shining;
dispel the darkness, we pray.

There is illness and sadness
among our own loved ones.
Lord, we pray for those feeling overshadowed
by the darkness of ill health,
depression or bereavement . . .
Through the touch of your healing hand,
may they experience the hope of your salvation.
Lord, the light of your love is shining;
dispel the darkness, we pray.

There are many of our friends
who have passed through the darkness of
death
and now rejoice in your eternal light . . .
Through following their example
of faith and courage,
may we one day share with them
the glory of heaven.
Lord, the light of your love is shining;
dispel the darkness, we pray,
for the sake of your kingdom. Amen.

All-age address 1

The Sermon on the Mount is arguably the
best-known piece of teaching Jesus ever gave,
combining great insight and profundity with a
simplicity and accessibility which anyone could
relate to. Jesus didn't use jargon or mindless
clichés. Instead, he took illustrations from
everyday life which were familiar to his hearers,
and told stories. This address outline develops
the pictures in this passage of Jesus' followers
being salt and light. Only a small amount of
preparation is required.

1) Bring out a salt cellar or grinder, and begin
   by asking one or two congregation members
   what they would use salt for. The most likely
   first answer is 'on chips'! Others may then
   mention vegetables, meat, or eggs. At this
   point bring out a hard-boiled egg in an egg
   cup, saying, 'Here's one I prepared
   earlier', and ask who likes boiled eggs. You
   could invite one of those who does to come
   and taste this one, or if you prefer, try it
   yourself. When the egg has been cracked
   open, sprinkle a little salt on it and comment
   on what effect this has. When salt is well
   sprinkled it brings out the taste of the egg,
   but if it's all stuck together in one place, not
   only will it taste horrible, but you will
   probably start coughing and need a long
   drink – have a glass of water handy! Before
   it was associated with health problems, salt
   had a vital function in preserving meat, so
   explain that Jesus wants those who follow
   him to do the same for their community
   and society, because if they don't, it'll start
   to go bad. Equally, if they all stick together
   they can't possibly bring out the good or
   prevent the bad.

2) Now produce a torch, and demonstrate some
   of its uses. A volunteer could shine it into a
   grubby corner or under a pew, for example,
   or use it to find their way into a dark area.
   It could be an aid for reading, or even act as
   a beacon. All these purposes show how
   Jesus wants his followers to be the light of
   the world. If his light is within us, it will
   shine out to others, showing up what needs
   to be cleaned up and put right; it will bring
   guidance in times of uncertainty; it will
   help us to see and do God's will; and it will
   be visible to everyone, drawing them to
   Jesus, the Light of the World.

Conclude by saying that the aim of the salt is
not to be salty, but to preserve and to bring out

the taste. Similarly, a torch is of use only when it shines on something else. We can only be used by God if we draw attention not to ourselves but to him.

All-age address 2

In the passage from Mark 1, we see two different aspects of Jesus. In the first part he's on the go all the time, healing first Peter's mother-in-law and then crowds of other people who'd come in all kinds of need. In fact, the pressure continues until well past bedtime. So the second part portrays him slipping away to a quiet place where he thought he could pray undisturbed. Eventually Peter finds him and they move on to other villages nearby to carry on with his ministry. This very simple outline uses two well-briefed volunteers to mime this contrast.

1) The first one is seated at a table or desk, on which there is a diary and telephone, together with plenty of scrap paper and a few pencils. He/she sits there scribbling away, answering the phone, getting up and going across the church and returning, leaving a pen where they went. As the phone keeps ringing they get more frantic, paper falls on the floor, the pen can't be found . . . Quote the old proverb 'more haste, less speed', and say that while this person does a good job and means well, he's just too busy. He's not taking time to think about what he's doing so everything starts to go wrong. Christians can easily allow themselves to get too busy, feeling guilty if they're not doing some-thing, but doing so much that none of it gets done well. Of course, there are times when all of us have more to do than time to do it in, but like Jesus we must recognise how important it is to stop and take time out with our heavenly Father.

2) Now bring on the second volunteer, dressed and equipped as a doctor. As he enters, the manager collapses in a heap on his desk, exhausted by his efforts. The doctor listens to his chest, takes his temperature and so on, and tells him he needs a good rest, at which point they can move across to a comfortable chair. He can't work effectively until he's sorted himself out. Say that if we just carry on doing things and never taking time for prayer or reflection, we'll end up doing nothing properly and becoming spiritually tired. When Jesus needed to spend time in quiet with his Father, he wasn't being idle, but getting the necessary rest and refreshment to continue with his ministry. We need to do this just as much as he did – a particularly useful point to bring out in the run-up to Lent.

PROPER 2

Sunday between 10 and 16 February inclusive
(if earlier than the Second Sunday before Lent)

In this Sunday's Gospel readings, Year A continues with Jesus' teaching in the Sermon on the Mount, focusing on his interpretation of the Law; Mark recounts the healing of a leper in Year B; and Year C parallels Year A as Luke records the 'Sermon on the Plain', a similar summary of Jesus' teaching.

Hymns

TRADITIONAL

- *Be thou my vision (70)*
- *Father, Lord of all creation (163)*
- *Fight the good fight (169)*
- *Give to our God immortal praise (203)*
- *I know that my Redeemer lives (311)*
- *May the mind of Christ my Saviour (447)*

CONTEMPORARY

- *Bind us together (72)*
- *Let there be love shared among us (386)*
- *Make way, make way (438)*
- *Colours of day (108)*
- *The kingdom of heaven (647)*
- *Where true love is present (743)*

CHANT

- *Ubi caritas (946)*

CHILDREN'S SONG

- *We're a bright light together (906)*

Readings

Year A   Deuteronomy 30:15-20;
             1 Corinthians 3:1-9; Matthew 5:21-37
Year B   2 Kings 5:1-14; 1 Corinthians 9:24-27;
             Mark 1:40-45
Year C   Jeremiah 17:5-10;
             1 Corinthians 15:12-20; Luke 6:17-26

Confession

We come to kneel in repentance
before our heavenly Father as we say,
Lord have mercy on us;
pardon and deliver us, we pray.

We repent of the wrong we have done:
hurtful gestures, careless behaviour
and selfish acts.
Lord, have mercy on us;
pardon and deliver us, we pray.

We repent of the wrong we have spoken:
insensitive conversation, harsh criticism
and cynical comments.
Lord, have mercy on us;
pardon and deliver us, we pray.

We repent of wrong thoughts and attitudes:
ill-disguised resentment, unfair judgements
and self-centred desires.
Lord have mercy on us;
pardon and deliver us, we pray.
Take away our sin, purify our hearts,
and make us holy as you are holy,
through Christ our Lord. Amen.

Absolution

Almighty God,
whose mercy is without end,
grant *you* pardon and forgiveness
for all *your* sins,
wisdom to speak and act rightly,
and confidence in *your* eternal calling,
through Jesus Christ our Lord. Amen.

Prayer

Remembering Jesus' love for the poor
and vulnerable,
we bring our prayers and requests
to our heavenly Father,
praying as he teaches: Your kingdom come,
your will be done.

Lord Jesus, we pray for those in need
who are forgotten by the rest of the world:
down-and-outs and street-children,
asylum-seekers and victims of exploitation . . .
Through the care and compassion we show

may they know they have a place in your heart.
Your kingdom come,
your will be done.

Lord Jesus, we pray for those
who hunger and thirst after righteousness:
carers and aid-workers,
peacemakers and campaigners for justice . . .
Through their devotion and commitment
may your love spread throughout the world.
Your kingdom come,
your will be done.

Lord Jesus, we pray for those
persecuted for their faith:
Christians in prison or at risk
for challenging wrong and doing right . . .
Through their boldness and courage
may the light of your goodness
overcome the darkness of evil.
Your kingdom come,
your will be done.

Lord Jesus, we pray for those
whose hearts are heavy:
the chronically and terminally sick,
the grieving, the anxious and the frail,
especially . . .
Through their suffering and pain
may they know the comfort of your presence.
Your kingdom come,
your will be done.

Lord Jesus, we pray for our own Christian
witness and service . . .
Through our decisions and actions,
may your kingdom come,
your will be done; for your name's sake. Amen.

All-age address

A recent TV commercial, inviting recruits to
the teaching profession, consisted of a number
of well-known figures simply saying the name
of their most inspiring teacher. All children are
familiar with the role of teacher, and there will
be very few adults who can't remember something of their schooldays, so this outline looks
at Jesus as one of the most memorable and
inspiring teachers of all time. Ideally a volunteer
can be progressively dressed up and equipped
as a schoolteacher to make the points visually,
but it would be just as effective to use a cartoon

drawing of one on an OHP slide, adding to it
with each point made.

1) We expect a teacher to know his or her
subject and to speak authoritatively about
it – an academic gown or mortar board will
do very well here. Jesus' authority came not
from academic studies but from his heavenly
Father, whom he listened to all the time and
obeyed implicitly. Our sharing of the good
news will be effective only if we too live in
trust and obedience to God our Father.

2) Teachers sometimes have to correct inaccu-
rate work or bad behaviour – a cane will
provide cartoon-style amusement value,
but, if you feel this conveys an unhelpful
message, a detention book or similar will
do just as well. Jesus also corrected people
when they misunderstood God, and made
it clear that wrong behaviour has inevitable
consequences.

3) Really good teachers inspire their pupils
and bring out the best in them, enabling
them to develop their full potential. The
simplest illustration may be a blackboard
and chalk, but a pile of erudite books will
be satisfactory, provided you make the
connection that depth of knowledge and
enthusiastic communication are essential to
good teaching. Explain how Jesus wanted
all his hearers not only to understand the
truth of what he was saying, but also to know
it as a reality in their personal experience.
Our heavenly Father isn't an academic
obscurity but our Creator who loves us and
wants us to enjoy life as he intended.

4) The best teachers make a difference to their
pupils not just in the classroom but for the
rest of their lives. Often our best subjects
at school are those that are taught most
enthusiastically. If possible, a couple of
enthusiastic volunteer pupils doing homework or research can help make this point.
Conclude by saying that as we learn from
Jesus, he will change the course of our
lives too, just as he did the disciples'. His
teaching is easy to understand, practical and
life-changing, and unlike a schoolteacher
we can carry on learning from him throughout our lives.

PROPER 3

Sunday between 17 and 23 February inclusive
(if earlier than the Second Sunday before Lent)

The readings for this Sunday will be among
the least used in the entire lectionary, since
they only appear when Easter falls so late that
there are five Sundays between Candlemas
and Ash Wednesday. The Gospel readings from
Matthew and Luke in Years A and C continue
with passages from the Sermons on the Mount
and Plain respectively, while Year B takes
Mark's account of the paralysed man lowered
through the roof to be healed by Jesus.

Hymns

TRADITIONAL

- *Christ is made the sure foundation (97)*
- *Dear Lord and Father (144)*
- *Immortal love, forever full (315)*
- *Jesu, priceless treasure (344)*
- *Praise to the holiest (572)*
- *The Lord is King! (650)*

CONTEMPORARY

- *Brother, sister, let me serve you (88)*
- *God forgave my sin (212)*
- *Healer of the sick (270)*
- *Lord, we come to ask your healing (422)*
- *O Lord, all the world belongs to you (509)*
- *We cannot measure how you heal (712)*

CHANT

- *Bless the Lord my soul (923)*

CHILDREN'S SONG

- *I'm accepted, I'm forgiven (830)*

Readings

Year A Leviticus 19:1-2, 9-18;
1 Corinthians 3:10-11, 16-23;
Matthew 5:38-48
Year B Isaiah 43:18-25; 2 Corinthians 1:18-22;
Mark 2:1-12
Year C Genesis 45:3-11, 15;

1 Corinthians 15:35-38, 42-50;
Luke 6:27-38

Confession

God of love,
your Son taught us that all your commandments
are summed up in the law of love.
We acknowledge that we have not loved you
with all our heart, soul, mind or strength,
nor our neighbours as ourselves.
We are sorry and ashamed,
and repent of the wrong we have done
and the good we have failed to do.
Have mercy on us, we pray,
cast out our sins,
and give us strength to obey you willingly
and courage to serve you joyfully,
for the sake of your Son,
our Saviour Jesus Christ. Amen.

Absolution

Almighty God,
source of all grace and mercy,
hear *your* cry of repentance,
pardon all *your* sin and wrongdoing,
and grant *you* the blessings of eternal life
both in this life and in the world to come,
through his Son, Jesus Christ our Lord.
Amen.

Prayer

We come to Jesus our Saviour,
casting all our burdens on him,
secure in the knowledge that he cares for us,
and saying,
Jesus, Master and Friend,
hear the prayer of our heart.

We bring our concerns for your Church
in every corner of the world,
for its preaching of the Gospel,
its care of the needy, and its unity.
May all your people set aside
differences of tradition and culture
to work together for your kingdom,
making your name known in every place,
and bringing your love into every situation.

In particular we pray for . . .
Jesus, Master and Friend,
hear the prayer of our heart.

We bring our concerns for the world we live in,
for its governments and political figures,
its mass media and communications systems,
its financial and commercial interests
and its many areas of intense suffering.
May all in leadership positions think wisely,
speak sensitively, and act compassionately
to promote justice and peace,
and counter corruption and evil.
Jesus, Master and Friend,
hear the prayer of our heart.

We bring our concerns for the sick and dying
and those who look after them,
for medical and nursing staff,
for carers and counsellors,
for rescue and emergency services,
and for care homes and hospices.
In particular we pray for . . .
May they experience your peace
and comfort in their suffering,
and feel your healing hand reaching out to them.
Jesus, Master and Friend,
hear the prayer of our heart.

We remember those who have died in faith,
and their friends and loved ones
who mourn them, especially . . .
May we follow in their steps
in our earthly pilgrimage,
so that one day we may also share with them
the joy of heaven.
Jesus, Master and Friend,
hear the prayer of our heart,
and guide us through this earthly journey
into eternal life,
through your risen Son,
Jesus Christ our Lord. Amen.

All-age address

This outline address is based on the passage from the Sermon on the Mount, though it could be used on other occasions too. The aim is to move away from the concept of the Christian faith as a set of regulations to adhere to or rules to keep, using instead Jesus' teaching to establish the 'rules' by which he wants us to live. A small amount of preparation is necessary to obtain suitable visual aids.

Begin by asking the congregation when they're required to obey certain rules. An early answer will almost certainly be 'when driving', while others might mention our obligations as citizens of our country, as employees of a particular organisation, or as students. From this it is easy enough to clarify that there are different kinds of rules and laws.

1) There are rules to keep us safe, for example on the roads. A copy of the Highway Code will exemplify this, as would a large copy of a road sign. If people disobey these there'll be a major accident.

2) There are rules to protect people and their property, which make burglary and violent behaviour, for example, serious offences. A copy of a legal document will reinforce this, or you could dress someone in a policeman's helmet to indicate enforcement of these rules.

3) There are rules to keep order, not least in school – if nobody kept them, there wouldn't be much learning going on! A detention book will again make this point. They may be unpopular, but such rules are for the benefit of all who come under them.

4) There are rules to ensure that everyone is treated fairly, by employers, traders, authorities and so on. A salary slip could be produced at this point.

5) There are rules to maintain society as we want it – paying taxes and following procedures, for example, come under this heading. Continue to use the salary slip here, or bring out instructions for water usage or something similar.

These laws are good and necessary, but the law of Jesus is quite different, because it emphasises good behaviour rather than the consequences of bad behaviour. You couldn't make laws about it, let alone enforce it! In this passage Jesus mentions four rules which are part of his law of love:

1) Love your enemies – not *like* them, it should be added. Love isn't a problem

when we find someone easy to get along with, but is altogether more demanding with those we find hard-going or downright awkward. As someone said, 'It's difficult to love God, because we haven't seen him, but far harder to love our neighbour because we have!' Jesus goes further than saying we're just to put up with them – he wants us to 'go the second mile' and put ourselves out for them.

2) Treat other people as you'd want them to treat you. Few people would disagree with the sentiment, but we all find it much harder to achieve in practice.

3) Do good without expecting a return. Our society is very short on generosity of spirit, or wallet, and often people will refuse to give anything if there isn't a possible pay-back. Jesus doesn't want us to think only of what we'll get out of acting generously, but to give freely as he does, without strings attached.

4) Be merciful to other people, because in so doing we're reflecting our heavenly Father's character. Our society and culture is often brutally harsh, unforgiving of failure and cynical about success. There seems to be little place for compassion or kindness, let alone unconditional giving. As followers of Jesus we're called not to be negative or judgemental, but forgiving and accepting (though explain that this isn't the same as being a doormat or tolerating wrong), sharing God's love without adding any small print.

SECOND SUNDAY BEFORE LENT

The Common Worship lectionary makes relatively few alterations to the Revised Common Lectionary which formed its basis, and this Sunday is the only one which goes its own way, making it one of the few Sundays in Ordinary Time with a distinctive theme. Creation was the primary ASB theme in the Sundays before Christmas, but since these have been superseded it was considered important to retain this focus elsewhere, and in a quite different way to Harvest Festival. Even outside the Christian community there is great concern at the damage being done to the environment by warfare, by corporate greed, and not least by the debris from our own domestic materialism. This Sunday therefore presents a great opportunity to teach about God as our Creator and Provider in a context most people will relate to. Year A's Gospel reading from Matthew contains some wonderful natural images from the Sermon on the Mount; Year B returns us to the Prologue from John's Gospel; and in Year C we have Luke's account of Jesus calming the storm.

Hymns

TRADITIONAL

- *Angel voices, ever singing (37)*
- *Blest Creator of the light (79)*
- *Eternal Father (153)*
- *God who made the earth (235)*
- *Let us with a gladsome mind (392)*
- *Thou whose almighty word (684)*

CONTEMPORARY

- *Christ triumphant (104)*
- *Dance and sing, all the earth (139)*
- *Inspired by love and anger (325)*
- *Jesus, stand among us (361)*
- *Moses, I know you're the man (451)*
- *Seek ye first (590)*

CHANT

- *Calm me, Lord (924)*

CHILDREN'S SONG

- *There are hundreds of sparrows (890)*

Readings

Year A   Genesis 1:1-2:3; Romans 8:18-25; Matthew 6:25-34
Year B   Proverbs 8:1, 22-31; Colossians 1:15-20; John 1:1-14
Year C   Genesis 2:4b-9, 15-25; Revelation 4; Luke 8:22-25

Confession

Father God, you created heaven and earth, and saw they were very good.
We are sorry that we have ill-treated them through our lack of care.
You put your life into each of us, and appointed us as stewards of Creation.
We are sorry that we have used its resources selfishly, and disregarded the need to share them with all people.
You created a garden of peace and delight, where people could live in harmony.
We are sorry that we have pursued our own ambitions, and brought about violence and bitterness.
Yet you long to restore us to yourself.
Please forgive our lack of concern and unwillingness to change.
Help us to live as good stewards of all you have entrusted to us, through Jesus Christ our Lord. Amen.

Absolution

Almighty God,
the Creator and Redeemer of all,
have mercy on *you*,
pardon and deliver *you*
from all selfishness and sin,
make *you* worthy servants of his kingdom,
and bring *you* at last to eternal life,
through Christ our Lord. Amen.

Prayer

We offer our prayers to God,
the Creator and Sustainer of all Life,
for this world and its needs, saying:

Lord of life,
in your mercy, hear us.

Father God, you have entrusted us
with caring for a wonderful world,
rich in beauty and resources,
yet scarred by human greed.
We pray for those whose livelihood and
welfare are threatened
by the drive for financial gain . . .
and for those who challenge the *status quo*
to act more wisely and carefully . . .
Lord of life,
in your mercy, hear us.

Father God, you command us
to treat each other with respect and care.
We pray for those caught up in violence and
conflict,
or who live under the threat of ill-treatment . . .
and for the peacemakers who build bridges
across the gulf that divides one group from
another . . .
Lord of life,
in your mercy, hear us.

Father God, you command us, your people,
to live in unity and work together
for your kingdom.
We pray for places where division and dispute
have undermined the Church's calling
to be one . . .
and for those who work to overcome
the barriers of past mistrust . . .
Lord of life,
in your mercy, hear us.

Father God, you desire us
to live as members of one body.
We rejoice with those who rejoice . . .
and we share the pain of those who suffer,
through illness of body, mind or spirit . . .
Lord of life,
in your mercy, hear us.

Father God, you promise all
who live by faith in you
a place in heaven with your saints.
We remember them with gratitude, especially . . .
Lord of life,
in your mercy, hear us.
**Receive our prayers and bring us in time with
them to your eternal home, where you reign
for ever. Amen.**

All-age address

People are probably far more aware today of
their environment than ever before, although
sadly we fall far short of God's ideal in our
stewardship of it. Children are especially
conscious of ecological issues, even at a quite
early stage of their education, while most adults
can now be persuaded to visit the recycling
bins! Schools and the media keep us informed
of the many issues involved, but this does
make it harder to cover the same ground in a
distinctively Christian way. This outline takes
a different approach, from the point of view of
God's involvement in Creation.

1) 'Big Bang' theories are widely propagated
   and largely accepted as an account of the
   start of the universe, though even the
   brilliant mind of Stephen Hawking accepts
   the possibility that some force or being
   may have caused such an event to occur.
   Whatever one's personal feelings about this,
   the Christian belief is clearly that, whatever
   the mechanism, creation was entirely God's
   initiative. A useful simple illustration of this
   is a pile of Lego bricks (or equivalent) which
   only take shape as a model if someone
   applies mind and hands to ordering them –
   a volunteer to do this will emphasise the
   point.

2) The trouble with Lego models is that they're
   basically static – they can only change if the
   modeller so decides. God has given the
   world the capacity to grow and develop,
   but this still depends on him, since he's the
   source of all life. A family pet is a better
   example of this (preferably one in a cage,
   owned by a child in the congregation).
   Animals may seem to have a mind of their
   own, but they need the care of their human
   owners to survive – if you ask, most children
   will be well aware of what's necessary to
   keep a pet healthy and happy. God has
   given us free will, but we still rely on him
   as the Author and Sustainer of Life.

3) In giving us free will, God knew the potential
   downside but was willing to take the risk
   that we would go our own way. Still using
   the pet as an example, ask what would

happen if it escaped or got lost. Whatever answers you receive, no one will argue with you that it might be at great risk if it's not found quickly. You may know a personal story along these lines, or you can use Jesus' parable of the lost sheep, but bring out very clearly the idea of God saving and healing those he created. Point out, too, that in Greek the word for 'saviour' and 'healer' is the same.

4) Conclude by explaining that when God saves and heals he also restores. When the lost pet is found, it may need veterinary attention, but thereafter it will resume its place in the home. God also brings us back to where we should have been, and enables us to start off again as he intended, and as Jesus showed us how.

SUNDAY NEXT BEFORE LENT

Common Worship retains the Transfiguration of Christ as a separate festival (on 6 August), but this is in the holiday season, and the story, common to all three synoptic Gospels, has an essential place in the approach to Easter, with its foreshadowing of Jesus' Passion. The ASB placed it on the Fourth Sunday of Lent, where it conflicted with Mothering Sunday and generally had to give way. The Revised Common Lectionary includes it on the Second Sunday of Lent, with an alternative suggestion of the Sunday before Ash Wednesday, so Common Worship adopts the latter and uses it as a springboard into the themes of Lent and Passiontide. All three Gospel readings describe the Transfiguration of Jesus, not necessarily the easiest of concepts to convey to an all-age congregation, but offering the chance to open our eyes to his glory and majesty, as well as his humanity.

Hymns

TRADITIONAL

- *Christ, whose glory fills the skies (105)*
- *God of grace and God of glory (225)*
- *Rejoice! The Lord is King (580)*
- *The Lord is King! (650)*
- *Thy kingdom come, O God (691)*
- *We hail thy presence glorious (714)*

CONTEMPORARY

- *Be still, for the presence of the Lord (67)*
- *He is exalted (273)*
- *Jesus, on the mountain peak (357)*
- *Jesus shall take the highest honour (360)*
- *Majesty (436)*
- *May the fragrance of Jesus (445)*

CHANT

- *Adoramus te, Domine (921)*

CHILDREN'S SONG

- *Jesus is greater (847)*

Readings

Year A   Exodus 24:12-18; 2 Peter 1:16-21; Matthew 17:1-9

Year B   2 Kings 2:1-12; 2 Corinthians 4:3-6; Mark 9:2-9

Year C   Exodus 34:29-35; 2 Corinthians 3:12-4:2; Luke 9:28-36 (37-43)

Confession

Coming into the presence of God's glory
as we see it in Jesus Christ,
we acknowledge our own unworthiness,
saying,
Merciful Lord, forgive our sins,
and make us worthy of you.

We have heard your words of life,
yet often our own lips have failed
to declare your glory.
Merciful Lord, forgive our sins,
and make us worthy of you.

We have seen your mighty works,
yet often our own hands have failed
to do your will.
Merciful Lord, forgive our sins,
and make us worthy of you.

We have seen your acts of compassion,
yet often our own hearts have failed
to respond
to the needs of those around us.
Merciful Lord, forgive our sins,
and make us worthy of you.

We have known your glorious presence,
yet often our own lives have failed
to be transformed.
Merciful Lord, forgive our sins,
and make us worthy of you.
Accept our penitence,
cleanse us of our sin,
and strengthen us in the service
of Jesus Christ, our Lord. Amen.

Absolution

God our Father,
whose glory is revealed in his Son,
have mercy on *you,*

grant *you* pardon for all your sins,
and restore *you* to the joy of serving him
in the sure hope of eternal life,
through Christ our Lord. Amen.

Prayer

We come to ask our heavenly Father
that the glory of Jesus may be seen
in our lives and in our world.
Lord of glory,
transform our lives.

We ask you to reveal your glory in the Church,
seeking to serve you,
yet discouraged by the pressures it faces . . .
Dispel the shadows of confusion,
and unite us in your love,
that we may shine as beacons of your good news.
Lord of glory,
transform our lives.

We ask you to reveal your glory in the world,
struggling with difficult issues
and overrun with sadness and misery . . .
Dispel the shadows of violence and want,
and give us the will to share equally
the good things you have given us.
Lord of life,
transform our lives.

We ask you to reveal your glory
to victims of inhumanity,
and to those who see no escape
from pain and fear . . .
Dispel the shadows of their despair,
and help them to trust in your unfailing love.
Lord of glory,
transform our lives.

We ask you to reveal your glory
to the unwell, the unloved,
and the uncared for . . .
Dispel the shadows of illness and sadness,
and bring them the warmth
of your healing touch.
Lord of glory,
transform our lives.

We ask you to reveal your glory
in us and through us

to those we encounter day by day . . .
May our lives reflect your majesty
and display your transforming power.
Lord of glory,
**transform our lives,
for the sake of your Son, Christ our Lord.
Amen.**

All-age address

The Transfiguration is arguably one of the most difficult accounts in the Gospels to get to grips with, let alone convey to an all-age congregation. Even the three disciples present showed some confusion in their reactions, Peter to the fore as ever! This outline address puts the emphasis on recognising Jesus as both human and divine, and how both could be present in the same person. By way of preparation you'll need to find a few magazine pictures of well-known people (sports or TV stars, perhaps) in unfamiliar situations or guises, and, if you or others are willing, some 'before and after' photos, showing the difference made by longer or shorter hair, a beard, or contrasting clothes styles. You could also take a magazine photo and 'doctor' it slightly with a moustache or beard in felt-tip pen. (It's helpful to have pictures pasted on to a piece of stiff card so that they can be manipulated more easily.)

If you've 'disguised' a well-known personality's image like this, start off by asking if anyone recognises who's underneath. It's likely someone will guess correctly fairly quickly, but others may be more confused, depending on the success of your artwork! When they've been identified, point out that the person underneath is still the same, however much you've defaced their picture – the change is entirely on paper. People have tried to reinterpret Jesus in all kinds of ways, to make him fit their own image of him, but however hard they may try, they can't get rid of the real person underneath.

Next bring out a picture of a famous personality, but not as they're normally seen – perhaps one taken in an unexpected context, or doing something far removed from their popular image – and ask for guesses as to who the celebrity is. Again, demonstrate that the person is just the same; it's simply that we have to revise our view of what they're like, having seen a different side of them. Jesus never tried to live up to people's expectations of him, but simply did his heavenly Father's will. If we force him to fit our own expectations we'll be disappointed, but by accepting him on his own terms we can see him for who he really is.

Finally, bring out the family photos, showing how much the subjects have changed over a number of years. It's still the same person, but we're viewing them at different stages in their lives, wearing different clothes or hairstyles, or standing in different places. We're seeing them 'in a different light'. That's how the disciples saw Jesus on the mountain. They knew he was still their teacher and friend, but now they recognised who he really was, God's own Son, the one he'd promised to send to put the world right. Occasionally, we catch a glimpse of the majesty and glory of God as we see him in Jesus, but we can't organise or force it. Only as we follow him and open our eyes, ears and hearts to him will we be able to experience him as he really is.

LENT and HOLY WEEK

Contrary to the impression an outside observer might get today from noting our retail behaviour, Easter is far and away the most important Christian festival. Perhaps we should be glad that, apart from chocolate eggs, Easter has been ignored by the marketing executives and retained to a large degree its spiritual qualities. The tide of secularism has inevitably left misapprehensions in its wake, however. One small boy informed me that Lent was 'a time when we all have to be miserable', a remark which made sense when it emerged that his family's devotional life meant he was deprived of chocolate and sweets for six and a half weeks! Since this enforced lack of glucose had only tenuous connections with faith ('we always give it up for Lent' was the sole explanation), the poor child's comment was entirely reasonable. In the past, Easter eggs, Easter bunnies and outlandish headgear were a celebration of the end of this period of self-denial, but while fasting can certainly have a spiritual benefit, restricting observance of Lent to food and drink downgrades its spiritual value to that of a typical diet.

A more helpful emphasis is on growth and development, paralleling what is happening in nature at this time of year. Our noisy society sees little value in meditation and reflection, but time invested in them invariably pays dividends in our Christian lives. Nor should we assume that small children are unable to keep silence and enjoy stillness. They may manage it for shorter periods but their capacity for awe and wonder is often far greater than that of the average cynical adult. As our thoughts are drawn towards the cross we can see the whole of Jesus' life, ministry and Passion in the context of God's overall plan to achieve salvation for all humankind. The period from Ash Wednesday to Easter Day is taken as a whole, with individual parts looking at it from a particular perspective. We journey with Christ through to his crucifixion and burial, so that on Easter morning we can rejoice with the first disciples, with Christians in every age and place, and with the powers of heaven, at the amazing reality that Jesus is alive, and has defeated for ever the power of sin and death. The aim is to 'relive' these momentous events, just as the Jews celebrate the Passover by 'reliving' it, because in doing so they become real to us and we can experience for ourselves the love, presence and the power of the risen Christ.

ASH WEDNESDAY

It's unlikely that many churches will want to include all-age worship on Ash Wednesday itself. Its themes and symbols don't seem very child-friendly, at least on the surface, though a significant proportion of Church Schools do observe it with an act of worship, either in the school or in the local parish church. However, much of the material is equally suitable for use on the First Sunday of Lent, and the symbolism of the burned ashes is as powerful for children as for adults, though safety considerations must be borne in mind if palm crosses are to be burned as part of the liturgy. This symbolises the destruction of our sinful life and all that damages our relationship with God our Father, and reminds us that all our past 'clutter' – wrong thoughts, words and actions – has been destroyed by his purity and love. Whether or not ashes are imposed on worshippers' foreheads, the essential Ash Wednesday/ Beginning of Lent themes of repentance and forgiveness should be highlighted. This leads on to the thought of God giving us a brand-new start, which fits in well with the wider Lenten theme of spiritual growth.

Act of Penitence. The traditional and most straightforward way of including the whole congregation in a liturgical act of penitence is for each member to come forward to the minister and have the sign of the cross imposed on their forehead in ash from a bowl of previously burned palm crosses mixed with a small amount of water. (Some like to do this during the liturgy itself, but apart from the inconvenience and safety concerns, palm crosses can take a long time to burn.) An alternative is to place the bowl of ash on a small table situated centrally, and invite two members at a time to impose the ashes on each other's foreheads, using a formula such as 'Repent, and believe the good news'. This can have considerable impact, though may not be as easy for children to relate to. If imposition of ashes seems unsuitable or out of keeping, a different approach is to invite everyone present (children included) to write on a slip of paper a sin or wrong attitude for which they are seeking God's forgiveness. They then bring these up and deposit them anonymously in a suitable container (an old ceramic bowl, or even a biscuit tin covered in foil will do), which is then set light to. Since no one knows what anyone else has written, the burning of the slips is a picture of how God's forgiveness and grace obliterate all that we've done wrong. This is a powerful symbol which can be used more widely than Ash Wednesday, though the usual safety precautions must be observed.

Hymns

TRADITIONAL

- *Come down, O Love divine (114)*
- *Forgive our sins, as we forgive (180)*
- *Just as I am (374)*
- *Lord, teach us how to pray aright (418)*
- *O for a closer walk with God (483)*
- *O for a heart to praise my God (484)*

CONTEMPORARY

- *Beauty for brokenness (60)*
- *Give thanks (202)*
- *God forgave my sin (212)*
- *Have mercy on us, O Lord (269)*
- *Lord, we know that we have failed you (423)*
- *Seek ye first (590)*

CHANT

- *You are the centre (951)*

Readings

Years A, B and C   Isaiah 58:1-12
2 Corinthians 5:20b-6:10
Matthew 6:1-6,16-21 or
Joel 2:1-2, 12-17

Confession

We come before Jesus our Saviour,
acknowledging our sin
and need of his forgiveness, saying,
Create in us clean hearts, O Lord,
and renew a right spirit within us.

We confess that we have done
what is evil in your sight,

and offended you in thought, word and deed.
Our lives have been spoiled
by our rebelliousness and pride.
Only you can save and restore us.
Create in us clean hearts, O Lord,
and renew a right spirit within us.

We confess that we have not obeyed
your commands,
and have failed to witness as we should
to your saving love.
Only you can forgive and strengthen us.
Create in us clean hearts, O Lord,
and renew a right spirit within us.

We confess that as members of your kingdom
we have not upheld your standards of peace
and justice in the world.
Our eyes have been closed to the suffering
and poverty around us.
Only you can pardon and deliver us.
Create in us clean hearts, O Lord,
and renew a right spirit within us.

We confess that as members of your family
we have not considered the welfare of others,
and have failed to show your compassion
and care to those in need.
Only you can cleanse and heal us.
Create in us clean hearts, O Lord,
and renew a right spirit within us.
Wash away our iniquities
and restore us to the joy of your salvation,
for your holy name's sake. Amen.

Absolution

Almighty God,
who receives with open arms
all who turn to him in penitence and faith,
have mercy on *you*,
forgive all *your* sin,
and open *your* lips to declare the praise
of him who died for us,
Jesus Christ our Lord. Amen.

Prayer

Let us pray to our Saviour Christ,
trusting in his mercy and grace as we say,
Lord, in your mercy,
hear our prayer.

We bring to the mercy of Christ our Church,
and God's people throughout the world . . .
As your body here on earth,
help us to bear witness to your saving love.
Lord, in your mercy,
hear our prayer.

We bring to the mercy of Christ our world,
with all its need and suffering,
and those who govern the nations . . .
As citizens of your kingdom,
help us to bear witness to your caring justice.
Lord, in your mercy,
hear our prayer.

We bring to the mercy of Christ
our community, its schools and institutions,
and our friends and neighbours . . .
As part of your family
help us to bear witness to your forgiving grace.
Lord, in your mercy,
hear our prayer.

We bring to the mercy of Christ
all who are suffering through illness,
loneliness or sadness,
especially any known to us . . .
As those you have called to share your love,
help us to bear witness to your healing power.
Lord, in your mercy,
hear our prayer.

We bring to the mercy of Christ
our own lives with their joys and sorrows . . .
As those you have called
to proclaim your good news,
help us to bear witness
to your coming kingdom.
Lord, in your mercy,
hear our prayer
and graciously answer us
when we call on your name,
through Jesus Christ our Saviour. Amen.

All-age address

If there is to be any kind of penitential act during the service, it's important to keep the address simple and well focused, so that it doesn't undermine what else is happening. This is a straightforward idea that needs only a moderate amount of preparation. Take a bulb that's starting to shoot (daffodils and tulips will be most readily available) and plant it in a reasonably large pot. Don't overfill it with soil, but leave room for several garden stones to cover the surface. These should be sufficiently large for you to paint on them the name of a sin or wrong attitude, such as anger, hatred, dishonesty, unkindness – poster paints work very well for this purpose. You can relate these to what the children are familiar with, especially in a school context (for example, sexual sin will be rather more relevant to teenagers than to under-elevens). Pile these stones around the plant until it's well obscured. Then bring up volunteers to remove and read out each stone. After saying a sentence or two about each one, explain that the plant won't be able to grow properly until it's free of the stones. Similarly, we need God to deal with our sins by forgiving and removing them completely so that we can know his forgiveness, grow in our faith, and rejoice in the new life he gives us.

First Sunday of Lent

Although the whole of Lent is a penitential season, the themes of repentance and forgiveness are particularly associated with its beginning. Traditionally the First Sunday of Lent has been marked by studying the temptations of Jesus. Unfortunately, society tends to see temptation exclusively as an external source of provocation to wrong behaviour, rather than an inner struggle between right and wrong. An old classic advert exemplified this perfectly, with its slogan 'Naughty but Nice!', encouraging us to give in without delay to instant pleasure in the form of a cream bun (naughty only from a dietary viewpoint, however, as evidenced by a flier for a local slimming club I spotted recently – simply headed 'Sin and Slim'!). But today's Lectionary readings go far deeper than the cosmetic impact of unhealthy eating.

Strange though they read at first to western eyes, Jesus' temptations were clearly those common to all humankind: the temptation to look for an instant solution, the temptation to run the gauntlet of fate, and the temptation to seek instant power. The lure of temptation is often subtle, hitting us when we're most vulnerable and masquerading as 'common sense'. Satan was trying to persuade Jesus away from the mission given him by his Father, but Jesus saw through this, and countered him each time, not with a clever riposte, but by drawing on the words of Scripture and his relationship with his Father in heaven. It should be emphasised that temptation is not a sin, unless we give way to it, and that in Christ's strength we can overcome it. And when we fail, as we often will, we know that he will always be there to forgive us if we sincerely repent and turn away from wrongdoing.

Hymns

TRADITIONAL

- *Father, hear the prayer we offer (161)*
- *Forty days and forty nights (190)*
- *Jesu, lover of my soul (343)*
- *Lead us, heavenly Father, lead us (379)*
- *Lord of our life (417)*
- *O the deep, deep love of Jesus (538)*

CONTEMPORARY

- *Be still and know (66)*
- *Forty days and forty nights in Judah's desert (191)*
- *I believe in Jesus (301)*
- *Inspired by love and anger (325)*
- *O let the Son of God enfold you (506)*
- *When God almighty came to earth (733)*

CHANT

- *Wait for the Lord (949)*

CHILDREN'S SONG

- *Jesus went away to the desert (852)*

Readings

Year A   Genesis 2:15-17, 3:1-7; Romans 5:12-19; Matthew 4:1-11

Year B   Genesis 9:8-17; 1 Peter 3:18-22; Mark 1:9-15

Year C   Deuteronomy 26:1-11; Romans 10:8b-13; Luke 4:1-13

Confession

Heavenly Father,
your Son Jesus Christ was tempted like us
in every way,
but without falling into sin;
yet we have allowed the tempter to deceive us
and lead us away from you into wrongdoing.
We ask you to have mercy on us,
forgive all our faults and failings,
and grant us strength to stand firm
against the power of temptation,
through Jesus Christ our Saviour. Amen.

Absolution

Almighty God,
who knows our weakness and frailty
but loves us still,
have mercy on *you*,
grant *you* pardon for all *your* sin,
and enable *you* to overcome the evil one
as *you* remain in his love,
through Christ our Lord. Amen.

Prayer

We come with confidence to Jesus,
our great high priest,
who sympathises with our weaknesses,
and listens to our requests and concerns, saying:
Lord, receive our prayer,
and keep us in your love.

Lord, you were tempted to put your trust
in the passing things of this world,
instead of obeying your Father's calling.
We ask for your help in resisting the pressure
to increase our possessions and wealth,
and pray for those who work in business
and commerce,
that they will deal honestly and fairly . . .
Lord, receive our prayer.
and keep us in your love.

Lord, you were tempted to exchange
your eternal glory
for the temporary power of this world.
We ask for your help in resisting the pressure
to seek social standing and popularity,
and pray for those whose work gives them
influence or authority,
that they will exercise it with justice
and compassion . . .
Lord, receive our prayer,
and keep us in your love.

Lord, you were tempted to leap from the Temple
to test your Father and achieve instant success.
We ask for your help in resisting the pressure
to seek attention and gain easy acclaim,
and pray for those who live in the public eye,
especially Christian leaders and ministers . . .
Lord, receive our prayer,
and keep us in your love.

Lord, you were tempted when you felt weak
and vulnerable,
and we pray for those who through illness or
circumstances
might feel tested and tempted to give up their
faith . . .
Lord, receive our prayer,
and keep us in your love,
watching and praying,
so that we are ready to meet you,
our Judge and our Redeemer. Amen.

All-age address

Many people today (including Christians!) are unclear about the true nature of temptation, and how we might experience it in the Christian life. The secular media focus almost exclusively on sexual indiscretions, addictive or uncontrolled behaviour, extravagant lifestyles or dietary excesses. To be fair, the Church itself has often paid more attention to limited matters of personal conduct rather than wider issues of attitude and the inner life. This outline takes the temptations of Jesus and places them in a twenty-first-century context to identify some of the more subtle distractions from following the way of Christ. Although relatively little physical preparation is needed, this outline more than most benefits from careful forethought and adaptation to the local situation.

1) Start by asking the congregation who's eaten breakfast that morning (unless it's an afternoon service!). Plenty of them are likely to have given it a miss, so follow up by finding out who's feeling hungry. The sight of food may well produce a reaction so bring out a fresh loaf (if possible from a home bread maker) and some butter, and ask who feels hungry. Then produce a cream bun (or a similar luxury food item) and ask the same question. The bottom line is that the hungrier we feel, the readier we are to eat. Emphasise that cream buns and the like are not inherently sinful (though hardly beneficial to the waistline). Jesus wasn't being tempted to a poor diet, but to trade in his relationship with and obedience to his heavenly Father for the very short-term satisfaction of his hunger. Some contemporary 'feel-good factors' could be illustrated here – a holiday brochure, a catalogue of expensive clothes or household items, a menu from an exclusive restaurant . . . None of these are wrong, but they can easily take up most of our time and energy and distract us from living God's way. Jesus was no doubt famished, but he didn't allow an understandable temptation to divert him from his mission.

2) Have a piece of solo instrumental music ready to play on a CD or tape. Ask an

experienced or accomplished musician to play a few bars on their instrument (they will need briefing to bring it with them) and say you can play like that too – then switch on the prerecorded music. This may well give rise to accusations of cheating! Switching on a machine isn't exactly rocket-science, and there's no substitute for hard practice if we want to play an instrument well. Jesus was tempted to go for the 'soft', short-term option of instant acclaim and power, with the hidden cost of having to give worship to Satan. It might have spared him the pain of the cross, but at the cost of his heavenly glory. Taking the easy way out may save us effort and win us popularity, but it's no substitute for obeying God's call and growing daily in faith.

3) Dress a member of the congregation in a suitable uniform that they aren't entitled to wear – failing other alternatives use a few robes from the vestry! However impressive it may look, it's all superficial, as uniforms alone don't confer experience or authority. Underneath the dressing up is a person like us. It's easy to show off and try to convince others of how spiritual we are, but saying and doing the right things in public means little if there's no underlying spiritual reality. Jesus contrasted a religious leader of this ilk with a despised tax-collector, one having the gall to tell God how good he was, the other conscious only of his sin and unworthiness. We may not attention-seek by jumping off high buildings, but 'spiritual one-upmanship' is just as dangerous. Faith has to be for real, not to impress others.

Finish by underlining how Jesus resists temptation, not by being 'strong' but by quoting Scripture and relying on his heavenly Father. That's the only way we can recognise temptation and stand firm against it.

SECOND SUNDAY OF LENT

The Second Sunday of Lent has three rather different sets of readings for each year. In Year A we read John's well-known account of Jesus' night-time encounter with Nicodemus, raising the issue of that grossly misunderstood concept of 'being born again'; Year B's Gospel from Mark contains Jesus' warning that those who would follow him must deny themselves and take up their cross; and for Year C Luke quotes Jesus' lament over Jerusalem. All three are connected by the thread of growth in the Christian faith, though you may need to be clear for the benefit of more occasional church-goers that 'born-again' Christians aren't a different or superior breed, and dissociate Jesus' use of the phrase from insensitive and aggressive 'Bible-bashing'. Much better to emphasise its links with the overall Lent theme of spiritual growth. Common Worship assumes that the Transfiguration will have been celebrated on the Sunday before Lent, but printed lectionaries include it as the Revised Common Lectionary alternative for this Sunday, not used two weeks earlier.

Hymns

TRADITIONAL

- *All my hope on God is founded (19)*
- *In heavenly love abiding (323)*
- *Put thou thy trust in God (576)*
- *Take up thy cross (626)*
- *The God of Abraham praise (642)*
- *To God be the glory (695)*

CONTEMPORARY

- *From heaven you came (195)*
- *I am a new creation (298)*
- *I lift my eyes (312)*
- *One more step (525)*
- *Take up your cross (627)*
- *To be in your presence (694)*

CHANT

- *The Lord is my light (944)*

CHILDREN'S SONG

- *Put your trust (882)*

Readings

Year A   Genesis 12:1-4a; Romans 4:1-5, 13-17; John 3:1-17 (or Matthew 17:1-9)

Year B   Genesis 17:1-7, 15-16; Romans 4:13-25; Mark 8:31-38 (or Mark 9:2-9)

Year C   Genesis 15:1-12, 17-18; Romans 3:17-4:1; Luke 13:31-35 (or Luke 9:28-36)

Confession

We acknowledge before God
our sins and failings
and seek his pardon, saying,
Father in heaven, forgive us
and bring us to eternal life.

We confess that we have followed
our own ways,
and not walked by faith with you.
Father in heaven, forgive us
and bring us to eternal life.

We confess that we have been distracted
by this passing world,
and not sought your kingdom above all else.
Father in heaven, forgive us
and bring us to eternal life.

We confess that we have thought
more highly of ourselves than we should,
and not considered the needs of others
above our own.
Father in heaven, forgive us
and bring us to eternal life.

We confess that we have not loved you
with all our hearts,
nor our neighbours as ourselves.
Father in heaven, forgive us
and bring us to eternal life.

Absolution

Almighty God,
who forgives all who truly repent,
have mercy on *you,*

wash away *your* sins
and bring *you* to eternal life
through Jesus Christ our Lord. Amen.

Prayer

God our Father invites us to bring him
the concerns of our hearts,
promising to answer in accordance with his will.
We respond: Lord of life,
may we grow in your love.

We bring you the Church,
your body here on earth,
praying for Christians whose faith
leads them into hardship or danger . . .
May we fulfil our obligation to support them,
and may their courage and commitment
inspire our walk of faith.
Lord of life,
may we grow in your love.

We bring you the Church in our local area,
both our own congregation
and Christians of other traditions . . .
May we lay aside our differences
and work with one heart and mind
for your kingdom.
Lord of life,
may we grow in your love.

We bring you the world
in all its pain and confusion,
its violence and despair,
with its victims of conflict and greed . . .
May we count their needs above our own,
and strive for the justice and peace
of your kingdom.
Lord of life,
may we grow in your love.

We bring you our friends and loved ones,
those who are unhappy or stressed,
unwell or anxious, grieving or lonely . . .
May we uphold them in our prayers,
and bring them your comfort and healing.
Lord of life,
may we grow in your love.

We bring you ourselves,
asking for your strength and love

to help us grow in faith day by day
as we worship and serve you.
Lord of life,
may we grow in your love,
and remain faithful to our calling,
for your name's sake. Amen.

All-age address

The three Gospel readings are not directly linked, but Jesus' encounter with Nicodemus, with his famous and frequently misunderstood picture of the need to be born again in order to enter God's kingdom, connects fairly well with the command to all his disciples to take up their cross and follow him and with his weeping over the state of Jerusalem. The ideal visual aids are children at various stages of childhood: a babe in arms, a toddler, an older schoolchild and maybe a teenager, with an added bonus if they're siblings. In the unlikely event of an all-age service having insufficient children available, you could cut out suitable large pictures from glossy magazines and paste them on to card.

1) Start by asking what evidence there is that the children are alive – the likeliest answers are that they eat, make a lot of noise and grow rapidly! Most parents complain about these signs from time to time on grounds of expense and aural discomfort, but they'd be far more worried if they were missing. Growth is the key indication that something is alive, and if the children are willing you could ask them about what sort of things they eat, and what sort of things they do to ensure they become healthy adults (for example, exercise, sleep, etc). As soon as a baby is born it starts that process of growing. As Christians, when we're 'born again' and become part of God's kingdom, we start growing in faith and the evidence of that will start to be seen in our lives.

2) Throughout childhood we learn how to do many things. A baby smiles, laughs, then sits up and crawls before it can take its first step (your toddler might oblige here!). A bit later it learns to read and write, to play games and sports, and do maths (a co-operative schoolchild will help you prove

the point). Some children find it easy to do these things; others find it hard. No one's good at everything. But watch a child learning to walk – usually it's very determined and won't give up at the first couple of falls, because it wants to reach something or somewhere. When Jesus talked about taking up our cross and following him, he was referring to the same kind of determination which refuses to give up at the first setback and keeps going to the very end, just as Jesus himself did. As we commit ourselves to serving God, so we grow in our faith and spiritual lives.

3) Finally ask your volunteers what upsets them. A baby cries because it needs feeding or changing. A toddler will cry when it falls over, or can't get its own way. An older child might get upset by an incident at school, or a teenager over a broken relationship. As adults, different things upset us – the loss of a loved one, maybe, or the pressures of work and family life. Jesus wept too. One of the strongest motivating forces for good is the tears shed over evil. As Christians we can look on the world as Jesus did Jerusalem, and weep over its pain and suffering. It's a sign of increasing spiritual maturity.

Conclude by briefly pointing out that it's worrying when a baby doesn't develop and grow on the path to adulthood. Similarly, when we're born again we start on that path to spiritual maturity which is finally fulfilled when we get to heaven.

THIRD SUNDAY OF LENT

Although there are again three rather different sets of readings for this Third Sunday of Lent, they are linked by the themes of recognition and being given another chance. In Year A a Samaritan woman comes to recognise Jesus as he sits by a well and offers her the living water which will transform her whole life; Year B's Gospel is John's account of the cleansing of the Temple, the recognition of evil and corruption and the possibility of a fresh chance through Jesus sweeping it away; Year C remains with Luke, who recounts Jesus' words on the 'signs of the times', to be recognised and responded to if new possibilities are to be opened up. In the middle of Lent, having identified our own sins and shortcomings, we now recognise who Jesus is and what he's done for us, and the ways in which he offers all people another opportunity to respond to his love.

Hymns

TRADITIONAL

- *I heard the voice of Jesus say (310)*
- *Jesus, grant me this I pray (342)*
- *Jesu, the very thought of thee (368)*
- *Jesu, thou joy of loving hearts (369)*
- *Praise him, praise him! (562)*
- *Rock of ages (584)*

CONTEMPORARY

- *As the deer (45)*
- *I am a new creation (298)*
- *Jesus, Jesus, holy and anointed one (353)*
- *Let us rejoice (389)*
- *O Lord, your tenderness (515)*
- *Only by grace (528)*

CHANT

- *Within our darkest night (950)*

CHILDREN'S SONG

- *I'm accepted (830)*

Readings

Year A   Exodus 17:1-7; Romans 5:1-11; John 4:5-42

Year B   Exodus 20:1-17; 1 Corinthians 1:18-25; John 2:13-22

Year C   Isaiah 55:1-9; 1 Corinthians 10:1-13; Luke 13:1-9

Confession

In penitence and humility
we kneel before our Father, saying,
Forgive our sins, merciful Lord,
and set us free to praise you.

We are sorry for disobeying your laws
and ignoring your will.
Forgive our sins, merciful Lord,
and set us free to praise you.

We are sorry for behaving
as though you did not matter,
and not honouring your name.
Forgive our sins, merciful Lord,
and set us free to praise you.

We are sorry for living in our own strength
and not trusting you to guide and lead us.
Forgive our sins, merciful Lord,
and set us free to praise you.

We are sorry for speaking and acting unkindly,
and not demonstrating your compassion
and love.
Forgive our sins, merciful Lord,
and set us free to praise you.
Cleanse our hearts from all that is wrong,
and fill them with your joy and peace,
through Jesus Christ our Lord. Amen.

Absolution

Almighty God, the source of all grace,
pardon all *your* sins,
release *you* from the oppression of guilt
and restore *you* to wholeness of life,
through Christ our Lord. Amen.

Prayer

We approach our Lord
with our prayers and concerns,

assured of his acceptance and welcome, saying,
Open our eyes, Lord,
we want to see Jesus.

You command us to spread the good news
of your kingdom
and bring people from darkness
into your wonderful light.
We pray for Christians across the world,
that your love may shine through their lives
in acts of reconciliation, peacemaking and care,
especially . . .
Show us how to recognise and take
every opportunity to shine as lights
in the surrounding darkness.
Open our eyes, Lord,
we want to see Jesus.

You command us to pray for those in authority,
so that under their rule
everyone can live in peace and harmony.
We pray for our leaders in Parliament
and in our local councils,
that their discussions and decisions
will uphold your kingdom, especially . . .
Show us how to act
in accordance with your laws,
bringing hope and joy
instead of despair and sadness.
Open our eyes, Lord,
we want to see Jesus.

You command us to care for those in need,
whether through illness and infirmity
or anxiety and stress.
We pray for anyone known to us
who is suffering at the moment
and in need of your healing touch
on their lives, especially . . .
Show us how to minister your love to them,
bringing your comfort and the reassurance
of your eternal presence.
Open our eyes, Lord,
we want to see Jesus.

You command us to walk with you by faith,
even when the direction is unclear.
May we know your presence beside us,
and recognise your hand at work
wherever you lead us.
Open our eyes, Lord,
**we want to see Jesus, in the world,
in our lives,**

**and then one day for ever in heaven.
We ask these things in his name. Amen.**

All-age address

In this outline, the theme of recognition running through all three Gospel readings is developed. It requires a certain amount of preparation in advance, and you'll need to collect a few glossy magazines and brochures for suitable material. Alternatively you could try downloading images from the Internet, though this might not have the same level of impact. First, gather together several pictures of places or objects seen from unfamiliar angles – a competent photographer might help with this. These should be pasted on to a large sheet of card. Next, on another sheet of card, paste some pictures of well-known personalities in a different context. Celebrity magazines can be a fruitful source on occasion – a shot of the singer Madonna and her family queuing up for tickets at a tourist attraction completely flummoxed our congregation!). Finally, perhaps taking your cue from sporting quizzes on TV, think up a description of a simple activity (such as baking a cake), and omit the final punchline (putting it in the oven), instead asking 'What happened next?'

1) Ask the congregation to identify the pictures of objects or places from unfamiliar angles, giving clues if necessary to speed the proceedings up! Point out that even as Christians we don't always see things as they really are and need to recognise evil when we meet it, as Jesus did in the Temple courtyard. Having recognised it, we then have to confront it, but at the same time our eyes must be open to see the good things God is doing in the world around us.

2) Next up is the unfinished description of an activity. In all probability the endings will be guessed fairly quickly, so move on to identifying the signs of the times. There are many evidences of evil all around us, and we need to be able to recognise its longer-term consequences as well as the short-term effect. Again it's important to stress the

good which is happening around us, and how we can see God at work in it.

3) Finally the well-known-people picture board. Recognition can depend on all sorts of details, not all of which are self-evident, but at the end of the day it boils down to 'who?'. The woman at the well recognised Jesus for who he was, the promised Messiah. When we recognise God revealed in Jesus we can then see him in the world around us and in the events of our lives.

FOURTH SUNDAY OF LENT

Although Mothering Sunday is always kept on the Fourth Sunday of Lent, they are two separate occasions. The Common Worship lectionary regards it as a Special Occasion, keeping the readings for Lent 4 in the main sequence. However, the majority of churches will prefer to celebrate Mothering Sunday as all-age worship, and the resource material here assumes this as the probable option, though the main readings are included for information.

Like a number of other annual 'occasions' (St Valentine's Day, Father's Day), Mothering Sunday is seen as a good marketing opportunity for greetings cards retailers and florists (usually under the modern secularised title 'Mother's Day', disconnecting it from its spiritual and liturgical roots). Everyone is agreed that mothers are wonderful and deserve to be celebrated, but doing so meaningfully in worship is not the most straightforward of tasks. The role of motherhood in society has changed massively in recent years. Until three or four decades ago mothers tended to remain at home, caring for everyone else and performing thankless tasks like warming slippers in front of the fire! But today many mothers, even of very young children, have a full-time job as well, in order to make ends meet and provide a few desirable extras – and where they're the main breadwinner, a new role of 'househusband' has been created. Women today have very different aspirations about their careers and status, which might well have shocked some of their pre-war counterparts, and along with other factors this has radically altered the nature of family life, giving it a higher standard of living, but maybe at the expense of relationships which survive and endure.

Many churches therefore like to use Mothering Sunday to provide a wider teaching base about the family in a Christian context. The biblical norm is the extended 'household' which embraced servants and slaves as well, which hardly sits comfortably with our smaller nuclear family units. The ideal of a stable Christian family is generally accepted, but we also have to be honest about the realities of life for many folk. Two in five marriages break down; one in four children lives with a single parent; the same number again live in a 'restructured' family. And it would be naive to think that families who remain together are necessarily 'happy', or that those who don't are automatically dysfunctional. Nor should we ever lose sight of the needs of many whose experience of family is poor or painful, or even non-existent – all of them may feel this day is one best forgotten. However, that's no excuse for not celebrating families and motherhood and thanking mothers and affirming their role (not least those who do so in a dual capacity) – despite the extremists, there's little evidence that the family is a man-made prison, or that motherhood is a social evil!

Hymns

TRADITIONAL

- *For the beauty of the earth (184)*
- *Help us to help each other, Lord (275)*
- *Jesus, good above all other (350)*
- *Now thank we all our God (474)*
- *Shall we not love thee (595)*
- *Sing we of the blessed mother (605)*

CONTEMPORARY

- *Brother, sister, let me serve you (88)*
- *I come with joy to meet my Lord (304)*
- *In an age of twisted values (317)*
- *Lord, we thank you (424)*
- *Morning has broken (450)*
- *Tell his praise (630)*

CHANT

- *In the Lord I'll be ever thankful (929)*

CHILDREN'S SONG

- *He's got the whole world (819)*

Readings

For Mothering Sunday
Old Testament: Exodus 2:1-10; 1 Samuel 1:20-28
New Testament: 2 Corinthians 1:3-7; Colossians 3:12-17
Gospel: Luke 2:33-35; John 19:25-27

or

Year A   1 Samuel 16:1-13; Ephesians 5:8-14;
          John 9:1-41
Year B   Numbers 21:4-9; Ephesians 2:1-10;
          John 3:14-21
Year C   Joshua 5:9-12; 2 Corinthians 5:16-21;
          Luke 15:1-3, 11b-32

Confession

Lord God, Father of all,
we confess that we have not followed
your commandments.
We have failed to honour parents;
we have not encouraged children;
we have not submitted to one another
out of reverence for Christ.
Lord forgive and heal us, we pray,
and help us to love unconditionally
those we live with,
as you have loved us, for Jesus' sake. Amen.

Absolution

Almighty God,
who wills us all to live together in harmony,
have mercy on *you*,
forgive all *your* sins
and bind *you* together in unity and love,
for the sake of his Son, Jesus Christ our Lord.
Amen.

Prayer

We join together in thanksgiving
to our eternal Father, as we say,
Father in heaven, receive our praise,
and hear your children's prayer.

We thank you, loving Father,
for your gift of love and family life . . .
Help us to live with our loved ones
in an atmosphere of peace and joy,
where your love reigns and your will is done.
Father in heaven, receive our praise,
and hear your children's prayer.

We thank you, mighty Lord,
that your love reaches out to everyone . . .

Help those who have authority in this world
to follow the ways of peace and righteousness.
Father in heaven, receive our praise,
and hear your children's prayer.

We thank you, gracious Spirit,
that your presence is within us day by day . . .
Help us to live in your strength,
which enables us to serve as you call us.
Father in heaven, receive our praise,
and hear your children's prayer.

We thank you, caring Saviour,
that you have compassion on all who suffer
in mind or body . . .
Help us to show your care to all in need,
and draw them into your presence.
Father in heaven, receive our praise,
and hear your children's prayer.
Make us one as you are one,
and build us up as your family,
brothers and sisters in our Lord Jesus Christ.
Amen.

All-age address

Given the varied experiences of and feelings about family life present in any given congregation, it's probably easier and more desirable to talk about parents rather than focus solely on mothers. A mother will still have plenty of chores to perform when she gets in from a day's work, but fathers are also doing more around the home so it makes sense, while prioritising mothers, to pay more attention to the whole family and what makes it tick. The following outline has worked well in trials, but does require a capacity for taking risks. You'll need a normal sized football (though you might feel less anxious using a softer one!), and two or three children to kick it around – don't forget that girls like to play too! The aim is to emphasise what makes the 'family team' work effectively by comparing it to a football team.

1) *'Families join together.'* Ask two or three volunteer children to go into a clear space (the central aisle of a nave can be effective!) and then tell them to kick the ball around. This they'll do, probably very amiably and

co-operatively, but as you talk to the rest of the congregation it will soon become obvious that they have no real purpose in doing it. An effective team has a common purpose that all its members strive for. The players have come together for a reason but there's no overriding purpose or sense of direction. When families lose that, they no longer function well as a team. Every member has to play their part, and mothers often have the same role as a central midfield player – holding the whole team together! And when a new member joins they have to be integrated too.

2) *'Families work together.'* Now ask the children to set up a goal and have a competition to see who can score most. As they do this, their activity will take on a sense of direction that was missing previously. Just as a successful team has to work hard together over a long season so families have to pull together over many years, by working together at their common tasks, by each person using their own skills and abilities without jealousy of the roles of other members, and by keeping sight of the main goals. One of these is making sure the younger members are properly trained for adult life, a role for both parents to share in, but one that mothers especially will take to heart and take to themselves.

3) *'Families celebrate together.'* If you can persuade your volunteers to indulge in a 'Match of the Day'-style goal celebration, it will help make the point that families celebrate different occasions and achievements together, be it a birthday with a nought at the end or an exam passed. Today is for acknowledging all that mums do in and for their family, and the celebration should be an appropriate recognition of that, even if less dramatic or over-the-top than certain Premiership teams! But everyone is part of the team and we can't leave it all to one member – point out what happens to football teams who try to.

Conclude by emphasising the importance of the day and the importance of the family unit not only joining together as a team, but working and celebrating together too. God wants families to be effective teams, not to fall apart or fall out, though he understands and cares when they do. He also wants the Church as his family to live in the same quality of love and care that we expect from a human family, and some will take on 'motherly' roles in the church family. As we grow in God's love spiritually, so we're called to reflect that to all around us.

Fifth Sunday of Lent

By the Fifth Sunday of Lent, known as Passion Sunday, we have entered Passiontide and our thoughts are by now firmly fixed on the cross and on Christ's impending death and crucifixion. The readings all reflect this, anticipating the cross and setting it in the wider context of God's saving purposes for humankind. All the Gospel readings are from chapters 11 and 12 of John's Gospel, and just as the disciples needed to understand that Jesus' passion and death were part of God's overall purpose, despite appearances to the contrary, no less do twenty-first-century Christians need to take in the reality of his final victory over sin and death, and allow this to transform their thinking and their journey of faith. On Passion Sunday we start to make that final journey with Jesus ourselves, as we relive the events of 2000 years ago which still resonate more powerfully than anything else in history.

Hymns

TRADITIONAL

- *Hail, thou once despisèd Jesus (258)*
- *I will sing the wondrous story (337)*
- *Once, only once, and once for all (522)*
- *Praise to the holiest (572)*
- *There's a wideness in God's mercy (662)*
- *We sing the praise of him who died (723)*

CONTEMPORARY

- *Come and see (109)*
- *Dear Christ, uplifted from the earth (142)*
- *Father, we love you (167)*
- *I am the Bread of Life (299)*
- *My Lord, what love is this (462)*
- *Open our eyes, Lord (532)*

CHANT

- *You are the centre (951)*

CHILDREN'S SONG

- *Step by step (885)*

Readings

Year A   Ezekiel 37:1-14; Romans 8:6-11; John 11:1-45

Year B   Jeremiah 31:31-34; Hebrews 5:5-10; John 12:20-33

Year C   Isaiah 43:16-21; Philippians 3:4b-14; John 12:1-8

Confession

Almighty God, King of all,
we come into your presence
recognising that we have fallen short
of your standards
and are not worthy to stand before you.
We confess the wrong we have done
and the good we have failed to do,
and ask your forgiveness.
Have mercy on us
and by your Spirit make us dead to sin
but alive to you,
in Jesus Christ our Lord. Amen.

Absolution

God our merciful Father,
the source of all life and love,
pardon and deliver you from all your sins,
fill you with his Spirit,
and grant you the blessings of eternal life,
through Jesus Christ our Saviour. Amen.

Prayer

Father God, Creator and Redeemer of the world,
as we offer you our prayers now,
we ask that the seeds of your love
may bear fruit in us.
Lord, transform our lives,
and help us live for you.

You call your people to witness together
to your saving love and power.
We pray for Christians involved in ecumenical
or evangelistic work,
or who are training for public ministry . . .
As we show the new life you give
in word and action,
and obey your great commission,
Lord, transform our lives,
and help us live for you.

You call your people to work together
to bring your light to the world's dark places.

We pray for Christians involved in political
and social action,
or working in high echelons
of business and commerce . . .
As we follow in your footsteps,
and share your compassion with the needy,
Lord, transform our lives,
and help us live for you.

You call your people to join together to share
joys and sorrows,
and care for one another in times of need.
We pray for Christians involved in healing
and caring,
or who rely on others for these ministries . . .
As we put your compassion into practice,
and act as channels for your healing and love,
Lord, transform our lives,
and help us live for you.

You call your people to deny themselves,
to take up their cross and follow you . . .
As we walk the way of the Cross
without counting the cost,
Lord, transform our lives,
**and help us live,
to your eternal praise and glory. Amen.**

All-age address

All three Gospel readings cover the same kind
of ground, which is hardly surprising since
John ordered his material in that way. It isn't
so much a question of there being life after
death, but more of new life springing from
death. The seed which has to die before the
wheat can grow is the most famous example of
this, and the jar of perfume also had to finish
its role as a container before its contents could
be used. The story of Lazarus is more than a
mere picture of what will soon happen to
Jesus, more even than a demonstration of his
power. Its centre is Martha's understanding of
eternal life. She believes that Jesus could have
healed her brother, and even that God will
hear his prayer for Lazarus to be restored to
life, but Jesus took her beyond that, to understand that he himself is the resurrection and
the life. There are many ideas around about
life after death, some stranger than others, and
these are fuelled by media fascination with the
subject. It's therefore very important to convey
the Christian belief that eternal life comes

through Jesus' death, and by 'dying' to our
former self-centred life. There are many potentially effective illustrations of this, most of
which have considerably more impact than
words:

1) Display a piece of fruit, and point out how
   beautiful it looks in terms of colour, smell
   and texture – even better when you see a tree
   or bush laden with them. It doesn't matter
   what fruit you choose provided you also
   have a drink made from it – for example,
   orange juice made from oranges, wine made
   from grapes. The point is that no benefit is
   gained from the fruit unless it's consumed
   in one way or another, however pleasing
   its appearance. The fruit has to 'die' in that
   form to be used either as food or drink.

2) Take an egg and extol the virtues of its
   appearance and shape, taste and goodness.
   Again this is interesting but useless, unless
   the egg is broken. However much protein
   it may contain, it can only be released by
   breaking the shell and destroying what
   was there before so that the contents can be
   scrambled, fried or put into a cake mixture.
   Although it's been broken the egg now has
   a far more useful life than when it was
   stuck inside the shell.

3) Finally bring out a packet of seeds. If you
   can obtain a specimen of the fully grown
   plant so much the better, because it's easy
   enough to show that the seed no longer
   exists. If it did, there'd be no growth and
   no plant, and it would end up as food for
   birds. The new life which exists in potential
   within that seed has to be released in the
   right conditions.

There's no resurrection without the crucifixion
coming first. Jesus' death, which he endured
through his obedience to his Father, released
in him, and therefore in us, eternal life.
Similarly we have to be prepared to give up
our old way of living and share in Jesus' resurrection life so that the potential for eternal life
within each of us is released. Only then do we
realise how much better is the existence for
which God created us, and that eternal life
isn't 'pie in the sky when we die' but something to start enjoying here and now.

PALM SUNDAY

For most people Palm Sunday marks the start of the Easter season, at least in practical terms, as schools break up, holiday plans are made and extra food purchased. In liturgical terms, while Easter Day itself is still seven days away, the activities and events of Holy Week have to lead up to the great climax of Easter morning and also set it in the wider context of God's saving purposes for humankind. Occasional churchgoers may well understand it more as a dramatic twist in the tail, a totally unexpected 'happy ending', than as the culmination of all that God had been accomplishing in and through his Son (indeed, throughout the history of his dealings with his people).

A procession marking Jesus' triumphal entry into Jerusalem has always been part of the Palm Sunday tradition, and if circumstances permit this can be an excellent opportunity for the Christian community to witness more widely to its faith. Many churches, at least in urban areas, can gain access to a suitable local venue, from which the procession can make its way to the main worship centre, although the distance should not be excessive, and more elderly or less mobile members of the congregation allowed to go straight to the destination venue (or offered a lift). A nearby school is sometimes a possible start point, and using this may help build links with the wider community, though a hall or other public place will work as well. Better still, why not co-operate with a local church of another Christian tradition and move from one building to the other? Failing all else the procession can simply circumnavigate the building, though this is unlikely to have as wide an impact.

If you are planning a procession, remember to arrange a wet-weather alternative, as March and April aren't always the most clement months, and if a busy road is to be crossed the police need to be informed – they are usually pleased to help if they can, and will generally offer a crossing patrol. Musical facilities may well be limited at the starting venue, and if there's to be singing en route, an instrumental group should be placed somewhere in the middle of the procession – though beyond a certain length it will be near impossible to keep everyone singing together. Palm branches to wave are very effective, and uniformed organisations often enjoy walking with their flags and banners, though give them plenty of notice as they will need to get written permission for young people to take part.

Palm Sunday is marked by the great contrast between the excited crowds who welcomed Jesus as he entered Jerusalem, and the baying mob who howled just a few days later for him to be crucified. Common Worship retains the tradition of two Gospel readings, one for each venue (or before and after the procession). *Lent, Holy Week and Easter* contains dramatised versions of each Evangelist's Passion narrative, and in many churches this replaces the sermon. There are considerations of audibility, and where the dramatised reading isn't possible (or even as an addition to it) an alternative address outline is included. Whatever kind of service is held on Palm Sunday, it will be the springboard for the rest of Holy Week and enable those who worship to enter into that journey through the pain and suffering which bursts into glorious new life on Easter morning.

Hymns

TRADITIONAL

- *All glory, laud and honour (14)*
- *A man there lived in Galilee (28)*
- *My song is love unknown (463)*
- *O dearest Lord, thy sacred head (482)*
- *Ride on, ride on in majesty (583)*
- *When I survey (738)*

CONTEMPORARY

- *From heaven you came (195)*
- *Hosanna, hosanna (290)*
- *I will enter his gates (336)*
- *Make way, make way (438)*
- *Meekness and majesty (448)*
- *You are the king of glory (762)*

CHANT

- *Stay with me (942)*

CHILDREN'S SONG

- *We have a king (905)*

Readings

Years A, B and C   Isaiah 50:4-9a
                            Philippians 2:5-11
Year A   Matthew 21:1-11; Matthew 26:14-27:66
Year B   Mark 11:1-11 or John 12:12-16;
                Mark 14:1-15:47
Year C   Luke 19:28-40; Luke 22:14-23:56

Confession

We kneel in penitence before the King of kings
to seek his forgiveness, saying,
Merciful Lord,
forgive us and cleanse us.

Sometimes we sing your praise,
but often our lips will not own you.
Merciful Lord,
forgive us and cleanse us.

Sometimes we bow to you as Lord,
but often our hands will not do your will.
Merciful Lord,
forgive us and cleanse us.

Sometimes we welcome you gladly,
but often our hearts will not find a place for you.
Merciful Lord,
forgive us and cleanse us.

Sometimes we hail you as King,
but often our lives show little evidence
of your reign.
Merciful Lord,
forgive us and cleanse us,
bring us back to the Cross
and fill us anew with your great love,
for the sake of your holy name. Amen.

Absolution

God, our heavenly Father,
have mercy on *you*,
grant *you* pardon from all *your* sin,
peace in *your* hearts
and assurance of his eternal love,
through Jesus Christ our Lord. Amen.

Prayer

We stand in the presence of Jesus our King
and ask his blessing on the world, saying,

King Jesus, we welcome you,
come and reign among us.

We ask you to bless this world
which you created,
and invade with your peace
the places where hatred and violence rule,
where lives are scarred with fear and misery . . .
King Jesus, we welcome you,
come and reign among us.

We ask you to bless this community,
and bring the joy of your salvation
to those whose lives are filled
with darkness and despair,
who feel rejected or exploited . . .
King Jesus, we welcome you,
come and reign among us.

We ask you to bless your worldwide Church,
and fill with your power
all who worship and serve you,
who show your compassion
and bring peace and relief in your name . . .
King Jesus, we welcome you,
come and reign among us.

We ask you to bless our homes and loved ones,
and reassure us of your presence
as we share our lives . . .
King Jesus, we welcome you,
come and reign among us.

We ask you to bless anyone who is suffering
or in distress,
to heal them in body, mind and spirit,
and strengthen their confidence in you . . .
King Jesus, we welcome you,
come and reign among us,
fill our lives with your joy
and our hearts with your love
as we cry 'Hosanna in the highest!'
to our Saviour Jesus Christ. Amen.

All-age address

The primary reason why Jesus was rejected
and executed by the authorities was that he
didn't conform to their expectations about the
promised Messiah. Instead of associating with
the *status quo* and upholding tradition, he

mixed with the poor and needy, and challenged the whole basis of established religion. If you're looking for an alternative to the dramatised Passion Gospel, the following idea is very effective at conveying the ways in which Jesus confounded expectations and stood against religious hypocrisy and self-righteousness. In effect, it's a tableau and will need thorough preparation and probably rehearsal for those participating. The main figure is a king who changes through the address, with the support of a number of other characters. There's no dialogue, so you'll need to keep the narrative moving so that the participants know when to do their bit.

1) At the outset the king should be regally attired – in purple cloak, crown, and anything else you can find which looks royal! He needs a retinue of servants, a cheering 'crowd' as he enters, and suitable props to suggest that a palace might be his usual residence. Explain that this is a proper king, powerful and revered, feared by his subjects and enemies alike, who dresses the part and lives in the appropriate style. If you can find a couple of trumpeters to provide a fanfare (or persuade the organist!) it will add to the effect. This is what we all think royalty should be like. But although Jesus was a king, he was a very unexpected one. He didn't live in a palace (pause for a moment while the trappings of palatial grandeur are removed); he didn't wear expensive clothes or accessories (remove the cloak, crown and any other royal touches); he didn't have servants to run round after him (at this point they leave); he didn't have much to do with the aristocracy (they too leave); in fact, he lived like the ordinary folk and at first glance you wouldn't know there was anything different about him. He was a completely unexpected king.

2) The trouble was that people were looking for a king who'd look impressive, who'd lead their army and fight for independence – the government could do without a troublemaker who'd been born into an ordinary family, had no money, got his support from the lower classes, and fought against corruption and evil. So they wouldn't have anything to do with him and tried to find ways to get rid of him (bring the retinue back, looking as though they're discussing and plotting how to cause his downfall). Ordinary people still flocked to hear his teaching (get them to crowd round him), much to the disgust of the hierarchy (who can look suitably disgusted at this point). Because he was an unexpected king, he became a rejected king.

3) He wasn't just rejected. Because he was a threat some people wanted him dead, and eventually they found a way to get him arrested, by bribing one of his friends (this can be mimed). He was tried (stand the king before a mock judge), and sentenced to death, before anyone realised what was happening (again this is easily staged). So he died like a criminal, and everyone thought that was the end. But it wasn't. When this king died he fought the battle himself, against evil and death, on behalf of everyone; and because he loved his people enough to do this, his Father raised him to life three days later. Now he still reigns in the hearts of those who accept him as king, and is Lord of the whole universe – greater than any monarch who lives in a palace, surrounded by wealth. He's the exalted king, before whom all other kings must bow.

MAUNDY THURSDAY

Maundy Thursday is not usually considered as all-age worship territory. There are practical reasons for this, but the rapidly increasing trend towards children being prepared to receive Communion long before they're confirmed has also given rise to the need for ongoing teaching about the sacraments and their significance. Maundy Thursday's worship is centred around thanksgiving for Holy Communion, and if children are not able to receive the bread and wine in your church it will be necessary for some other arrangement to be made, or at least an explanation given, so that they don't feel excluded. (Please note that children who are allowed to receive the elements in their own church may receive them anywhere.)

Restrictions invite children to ask 'Why?', and barriers to their understanding will be erected if the reasons given don't satisfy them. Children have many questions about the Eucharist, and it's more important to tackle these than dwell on the 'qualifications' for receiving the sacrament. What's the relevance today of these events 2000 years ago; why bread and wine; why can only a priest consecrate them; why does he wear vestments (where that's the tradition)? Different traditions will give slightly varying answers to these, but all Christians share the same belief about the significance of the sacraments, which only makes more scandalous the barriers born of past disputes about this.

The material offered here aims to help in the process of increasing awareness and could be used on other occasions when the church is offering thanks and praise for this central part of its worshipping life. Some churches follow the traditions of the foot-washing, the stripping of the altar and the Maundy Watch, all of which are highly visual and can involve children actively – they have a profound effect on most adults, too. There's also the possibility of preceding this service with a passover meal, or a fellowship supper, to emphasise its context. Although these normally take place in the evening, which would limit the number of young children present, if there's a sufficiently wide age-range the opportunities engendered fully justify adopting an all-age worship approach.

Hymns

TRADITIONAL

- *And now, O Father, mindful of the love (34)*
- *An upper room (38)*
- *At the Lamb's high feast (53)*
- *My God, and is thy table spread (456)*
- *O thou, who at thy Eucharist (540)*
- *We hail thy presence glorious (714)*

CONTEMPORARY

- *A new commandment (35)*
- *Among us and before us (30)*
- *Broken for me, broken for you (87)*
- *Gifts of bread and wine (200)*
- *Here is bread (277)*
- *Jesus took a piece of bread (366)*

CHANT

- *Eat this bread (926)*

CHILDREN'S SONG

- *In the upper room (835)*

Readings

Years A, B and C   Exodus 12:1-4 (5-10), 11-14;
1 Corinthians 11:23-26;
John 13:1-17, 31b-35

Confession

God our Father, your Son Jesus Christ came,
not to be served but to serve,
and to give his life as a ransom for many.
We are sorry for acting out of self-interest,
and failing to walk his way of sacrifice
and service.
Forgive our selfish attitudes,
and deliver us from narrow prejudice,
that we may follow the example of our Saviour,
and live to your praise and glory. Amen.

Absolution

Almighty God,
whose love is everlasting,
have mercy on *you*,
pardon and deliver *you*
from *your* sins and failings,
and give *you* the humility and strength
to follow the way of the Servant King,
through Christ our Lord. Amen.

Prayer

We bring to God our sacrifice
of praise and thanksgiving
and offer our requests to him, saying,
Lord, accept our praise,
and receive our prayers.

We thank you for the gift of creation,
reflecting your nature,
and for making us stewards of its resources.
In gratitude may we treat it wisely
and with care.
Especially we pray . . .
Lord, accept our praise,
and receive our prayers.

We thank you for the gift of your Son Jesus,
who lived as one of us
and gave his life for our sake.
In gratitude may we share his love
with all whom we meet.
Especially we pray . . .
Lord, accept our praise,
and receive our prayers.

We thank you for the gift of forgiveness,
freely available through Jesus' death
on the cross.
In gratitude may we live as those
whose guilt has been taken away
and extend your saving love
to those around us.
Especially we pray . . .
Lord, accept our praise,
and receive our prayers.

We thank you for the gift of new life,
ours because Jesus was raised from death,
victorious over all the forces of evil.

In gratitude may we witness
to the hope of eternal life you set before us.
Especially we pray . . .
Lord, accept our praise,
and receive our prayers.

We thank you for the gift of bread and wine,
the symbols of your complete salvation
and unending love for us.
In gratitude may we remember
your death and resurrection
until you return in glory,
and be strengthened to follow and serve you.
Lord, accept our praise,
and receive our prayers,
for the sake of the one whose death
opens the gates of eternal life,
Jesus Christ our Saviour. Amen.

All-age address

Begin by asking the congregation what events they would mark by having a special meal. You may find it helpful to write these up on an OHP or flip-chart. Birthdays and Christmas will probably head your list, followed closely by anniversaries, christenings, housewarmings, reunions or notable achievements. Usually we celebrate something that's happened already which we want to remember. Most people enjoy a good party or celebration, but it would be considered very odd if we wanted to make merry on our own! We invite special friends for the occasion, and prepare the sort of food we wouldn't normally eat. If you can find a couple of volunteers (this may be best organised in advance!) they can illustrate the point by sitting at a table, on which you place Christmas crackers, then a wrapped present, followed in turn by a bottle of champagne, an old photograph, party hats and finally a cake (if you don't want to use a real cake, a local bakery may let you borrow a 'dummy' used for sales purposes).

Explain that the Jews always remembered the Passover in a special meal, as God had commanded them. It was shared by the whole family, and acted out as a way of making sure no one forgot the most important event in Israel's history. In a way, we do the same – a couple celebrating their anniversary are reliving the day they got married, for example, or when they first met, and entering into the emotions and excitement they felt then. The evening before his death Jesus celebrated the Passover with his friends, the disciples, and during the meal he drew some obvious parallels between that event and what was about to happen to him. He instructed them to carry on with this way of remembering him after his death, resurrection and ascension, so Christians have done this ever since.

Conclude by saying that Jesus invites all of us to this special meal to celebrate what he's done for us, and because he wants us to experience the reality of it ourselves. As we take the bread and wine, just as Jesus and the disciples did to remember God's great act of releasing them from slavery in Egypt, so we enter into the events of his death and resurrection and they become real to us. We know the bread and wine are symbols of his body and blood, but as we take and eat them we too can experience the presence of Christ, and share more deeply in his risen life.

GOOD FRIDAY

Although legally still recognised as a Public Holiday, Good Friday has largely become indistinguishable from any other Friday. Shops open, many employees have little choice about working, and the media barely notice it. Ironically, Easter Day is now the only day when trading is prohibited! Sadly the connection between the two is barely recognised in most communities, though logic alone dictates that the resurrection could not have taken place without the crucifixion. But this is the heartland of the Christian faith, and Easter is its principal Feast. The celebration of Palm Sunday leads on to Good Friday as its inevitable culmination and the whole congregation should be involved in this.

Many churches are now finding ways to integrate the traditional observance of the 'Three Hours' Devotion' with worship suitable for all age-groups, essential if younger members are to develop an appreciation of its importance. Young people's leaders sometimes offer a Good Friday 'workshop' of activities which are part of the whole church's observance, and even if the full three hours is rigorously kept, some time should be devoted to worship which encompasses all ages and groups. Our church has tried various patterns, and one that works well is to offer more devotional worship for adults while the children have their own activities for a couple of hours, and then to conclude the occasion with an all-age service centred around various symbols of Jesus' Passion and the events of Holy Week. We also prepare collages made up of newspaper and magazine pictures and headlines relating to suffering and crucifixion, which aim to earth the teaching in contemporary events and issues. All of this needs careful preparation, but is well worth the effort.

It may seem regrettable that a supposedly Christian people can be so ill-informed about and disinterested in the events which shaped our faith, but Good Friday is not about rectifying the information gap. On the Cross Jesus confronted and defeated for ever the evil which has so damaged the world. His final cry, 'It is finished!' referred not to his life, but to the mission he had come to fulfil in obedience to his heavenly Father. As the Church celebrates Easter it shares in the victory of Jesus over sin and death, and its worship is directed at enabling everyone present to know that as their own experience.

Hymns

TRADITIONAL
- *In the cross of Christ I glory (327)*
- *It is a thing most wonderful (333)*
- *On a hill far away (520)*
- *O sacred head, surrounded (535)*
- *There is a green hill (657)*
- *The royal banners forward go (663)*

CONTEMPORARY
- *A purple robe (39)*
- *I do not know the man (306)*
- *Mary, blessed grieving mother (441)*
- *My Lord, what love is this (462)*
- *There is a Redeemer (658)*
- *Were you there (721)*

CHANT
- *Jesus, remember me (931)*

CHILDREN'S SONG
- *Lord, you've promised (864)*

Readings

Years A, B and C   Isaiah 52:13-53:12; Hebrews 10:16-25 or 4:14-16, 5:7-9; John 18:1-19:42

Confession

Lord Jesus,
though we claim to be your friends
we have often let you down.
We confess that we have turned away
from your suffering,
kept silent when you are mocked and ill-treated,
and pretended we do not know you.
Forgive us and help us, we pray,

and in your mercy
bring us the joy of your salvation,
through Jesus Christ our Lord. Amen.

Absolution

May God our Father,
whose Son Jesus Christ has won the victory
over evil and death,
have mercy on *you*,
pardon and deliver *you* from all *your* sin,
and release *you* from fear
into freedom and peace,
through Jesus Christ our Lord. Amen.

Prayer

As our Saviour lays down his life for us
on the cross,
we recognise him as the Redeemer of all, saying,
Lord, hear our prayer,
and let our cry come to you.

We thank you, Lord, that on the cross
you willingly forgave those who hated you
and condemned you to death.
Please help those who exploit others
for personal gain
to realise that only in accepting your love
will they find true satisfaction.
Especially we pray for . . .
Lord, hear our prayer,
and let our cry come to you.

We thank you, Lord, that on the cross
you showed compassion and care.
Please help those who seek to share your love
with the needy, lonely and suffering,
wherever they are in the world,
and give them strength and encouragement
in their service.
Especially we pray for . . .
Lord, hear our prayer,
and let our cry come to you.

We thank you, Lord, that on the cross
you showed mercy and forgiveness
to the penitent thief
who recognised you as King.
Please help those who feel rejected
or unworthy of your love

to know that you accept them as they are
and give them true peace.
Especially we pray for . . .
Lord, hear our prayer,
and let our cry come to you.

We thank you, Lord, that on the cross
you obeyed your Father even to death.
Please help us who follow in your footsteps
to demonstrate in our lives
your willing obedience and selfless love.
Especially we pray for . . .
Lord, hear our prayer,
and let our cry come to you.
As you have loved us,
so may we love one another,
that all people will know we are your disciples
and be drawn to you as Saviour and King.
In your name we ask this. Amen.

All-age address

The basis of this address comes from *For All the Family* (Kingsway, 1984), a pioneering book of ideas for all-age talks. Beforehand take either an acetate sheet for an OHP or a large square piece of card, and on it draw a cross, with the lengths of both lines equal. To begin, hold this up and slowly rotate it through 45 degrees, asking as you do so what this symbol might mean. Four answers are likely to emerge.

1) In mathematics it's either an addition sign, or, if turned round, a multiplication sign, both of which indicate an increase in value. Emphasise that God doesn't regard us as valueless, but that without him our lives can't be as fulfilled or purposeful, because he created us for himself. Jesus said he came so that we might 'have life in all its fullness'. When we respond to his love, accept his forgiveness and follow his ways, we find the Cross gives our lives a new 'value' – eternal life.

2) A cross is also used by teachers to indicate when a question's been answered wrongly. A card with a simple miscalculation marked as wrong will help make the point more effectively. No one likes to get things wrong, but we need to be told, so that we

can learn how to put it right next time. The cross tells us we've got something wrong – unkind words, selfish actions, unpleasant thoughts. On our own we haven't got a hope of doing anything about it. We'd much prefer not to admit we're wrong and need help, but nothing will change unless we do. The cross does far more than tell us we're wrong. Because Jesus was the only person who did get it right, God accepts us through him, just as we are, forgives us for all we've done wrong, and gives us strength to live for him from then on.

3) Another use of the cross symbol is at the end of a letter or on a Valentine's card. We might write, 'I love you. xxxxx' – here you could display the inside of a card with a couple of red hearts and a suitable inscription. The cross is a sign of Jesus' great love for us, too. There's nothing he would stop at to bring us back to himself, even death as a criminal. When someone says they love us, we want to see some evidence that they mean it (you could produce a box of chocolates or a bunch of flowers). God didn't just *say* he loves us – the cross proves it beyond doubt.

4) Finally display on a card a red triangle with a cross inside. Someone may already have mentioned its use to mark a crossroads. When we come to one, we know we have to make a decision about which way to go, and if we're not sure we consult an atlas. The cross of Jesus forces us into deciding which way we're going in our lives. We can choose to go our own way or to follow him. He doesn't force us because he wants us to make our own minds up, but when we see his cross we're faced with a decision we can't avoid.

EASTER to PENTECOST

Six and a half weeks after Ash Wednesday we arrive at Easter Day, the single most important feast of the Church's year – and for those who gave up some food or drink for that time, it no doubt feels like a feast! Joanne Harris' entertaining and thought-provoking novel *Chocolat* (Black Swan, 1999) contrasts the negative, life-denying, controlling behaviour of the local church with the joyous, colourful, chocolate-flavoured festival inaugurated by the main character, Vianne. Sadly the Church has often given this kind of impression, but with no justification. Our celebration of Easter is far more than an affirmation of the life we enjoy here, important though that is. We can be affirmative of it because in Christ's death and resurrection we have the promise of a new life, eternal life which starts here on earth, and continues in heaven when we die. Surely of all people we should be celebrating most extravagantly and vibrantly the good news that Jesus is alive! Our own church enjoys a splendid cooked breakfast between our two Easter morning Eucharists – and a small choco-fest after the second one! But that's only part of the story. Our worship should also be radiant and full of joy – if possible sending worshippers out as glowing and excited as Jesus' followers that day. And not just for one day, either. Eastertide is as long as Lent, and that celebratory atmosphere should pervade the whole period up to Pentecost, which is both the culmination and logical conclusion of Easter and Ascensiontide. It's also the beginning, both of the Christian Church, and of our own walk of faith as the Holy Spirit comes into our hearts and lives.

EASTER DAY

Forty-seven days after Ash Wednesday we arrive at the greatest day in the Christian year! The forty days of Lent finish on Palm Sunday, but these lead straight into Holy Week and Jesus' trial, crucifixion and burial. Then suddenly the darkness and sorrow of the Passion are swept away by the light and joy of Easter. For the Early Church, however, it wasn't just an amazing and unexpected happy ending. Those first Christians realised that the resurrection was God's total vindication of his Son's obedience and achievement – the final, clinching part of his plan to save humankind. It was the fulfilment of all that the Old Testament had foreshadowed, the culmination of Jesus' entire life and ministry.

Everyone enjoys Easter with its springtime emphasis on new life appearing after the 'death' of winter. Schools are busy with Easter bunnies and chickens, and shops are full of chocolate eggs. All of this is enjoyable and worth celebrating, but it can also be a major distraction from the Christian message of Easter. The resurrection wasn't just a happy ending to what would otherwise have been a tragic ending to a noble story. Its significance certainly wasn't lost on the disciples, or the other apostles of the earliest Church, for whom it was the key belief, the validation of their faith – from Peter's sermon on the Day of Pentecost onwards it was the bedrock of their teaching. Without the resurrection there wouldn't be a Christian faith at all!

The joy and celebration must be tempered by sensitivity to those for whom this is a time of unhappy memories or distressing circumstances, but the resurrection speaks equally to them, because the light of the risen Christ penetrates even the darkest situation. We can't deny the world is full of suffering and hurt, but the resurrection helps us challenge the cynicism and hopelessness all around with the news of Jesus' final victory over all the forces of evil and death. There's no need to apologise for being joyful!

Common Worship gives readings for the Easter Vigil, if this is kept, and for a main eucharistic service later on Easter Day, as well as a principal (morning) service. Since most churches make this a Eucharist, the Gospel reading is assumed, but two additional readings are encouraged, with the possibility of a reading from Acts either as an alternative to the Old Testament, or as the New Testament reading in place of one from an epistle. The material outlined here could be used at any time on Easter Day.

Hymns

TRADITIONAL

- *A brighter dawn is breaking (3)*
- *Alleluia, alleluia (9)*
- *Jesus Christ is risen today (348)*
- *Now the green blade rises (475)*
- *The day of resurrection (637)*
- *Thine be the glory (672)*

CONTEMPORARY

- *Alleluia, alleluia, give thanks (8)*
- *All heaven declares (17)*
- *From the very depths of darkness (198)*
- *I danced in the morning (305)*
- *Led like a lamb (380)*
- *We will lay our burden down (726)*

CHANT

- *Surrexit Christus (943)*

CHILDREN'S SONG

- *All in an Easter garden (768)*

Readings

Year A   Jeremiah 31:1-6*; Colossians 3:1-4*; John 20:1-18 (or Matthew 28:1-10)

Year B   Isaiah 25:6-9*; 1 Corinthians 15:1-11*; John 20:1-18 (or Mark 16:1-8)

Year C   Isaiah 65:17-25*; 1 Corinthians 15:19-26*; John 20:1-18 (or Luke 24:1-12)

* Acts 10:34-43 may be used as an alternative to one of these

Confession

Living Lord, conqueror of evil and death, we confess to you our sins and failings.

Our faith has been clouded by doubt,
our witness weakened by fear,
our service diminished
by lack of commitment to you.
We are truly sorry, and ask you to forgive us.
Help us to trust the power of your risen life
and set our minds on the things
which last for ever,
that our lips may declare
the truth of your resurrection,
and our lives show forth its glorious light,
for your name's sake. Amen.

Absolution

Almighty God our Father,
who raised his Son from death to life in triumph,
have mercy on *you*,
forgive all *your* wrongdoing
and raise *you* from the death of sin
to the joy of eternal life,
through the same Jesus Christ our Lord. Amen.

Prayer

Knowing the presence of Jesus with us,
we bring him our prayers and concerns, saying:
Risen Master,
live in our hearts for ever.

Jesus, our risen Lord, we pray for the world,
which you died to save,
asking you to transform its brutality and violence
with your eternal peace . . .
Equip us to be peacemakers for your kingdom.
Risen Master,
live in our hearts for ever.

Jesus, our risen Saviour,
we pray for the suffering,
who you came to heal,
asking you to transform their pain and despair
with your eternal hope . . .
Strengthen us to be faithful servants
of your kingdom.
Risen Master
live in our hearts for ever.

Jesus, our risen King,
we pray for governments and leaders,
whose authority comes from you alone,
asking you to transform their decisions
and actions
with your eternal wisdom . . .
Enable us to be wise stewards
for your kingdom.
Risen Master,
live in our hearts for ever.

Jesus, our risen Master, we pray for the Church,
who you called to be your followers,
asking you to transform our worship and service
with your eternal love . . .
Make us worthy ambassadors
for your kingdom.
Risen Master,
live in our hearts for ever.

Jesus, our risen Friend,
we pray for the sick and dying,
who you embrace with your love and care,
and ask you to transform those
troubled by doubts
with your eternal comfort and healing . . .
Help us to be compassionate friends
for your kingdom.
Risen Master,
live in our hearts for ever.

Jesus, our risen Lord, we offer you ourselves,
fallible and sinful as we are,
trusting in your mercy,
and asking you to transform our lives
with your eternal presence . . .
May your joy and peace be seen
in all we say and do.
Risen Master,
**live in our hearts today,
and until we praise you for ever in heaven.
Amen.**

All-age address 1

Most people will pay lip-service to the concept of open-mindedness, but when it comes to the crunch they are fairly choosy over what they're prepared to be open-minded about! It's one thing to be open to the possibility that the resurrection really happened, but quite another to be open to the transforming power of the risen Jesus. This address aims to encourage the congregation to move from the former to the latter.

If you have the services of someone who's good at artwork, pictures of the four scenes will help convey the points, but a few volunteers will be even more effective. You'll also need enough chocolate eggs to distribute afterwards.

1) Ask the first volunteer to go to the furthest end of the church and then say something in a fairly low voice (don't forget to switch off the microphone!). He or she probably won't hear you at first, and you'll need to repeat yourself a bit louder. The volunteer will probably have to come a lot nearer to hear you properly. All sorts of factors prevent us hearing clearly – from deafness to distance – but sometimes we don't hear properly because our minds are elsewhere. Mary Magdalene might have been like that in the garden that first Easter morning. She was the first person to see Jesus alive, but thought he must be the gardener. Her eyes were blurred with tears, but her ears were open, and as soon as she heard him speak her name she recognised him. Often we fail to hear Jesus calling us because our minds are on other things – we need to have open eyes and ears to recognise and hear him as Mary did.

2) The second volunteer has to emulate Simon Peter. Try to make sure a door is left open where most people wouldn't go, to the vestry perhaps, and then invite the person to go through and see what's on the other side. You could even leave the chocolate eggs (from section 4 below) on a table to be collected. John was a bit anxious and remained outside the tomb, but Peter, true to form, rushed straight in and saw the folded graveclothes. The open tomb was an open door. Jesus' resurrection is like an open door to new and eternal life for anyone who's prepared to go through it.

3) The third volunteer is a bit like Thomas. Before the service hide a pound coin in the most unlikely place you can think of. Ask the volunteer if they believe a coin is hidden there. Hopefully they'll say no, in which case you can 'reprimand' their lack of faith in your honesty! Thomas wasn't prepared to believe what the rest of the disciples told

him – he wanted to see Jesus alive for himself. At first he didn't have an open mind, and it was only when he experienced Jesus' risen presence for himself that he believed. We too need to have open minds, not just to the fact of the resurrection but to its reality in our lives here and now.

4) The last part needs no volunteers. Briefly recount how the disciples, fed up and worn out after a long night of unsuccessful fishing, saw Jesus by the lakeside. They had to open their hands to receive the huge catch of fish that he gave them. We have to open our hands to receive the blessings of eternal life which are ours through Jesus' resurrection. Conclude by offering the chocolate eggs to all those whose hands are open to receive them – though it might be more convenient and less distracting to delay the distribution until the end of the service!

All-age address 2

The aim of this address is similar to the previous one but focuses more on the element of belief. I took the idea from TV's favourite grumbler, Victor Meldrew (*One foot in the grave*), who frequently expostulated 'I don't believe it!' A few simple props need to be gathered beforehand – you may well find other unlikely facts or circumstances to relate. A simple illustration is a can of baked beans. Ask for guesses as to how many of these are eaten each year in Britain – I've never yet had an answer near the correct one, which is 400,000,000! When you give the answer, someone's guaranteed to say, 'I don't believe it'. I also use an eighteenth-century picture of Hereford Cathedral in its original state. Few people believe it had a spire but it did until the nineteenth century when it was blown down in a storm. Nor do many believe that the Oval cricket ground was used during the Second World War as a prisoner-of-war camp. You can use a variety of surprising facts, so long as the response is 'I don't believe it'.

When Jesus was crucified, many of his friends said, 'I don't believe it'. It didn't seem possible that all their hopes had been dashed so completely, that their Master had been killed. So on the day after the Passover festival, the women wanted to treat Jesus' body with oils and spices in the proper way. They found the stone rolled to one side and the tomb empty apart from the graveclothes, and they also said, 'I don't believe it'. An angel reassured them that Jesus was alive, exactly as he'd promised, so they rushed back to the disciples, who also said, 'I don't believe it', as did the two who were walking to Emmaus, and many others – that is, until they saw Jesus for themselves. Then they had to believe it. Finally Thomas, who'd been out when Jesus appeared to the other disciples, refused to believe what they told him until he'd seen and touched the Lord himself. Then he said, 'I do believe; you're my Lord and my God.'

Conclude by saying that many people react to the idea that Jesus is alive now, or that the resurrection really happened, by saying, 'I don't believe it!' But when they encounter the risen Jesus themselves, and experience the reality of new life in him, their lives are transformed, just like the disciples'. For two thousand years ever since the first Easter Day, people all over the world, from every different culture and tradition, have witnessed to the truth that Jesus really is alive for evermore, and wants us to share his risen life that never ends.

SECOND SUNDAY OF EASTER

The Sunday after Easter has long been known as 'Low Sunday', usually an apt description of attendances, which can dip markedly as congregations use the post-Easter break to visit relatives or take a short break. Since this is likely to include young people's leaders, all-age worship may be the most viable option. However, 'low' should not signify 'depressing'! Only a week into Eastertide the Church should still be radiant with the joy of the risen Christ, regardless of how many are left in the congregation, and there will be plenty of joyful Easter hymns left to sing. From now until Pentecost, the Common Worship lectionary gives precedence to the reading from Acts (i.e. if the Old Testament reading is used, Acts becomes the New Testament reading). On this Second Sunday of Easter the Gospel reading is common to all three years, concluding John's Resurrection Narrative with Jesus' appearance to Thomas and the other disciples.

Hymns

TRADITIONAL

- *Love's redeeming work is done (433)*
- *Low in the grave he lay (435)*
- *The Lord is risen indeed (652)*
- *The strife is o'er (667)*
- *This joyful Eastertide (680)*
- *Ye choirs of new Jerusalem (754)*

CONTEMPORARY

- *Among us and before us (30)*
- *Bless the Lord, my soul (76)*
- *Dance and sing, all the earth (139)*
- *Praise him on the trumpet (561)*
- *Shout for joy and sing (596)*
- *This is the day (676)*

CHANT

- *Confitemini Domino (925)*

CHILDREN'S SONG

- *O give thanks (870)*

Readings

Year A   Acts 2:14a, 22-32; 1 Peter 1:3-9; John 20:19-31

Year B   Acts 4:32-35; 1 John 1:1-2:2; John 20:19-31

Year C   Acts 5:27-32; Revelation 1:4-8; John 20:19-31

Confession

Risen Lord,
we confess that we have not followed
or obeyed you as we should.
We have hidden our faith
from the sight of others;
we have not trusted you with all our hearts;
and our lives have not been filled
with your peace.
Forgive us we pray,
and open our eyes to the hope of eternal life
which you promise us
through your mighty Resurrection.
Amen.

Absolution

God, who raised our Lord Jesus
from death to eternal life,
have mercy on *you*,
pardon all *your* sins and failings,
and fill *your* hearts with the power and joy
of his risen Son, Christ our Lord. Amen.

Prayer

The risen Lord comes to us
in our fear and doubt,
inviting us to leave with him our prayers
and troubles.
We respond in faith: Lord, give us your peace,
and accept our prayers.

We live in an uncertain and confused world;
creation is plundered, people are devalued,
society is dominated by fear and malice.
Lord, we pray for all whose lives are scarred
and broken . . .
By your risen presence, fill them with hope.
Lord, give them your peace,
and accept our prayers.

We live in a society of broken relationships;
sadness and loneliness are rife,
and many are suspicious and fearful.
Lord, we pray for all who feel isolated
or rejected . . .
By your risen presence, fill them with
confidence.
Lord, give them your peace,
and accept our prayers.

We live among homes and families under
pressure;
social and financial concerns create tension,
family life is fragmented and fraught.
Lord, we pray for all who feel they've lost
their grip . . .
By your risen presence, fill them with courage.
Lord, give them your peace,
and accept our prayers.

We live in a world needing to be made whole
again;
medical research has advanced knowledge,
but many long for wholeness in body and mind.
Lord, we pray for those who need healing
of any kind . . .
By your risen presence, fill them with comfort.
Lord, give them your peace,
and accept our prayers.

Our lives are full of joy and sorrow,
light and shade;
Lord, we pray that everything we do
may radiate the joy of your Resurrection.
By your risen presence, fill us with joy.
Lord, give us your peace,
**and accept our prayers, for your name's sake.
Amen.**

All-age address

Rather like the second of the Easter Day
addresses, this one focuses on the question of
what we believe. Although very simple in
approach, it needs some thought in advance,
together with a little shopping! Obtain three
tubes with various substances in, at least one
of which should be edible and one thoroughly
inedible – examples might be toothpaste, cream
cheese and instant glue, though others will
spring to mind and may be more appropriate.

Cover these with plain paper, ideally of different colours, so you know which is which! Also
buy a box of wrapped chocolates (for example,
Roses or Quality Street) and empty its contents into a cardboard box previously used to
hold something completely different. Retain
the empty box for display.

1) To start off, hold up the three tubes for
inspection, informing everyone that the
contents of only one are edible. Ask if they
believe you. A few will be cynical, a few will
be trusting, but it's likely that most will be
unsure. Now ask people why they believe
or have doubts. What will emerge is that
no one can possibly give the correct answer
unless they investigate for themselves. You
could now allow three volunteers to unwrap
the tubes and discover what they contain.
Point out that Thomas was rather like this.
He wasn't prepared just to accept what
somebody else had said about Jesus being
alive again – he wanted to prove it for himself. So Jesus allowed him to see the wounds
and realise that what he'd heard was true.
Believing what's said by someone else is all
very well, but it is no substitute for finding
out personally.

2) Now show the two boxes which at first
glance speak for themselves, unlike the
tubes. Again tell people that one contains
something edible and the other doesn't. This
time more people may take your words at
face value, though a few at least will recognise the ambiguity of that statement, and
query which box has the chocolates. You
could continue by inviting one or two to
come and dip into the second box for themselves, and eat what they find in there – this
is very effective if the box formerly contained something with a 'ugh-factor'! When
one or two have proved that there really are
chocolates in the second box, you can conclude by saying that Thomas believed what
he'd been told, unlikely as it must have
seemed at first, once he'd experienced the
risen Jesus for himself. Just as the only way
to experience the chocolates is to taste one
and enjoy it, so the only way to know the
truth of the Resurrection is to experience
the living presence of the risen Jesus in our
lives day by day.

THIRD SUNDAY OF EASTER

This week we move on to the subsequent Resurrection appearances of Jesus to his followers, with Luke's account of the Emmaus Road encounter and the appearance just before the Ascension, and John's narrative by the lakeside. All of these dwell on the disciples recognising Jesus and responding to his presence – if, in two cases, rather slowly! Believing something to be true on an academic level is one thing, and scientifically proving it to be true is another, but recognising on a personal level that it is true depends not just on acceptance or proof but also personal experience. Although there are three different Gospel readings they have the same theme, so the all-age address can be adapted to whichever one is read.

Hymns

TRADITIONAL

- *Come, risen Lord (126)*
- *Come, ye faithful, raise the anthem (131)*
- *Good Christians all, rejoice and sing (241)*
- *Jesu, thou joy of loving hearts (369)*
- *Now is eternal life (470)*
- *Praise to the Lord, the Almighty (573)*

CONTEMPORARY

- *Bread is blessed and broken (81)*
- *Christ's is the world (101)*
- *Jesus, Prince and Saviour (358)*
- *Jesus, stand among us at the meeting of our lives (361)*
- *Lamb of God, Holy One (377)*
- *One more step along the world I go (525)*

CHANT

- *O Lord, hear my prayer (938)*

CHILDREN'S SONG

- *Thank you, Lord, for this new day (887)*

Readings

Year A   Acts 2:14a, 36-41; 1 Peter 1:17-23; Luke 24:13-35

Year B   Acts 3:12-19; 1 John 3:1-7; Luke 24:36b-48

Year C   Acts 9:1-6 (7-20); Revelation 5:11-14; John 21:1-19

Confession

Living Lord Jesus,
you appeared to your followers
after your Resurrection,
yet they failed to recognise you.
We acknowledge that we too
have not always opened our eyes to see you,
nor our ears to listen to your voice.
Forgive our blindness and slowness,
and give us the vision to recognise
and welcome you with joy into our lives,
in your name. Amen.

Absolution

Almighty God,
who raised from the dead our Lord Jesus,
forgive all *your* sins
and strengthen *you* to walk with him
in joy and confidence. Amen.

Prayer

In confidence and hope
we come with our prayers
to our Saviour, saying,
Risen Master,
in your mercy hear us.

We ask you to fill us
with the truth of your Resurrection life.
May we and all your people
be bold both in word and action
to declare the good news of eternal life
to the world around.
We pray for all ministers
and Christian leaders . . .
Risen Master,
in your mercy hear us.

We ask you to fill us
with the power of your Resurrection life,
especially those Christians who are suffering
because of persecution, isolation or poverty.
We pray for all mission and aid workers
in the world's neediest
and most dangerous places . . .
Risen Master,
in your mercy hear us.

We ask you to fill us
with the peace of your Resurrection life,
especially those living in conditions of fear,
violence, exploitation or injustice.
We pray for the leaders of the nations
and all politicians and financiers . . .
Risen Master,
in your mercy hear us.

We ask you to fill us
with the wholeness of your Resurrection life,
especially those who are unwell
in body or mind.
We pray for all who endure the pain
of bereavement and loneliness,
or whose lives are darkened by anxiety
and depression . . .
Risen Master,
in your mercy hear us.

We ask you to fill us
with the joy of your Resurrection life.
May our hearts and voices be alive
with praise and rejoicing.
Risen Master,
**in your mercy hear us
and receive our thanksgiving and prayers,
for your name's sake. Amen.**

All-age address

The theme of recognition runs through all the Gospel readings for this Sunday, and highlights the fact that the disciples' belief in the Resurrection, while certainly rooted in Old Testament teaching, was primarily based on personal experience. Interestingly, they didn't invariably recognise Jesus at first, and in two cases recognition came as a result of what he did. This address repays the moderate amount of preparation needed in advance.

1) Cut out some fairly large pictures from glossy magazines of well-known celebrities (sporting or showbiz) and either 'disguise' them heavily with a thick felt-tip pen or cover the most obvious features with blank paper. Hold a few of these up and ask the congregation to identify them – the success of this will depend on the effectiveness of the 'artwork', but beware it doesn't become the most memorable bit of the service! When at least one or two have been correctly guessed, discuss the ways in which we recognise people – such as facial features, hairstyle or colour, and choice of clothes. Point out that if we haven't seen an old friend for several years, the grey hairs or increased girth can cause considerable surprise, and we may take a moment or two to realise who we're talking to. After his Resurrection Jesus had changed physically, so the disciples needed to find other ways to recognise him.

2) Prepare an audiotape of three or four well-known voices from the radio or CDs, speaking or singing, and again ask for identification. It's not so easy to define how we recognise someone by their voice, and their use of language may give away as much as timbre or pace. Some people have a quite unmistakable way of speaking, even on the telephone, and the disciples may have thought there was something familiar about the voice they could hear, though they couldn't quite put a finger on it.

3) The disciples finally knew it was Jesus from what he did – the catch of fish, the breaking of bread. They didn't have to take any notice of the apparent stranger, but when they did they realised he wasn't a stranger at all. We recognise people most of all because of our relationship with them. It's not just what they look like or how their voices sound, but more the sort of person we know they are. We may see evidence of Jesus at work in our own lives or the lives of others, or hear his voice speaking to us. When we live in relationship with him we truly realise who he is.

FOURTH SUNDAY OF EASTER

At this point in Eastertide the Common Worship lectionary moves away from the Resurrection narratives and into John's Gospel for a few weeks. For the Fourth Sunday of Easter John 10 is divided between the three years, though the theme of the Good Shepherd remains constant. In Year A (vv. 1-10) the emphasis is on Jesus as the 'Gate for the Sheep', and distinguishing good from bad shepherds; Year B (vv. 11-18) contrasts the bad shepherds with Jesus' role as the Good Shepherd and includes his comment about 'sheep from other folds'; finally, Year C (vv. 22-30) tackles the controversy with the Jewish leadership over Jesus' words. The all-age address takes the theme as a whole, though the particular perspectives can be drawn out as appropriate. Twenty-first-century urban society tends to view the countryside more as a giant theme park than as a working environment, with disastrous detrimental consequences, and the role of shepherd is rarely considered by most people. But it is fundamental to Jesus' understanding of his purpose and mission, and we have to accept this on its own terms, allowing that first-century Palestinian sheep-farming is very different from what's now done in western Europe. The basic themes are universal, however, and simply need reinterpreting for the twenty-first century.

Hymns

TRADITIONAL

- *Faithful shepherd, feed me (156)*
- *Jesus, where'er thy people meet (367)*
- *The God of love my shepherd is (643)*
- *The King of love my shepherd is (649)*
- *The Lord my pasture shall prepare (653)*
- *The Lord's my shepherd (654)*

CONTEMPORARY

- *All heaven declares (17)*
- *As we are gathered (47)*
- *Be still and know (66)*
- *For the healing of the nations (186)*

- *In you, my God (328)*
- *Only by grace can we enter (528)*

CHANT

- *Nada te turbe (937)*

CHILDREN'S SONG

- *Step by step (885)*

Readings

Year A   Acts 2:42-47; 1 Peter 2:19-25; John 10:1-10

Year B   Acts 4:5-12; 1 John 3:16-24; John 10:11-18

Year C   Acts 9:36-43; Romans 7:9-17; John 10:22-30

Confession

Lord Jesus, loving Shepherd,
we are sorry that we have failed
to listen to your voice
or follow in your steps.
We have wandered astray and become lost
in the paths of disobedience and self-will,
and ask you to forgive us.
Bring us back
under your protecting hand, we pray,
heal the wounds of sin,
and restore us to your eternal presence,
for your name's sake. Amen.

Absolution

Almighty God,
who is more ready to forgive
than we are to repent,
have mercy on *you*,
forgive and deliver *you* from all sin,
and grant *you* strength to walk with him
by faith to eternal life,
through Jesus Christ our Lord. Amen.

Prayer

We respond to our risen Saviour Jesus,
who calls us to his service, saying:
Good Shepherd, may we hear your voice;
help us to follow where you lead.

Lord Jesus, we ask you to guide your Church
through the many perplexing and difficult
changes it faces,
and the conflicting pressures
which pull it different ways.
Give us courage to trust your word
and remain true to you . . .
Good Shepherd may we hear your voice;
help us to follow where you lead.

Lord Jesus, we ask you to have mercy
on this world,
with the many different crises it faces,
environmental, social and political.
Give the world's leaders wisdom
and humility in their decision-making . . .
Good Shepherd, may we hear your voice;
help us to follow where you lead.

Lord Jesus, we ask you to comfort
those who find life stressful and difficult,
with the increasing problems of old age,
and the desperation of troubled young people.
Give patience to workers in medicine,
counselling and caring . . .
Good Shepherd, may we hear your voice;
help us to follow where you lead.

Lord Jesus, we ask you to guide us
through this wonderful yet disturbing world.
May we not be discouraged or despairing,
nor become too comfortable as we are,
but stand firm against the attacks of the evil one,
fulfilling our calling,
and trusting you for strength to endure and
hold fast.
Good Shepherd, may we hear your voice;
**help us to follow where you lead
along the narrow path that leads to eternal life.
Amen.**

All-age address

There are many points which can be raised
from this profound chapter, but you can't
make them all in one address! In traditional
preaching style, three are highlighted here, but
these can be given different levels of emphasis
depending on what you're particularly wanting to bring out. If you're brave enough, the
most effective illustration is a family dog

(your own or borrowed), but you need to be
sure that it has a placid temperament and will
react well to the situation! (Bear in mind that
some people, especially small children, aren't
easy with dogs, and their unease won't decrease
if the animal concerned isn't under complete
control.) If you feel that working with animals
is of doubtful wisdom, a smart bicycle with its
owner (previously primed) can also help bring
out the same points.

1) Shepherding was rather different in
   Palestine two thousand years ago, but don't
   let this restrict Jesus' message to those
   times. The shepherd's relationship with his
   sheep could well have been similar to ours
   with a family pet – he would be distressed
   if any were to come to harm, and he cared
   for them on the same level. A dog can bark
   or growl but it's still vulnerable compared
   to other larger animals, and needs to be
   protected. At this point allow the dog to
   enter, and after a short time to allow the
   reaction to subside, explain how most dogs
   have to be on a lead to prevent them running into a busy road or finding some
   other dangerous situation. The shepherd
   needed to do the same, so at night the
   sheep were penned in to protect them
   against attackers. Jesus the Good Shepherd
   looks after his flock too and whatever happens physically will keep us from being
   harmed by the forces of evil (though don't
   let the idea develop that being a Christian
   provides an automatic insurance policy
   against things going wrong). If you opt for
   the bicycle, stress the importance of keeping it chained up and protected against the
   elements.

2) Dogs also need to be cared for – feeding,
   grooming, exercising, obedience training.
   These are all important, even if the dog
   isn't happy about it! A short demonstration
   of one of these would be suitable, though
   avoid food – dogs get quite excited at the
   prospect, so it's better to say that dogs will
   overeat if allowed, and feeding has to be
   controlled. Jesus cares for his flock too, even
   though sometimes we don't like it much.
   We too need to be fed spiritually, to learn to
   obey, to develop our faith. With a bicycle,

emphasise the need for oiling and regular maintenance, and not allowing it to go rusty through lack of use.

3) Dogs also need to be led. They'll go rushing off all over the place unless they are on a lead to keep them under control and in the right direction, though it's best not to demonstrate this! Without a caring owner they'd soon be lost. The same point can be made with a bicycle, demonstrating the need for a careful rider to steer it in the right direction. Jesus the Good Shepherd wants to guide us in the right paths, following his ways and keeping us away from danger and distraction. We too must be willing to let him lead us, and submit to his control.

FIFTH SUNDAY OF EASTER

As we approach Pentecost, the Gospel readings continue in John, with Year A incorporating Jesus' statement that 'I am the way, the truth and the life'; Year B focuses on 'I am the true vine'; while Year C follows on from his washing the disciples' feet with his command that they love one another. The common factor in all three is Jesus' talking about what the disciples must do after his death, resurrection and ascension, when they no longer have his physical presence. With them we too are called to continue the works of Jesus by faith, to bear fruit by remaining in him, the true vine, and to love one another as he has loved us. Only with the gift of the Spirit will it be possible for us to achieve this, however.

Hymns

TRADITIONAL

- *How sweet the name of Jesus sounds (297)*
- *O Jesus, I have promised (503)*
- *O praise ye the Lord (534)*
- *Thine for ever, God of love (673)*
- *Thou art the Way: by thee alone (682)*
- *Who is this so weak and helpless (748)*

CONTEMPORARY

- *Let us talents and tongues employ (391)*
- *Love is his word (429)*
- *Peace, perfect peace, is the gift (555)*
- *Take up your cross, he says (627)*
- *This is my body (674)*
- *You are the light (763)*

CHANT

- *Ubi caritas (946)*

CHILDREN'S SONG

- *God made a boomerang (806)*

Readings

Year A   Acts 7:55-60; 1 Peter 2:2-10; John 14:1-14

Year B   Acts 8:26-40; 1 John 4:7-21; John 15:1-8

Year C   Acts 11:1-18; Revelation 21:1-6; John 13:31-35

Confession

We humbly confess our sins and shortcomings to God our Father, saying,
Merciful Lord
forgive us and help us.

For doing only what we want to
rather than obeying your law of love,
Merciful Lord
forgive us and help us.

For sitting in judgement on others
rather than acknowledging our own faults,
Merciful Lord
forgive us and help us.

For looking after our own interests
rather than attending to the needs of others,
Merciful Lord
forgive us and help us.

For promoting our own image
rather than considering others before ourselves,
Merciful Lord
forgive us and help us.

For ignoring Jesus' command
to love one another
rather than showing the world
we are your disciples,
Merciful Lord
forgive us and help us,
so that we may remain in your love
and bear fruit for your glory,
through your risen Son,
our Saviour Jesus Christ. Amen.

Absolution

Almighty God,
who is able to save completely
those who call on him,
have mercy on *you*,
pardon and forgive all *your* sins,

and strengthen *you* to fulfil his commands
and display his love for the sake of his Son,
Jesus Christ our Lord. Amen.

Prayer

Jesus, our Saviour and Friend,
we come to you with our requests and concerns,
saying:
You are the vine and we are the branches;
make us fruitful in your service.

Bless and guide all your people,
as we work and witness to your saving love.
Cut away from us anything that is unfruitful,
and make us obedient to your commission
to worship you in spirit and in truth,
and to make disciples of all peoples . . .
You are the vine and we are the branches;
make us fruitful in your service.

Bless and guide those in authority,
over us and over the world.
May they act against evil and dishonesty,
promote what is good and right
and root their laws in your compassion
and love . . .
You are the vine and we are the branches;
make us fruitful in your service.

Bless and guide those who bring comfort,
as counsellors, carers, and aid-workers.
May their work be governed by compassion
and strengthened by faith,
as they minister to old and young,
the elderly and terminally ill,
the homeless and drop-outs . . .
You are the vine and we are the branches;
Make us fruitful in your service.

Bless and guide those who suffer
through illness or infirmity,
lack of purpose or lack of resources . . .
May they be reassured by your risen presence,
that your love remains in them,
and that in all their sorrow,
You are the vine and we are the branches;
make us fruitful in your service.

Bless and guide us
as we continue our earthly pilgrimage.

As we remain in you, the true vine,
so may your life be seen in us,
**and in the fruit we bear for your Kingdom,
through Jesus Christ our Lord. Amen.**

All-age address

Although this address picks up on the theme of 'fruit', it can be applied to any of the Gospel readings. All of them are about how the life of Christ within us affects our lives day by day, and can be seen in our words, actions and relationships. Many people seem to understand the Christian life as a kind of Sunday pastime, to be indulged in when time allows. If it starts to invade other areas of life it becomes more challenging, even threatening. But the Gospel is just another philosophy of life if it only affects an hour every Sunday. Its fruit is evident in the lives of those many Christians who allow their faith to inform their work and leisure, their families and friendships, and above all their priorities. Little physical preparation is needed for this address, other than a bit of strategic shopping!

1) Take an apple or another fruit and show it to the congregation. It needs to be in good condition, so that people will find it attractive. Ask for suggestions about what makes it desirable, and if possible write these up on an OHP. Appearance, smell and colour will all be mentioned, but if taste is suggested point out that no one's yet taken a bite from it, to see if it's as good as it looks. Use this to make the point that, however nice something may appear on the surface, the real test is what happens when you sink your teeth in and the taste buds start to operate. Jesus wants us to bear fruit in our lives which isn't just pleasant on the surface but is good all the way through – it's no use looking good if what people experience is unpleasant. The Christian life is attractive on the outside because it's good on the inside.

2) If possible, now produce an unripe example of the same fruit. It won't taste very good because it's not ready to eat yet, but give it time. . . . Just as we don't expect to find

fully formed fruit suddenly appearing on trees, neither do we expect new Christians to turn up with a clerical collar! But if there's no sign of fruit growing at all we assume something's not quite right. The fruit of the Spirit takes time to develop and mature, and it shouldn't be used before it's ready, but all the time God's life is flowing through us it will grow. As Christians we carry on bearing fruit for God's kingdom only as we remain in him and he in us.

3) Now bring out a few more examples of the same fruit. We'd be a bit disappointed if a tree only produced one apple or pear in a year. Trees go on producing fruit, maybe more in some years than in others, until the mature tree produces a regular harvest from all its branches. Our Christian lives should bear fruit in the same way – God's Spirit should be seen at work in every part of our lives, not just one small aspect.

4) Finally display a selection of different fruits and reassure everyone that they don't all come from the same tree! We enjoy a wide variety of fruits (you might like to include one or two exotic varieties at this point), and sometimes blend their tastes in a fruit salad. God doesn't want us all to be the same, but he does want us to be fruitful for him and to bring our different gifts and personalities together to show the world his love in action. John's Gospel emphasises time and again that the evidence or 'fruit' of God's love remaining and growing within us is the love that we show one another and to those around us, even if we find many different ways to express it.

SIXTH SUNDAY OF EASTER

As Pentecost approaches, the readings reflect increasingly the role of the Holy Spirit in the lives of those who follow Jesus. All three Gospel readings follow on from the previous week's, and in two of them Jesus specifically refers to the Holy Spirit. In Year B, which continues the discourse on the true vine from chapter 15, the Spirit isn't mentioned until after the set verses, but both context and content imply that Jesus' presence will continue with the disciples into the future and give them the strength to obey his commandments. Very shortly their lives would be turned upside down, first by the events of the Crucifixion and Resurrection, and then by Jesus' return to be with his Father. As they heard these words they must have been confused and scared, and Jesus didn't give them false comfort – they would have to live through the feelings of sadness and joy, of uncertainty and vulnerability, which would characterise their experience of the next few weeks. The Holy Spirit would not only be their 'Comforter', but he would also lead them into all truth. Without his presence they wouldn't be able to make sense of all this; with it they were able to grasp the wider picture of God's purposes. The underlying unifying theme is God's promise to all his followers, a promise to be fulfilled at Pentecost.

Hymns

TRADITIONAL

- *City of God, how broad and far (106)*
- *Come, thou Holy Spirit, come (127)*
- *Finished the strife (173)*
- *Holy Spirit, come, confirm us (288)*
- *Love divine, all loves excelling (428)*
- *O King enthroned on high (504)*

CONTEMPORARY

- *Bless and keep us (73)*
- *Follow me (176)*
- *Heaven shall not wait (272)*
- *O Lord, all the world belongs to you (509)*

- *Sing to God new songs of worship (603)*
- *This is my will (675)*

CHANT

- *In the Lord is my joy (930)*

CHILDREN'S SONG

- *Christ is our King (784)*

Readings

Year A   Acts 17:22-31; 1 Peter 3:13-22; John 14:15-21

Year B   Acts 10:44-48; 1 John 5:1-6; John 15:9-17

Year C   Acts 16:9-15; Revelation 21:10, 22-22:5; John 14:23-29

Confession

Heavenly Father, we come into your presence in sorrow,
to repent of all that is unworthy of your love.
We have spoken unkind words
and acted thoughtlessly;
**we have been swift to criticise
and harsh in judgement;**
we have harboured selfish and dishonourable thoughts;
we have disregarded the concerns and well-being of all people.
Have mercy on us Lord;
forgive all our sins;
help us to obey your commandments,
**and to love one another as you love us,
for the sake of your Son, our Saviour Christ.
Amen.**

Absolution

Loving God, forgive all *your* sins,
restore and renew *you* from within,
and keep *you* remaining in his love,
through our Saviour Jesus Christ. Amen.

Prayer

We bring our concerns and prayers
to our Saviour Jesus,
confident in his promise

that he will hear and answer us, saying,
Lord, we ask this in your name;
receive and answer our prayers.

Lord, your world is full of sadness and fear.
Creation is damaged and spoiled;
crime and violence dominate the lives of many;
people made in your image
are exploited and degraded.
We pray for all national governments
and leaders,
as they address the problems
of poverty, abuse and exploitation;
especially . . .
Lord, we ask this in your name;
receive and answer our prayers.

Lord, your Church is hard-pressed
and often discouraged.
Opposition and conflict are ever present;
resources are stretched to breaking point;
churches struggle to survive.
We pray for those Christians
whose faith puts them at risk of persecution;
for those who willingly risk their own safety
to bring aid and relief to the needy;
for those who refuse to take the easy path
of compromise;
especially . . .
Lord, we ask this in your name;
receive and answer our prayers.

Lord, many people are suffering
through illness, anxiety or depression.
The pressures of daily living burden them down;
damaged relationships fill them with despair;
the temptations of this world
lead them to a dead end.
We pray for anyone we know
who is enduring a time of darkness
or difficulty, whatever its cause; especially . . .
Lord, we ask this in your name;
receive and answer our prayers.

Lord, you have promised to hear
the prayers of your people.
Help us to remain in you
so that we pray not out of self-interest
but in accordance with your will,
and answer us not as we would wish
but as you know is best.

Lord, we ask this in your name;
**receive and answer our prayers,
for the sake of your eternal kingdom. Amen.**

All-age address

In tackling the promises made by Jesus, it may well be important to mention what he didn't promise. The idea often surfaces that accepting the Christian faith somehow short-circuits problems and suffering, or that God is obliged to answer every prayer, no matter how selfish or insensitive to the needs of others. The 'prosperity gospel' also lurks in the recesses of our materialistic culture, with its false bridge between faith and financial benefit. Jesus never made or implied any such promises. On the contrary, he made it quite clear that following him was no easy option – Christians are called to tread the narrow path that leads to eternal life.

However, he did promise that we don't have to go it alone, that his presence will always be with us to give strength and courage, and that he will guide us throughout the journey ahead. This address requires a couple of willing volunteers, who won't mind not being primed in advance about what's going to happen.

1) Having found a suitable volunteer, inform them that you'd like them to do a small job for you, and that you'll reward them on its completion. Assuming they agree, send them to perform a simple and non-time-consuming task, such as fetching a glass of water. When they return reward them with a small bar of chocolate or something similar. Explain that our society usually organises work in that way, paying an appropriate amount for jobs done properly. However, Jesus' promises to his disciples just before he died weren't like that; they didn't come with any small print. He simply promised that when he'd returned to his Father in heaven, he would send the Holy Spirit to be with all his followers. They didn't have to finish their tasks first.

2) Now offer someone a similar small bar of chocolate, this time without any strings attached – beware too many takers at once! Give it to a volunteer but then ask them to

go and do another small job, such as switching a light off, or taking something to another part of the building. While this is happening say that Jesus doesn't manipulate or bribe us to do certain things. He gives us his Spirit, but wants us to serve him in response to his love for us, not because we think we'll get something out of it.

3) This time ask a volunteer if they'll go and find something for you (another bar of chocolate will do very well). Make sure this is well hidden in advance, so they can't find it without your help. Since they'll almost certainly ask for help, offer to go with them and help them locate it. Jesus knows we can't fulfil the tasks we've been given on our own, so he promises to go with us every step of the way. His presence is its own reward as we serve him, and while we don't do so for personal gain, we experience his blessings along the way (though not necessarily material ones!).

Conclude by saying that while Jesus never promised that we'll avoid suffering or enjoy non-stop prosperity, he did say that following his way would be far more rewarding or fulfilling than anything this life can offer. The promises of materialism are at best short-term; Jesus' promises are valid for ever.

ASCENSION DAY

Ascension Day always falls on a Thursday, since it's forty days after Easter, so logistical problems may reduce the likelihood of all-age worship being included on that day. The material can easily be used on the following Sunday, however, and it may help all the Church community to share in celebrating the Ascension. In one sense it's the conclusion of a journey that started back in Advent with God's promises, but it also completes the story of Christ's earthly ministry as he returns to the glory of heaven. He has achieved everything his Father had sent him to do, has been vindicated by the resurrection and is now glorified in heaven by his ascension. The disciples must have felt confused; after witnessing Jesus' crucifixion and experiencing his resurrection they still had no idea of who the promised Holy Spirit was, or how they would recognise him – and it was barely three years since they'd first met Jesus! If it felt like the end of a drama they'd been taking part in, they would soon discover that for them it marked a beginning as much as a conclusion. But Jesus had also promised he would one day return in glory, so in every sense this is a day for looking forwards rather than back. Although few churches now make much of it, Ascension Day is a good opportunity for outdoor worship, ideally on a hilltop – some local schools do this too, though it needs careful planning and explaining.

Hymns

TRADITIONAL

- *Alleluia, sing to Jesus (12)*
- *All hail the power of Jesus' name (16)*
- *At the name of Jesus (54)*
- *Come, let us join our cheerful songs (120)*
- *Hail the day that sees him rise (255)*
- *Rejoice, the Lord is King (580)*

CONTEMPORARY

- *Christ triumphant (104)*
- *He is exalted (273)*
- *Jesus shall take the highest honour (360)*
- *Majesty (436)*

- *My Jesus, my Saviour (461)*
- *Name of all majesty (465)*

CHANT

- *Laudate Dominum (933)*

CHILDREN'S SONG

- *He is the King (818)*

Readings

Years A, B and C   Acts 1:1-11
                      Ephesians 1:15-23
                      Luke 24:44-53

Confession

Lord Jesus, reigning now in heaven,
you gave your life for us on the cross,
yet we have not loved you with all our hearts;
you were raised from death victorious over sin,
yet we have not lived in the light of eternal life;
you returned to the Father in glory,
yet we have not owned you as King.
We acknowledge our sin before you,
asking you to pardon and deliver us.
Fill us with a new joy in worship
and new commitment to your will,
for your name's sake. Amen.

Absolution

God the Father of all mercies,
grant *you* forgiveness of all *your* sins,
strength to live
according to his commandments
and the joy of his eternal kingdom,
through Jesus Christ our Lord. Amen.

Prayer

We approach our sovereign Lord,
the Creator and Ruler of all,
bowing before his majesty
yet certain that he will listen to us, saying,
Lord of glory,
hear your people's prayer.

We ask you to bless your Church
and all Christian people throughout the world.

Whether in joy or sorrow,
in peace or turmoil,
in poverty or plenty,
may we worship and serve you together.
Especially we pray for . . .
Lord of glory,
hear your people's prayer.

We ask you to bless your world
and all who have been given authority
over nations or local communities.
Whatever conflicts they have to confront,
whatever problems they must overcome,
may they work for justice and peace
so that your kingdom is seen on earth.
Especially we pray for . . .
Lord of glory,
hear your people's prayer.

We ask you to bless our local community
and all who work for its best interests.
In nurseries and schools,
in places of work and trade,
in homes for the elderly and day centres,
may they show your care
for the vulnerable and exploited.
Especially we pray for . . .
Lord of glory,
hear your people's prayer.

We ask you to bless our families,
friends and loved ones,
and all who are enduring pain,
anxiety or loneliness.
Whether in illness or infirmity,
in depression or sadness,
in grief or emptiness,
may they feel your healing touch on their lives,
reassuring them
and restoring them to wholeness again.
Especially we pray for . . .
Lord of glory,
hear your people's prayer.

We ask you to bless us
as we commit our lives to you.
As our hearts are filled with your praise,
may we be obedient to your sovereign will
and live as faithful servants
of your eternal kingdom.
Lord of glory,

**hear your people's prayer
and reign among us as King of kings,
through our risen and ascended Lord,
your Son Jesus Christ. Amen.**

All-age address

The basis of this address is not Jesus' departure from this earth, but the words he spoke to the disciples before this happened. You could call it 'famous last words'! Some people just have to have the last word in any discussion, mainly because they want what they've said to be remembered. A bit of preparation is needed for this in the form of two or three cards, each containing some famous last words. These could be amusing or serious. A particular favourite is Lord Palmerston's final comment, 'Die, my dear doctor? That's the last thing I shall do.' Oscar Wilde's parting shot at the poor state of his room usually makes an impact too: 'Either that wallpaper goes or I do!' On a more literary level, the end of King Lear is particularly apposite, as are the final words of Becket's Christmas sermon in *Murder in the Cathedral*. There are plenty of alternatives, of course, but whatever you decide on, make sure you've got enough volunteers to read these out at the right time.

1) Begin by asking if anyone was given an instruction as they left home. Children are usually told by parents to behave themselves or be good; adults might be asked to pass on a message and told not to forget under any circumstances! We usually receive these instructions just as we're leaving because the speaker wants us to remember this above all else. Jesus wanted his followers not to forget what he'd said, so he left them with a command (to go into the world and make disciples of all nations) and a promise (that he'd always be with them for as long as time endures).

2) If you've chosen some amusing lines have these read out now with a good build-up. We don't know if these really were the final words of the people concerned, but if so, they may not have meant them to be funny. Jesus always said exactly what he meant –

there was never much doubt about what he was saying, which was why the religious leaders wanted to get rid of him. His instructions to his followers were quite clear.

3) Now have read one or two more serious quotes. The speaker (or writer) wants us to take on board these final words as they sum up what's been said in a memorable way, and give a clue to the underlying significance of the book or play. Jesus' last words sum up his ministry too, and indicate that it wasn't an isolated burst of miraculous events but the start of God's kingdom breaking in on human affairs, which his followers are to continue.

Parents, writers and speakers, even people on their death-beds, often use their last words to impress on us the importance of all they've been saying. Jesus went further by sending the Holy Spirit to enable us to fulfil his instructions.

SEVENTH SUNDAY OF EASTER

Since we're now in Ascensiontide, today is also known as the Sunday after Ascension Day. The themes are very similar as the disciples have seen Jesus return to heaven but haven't yet received the gift of the Holy Spirit. It must have been a rather uncertain time for them as they waited for what had been promised without much idea of what it would be or how they'd recognise it. They trusted Jesus' words but couldn't quite see how the whole picture would fit together. In western society we've become very used to 'instant' products and services – coffee, electric power, banking, information and so on. As a result, we're not very good at waiting, and become impatient when God refuses to function as a consumer service and give us what we want straight away. The disciples had to sit and wait for God's timing, and in the meantime prepared themselves by making the eleven up to twelve again and voting in Matthias. The Gospel readings are all taken from Jesus' high-priestly prayer in John 17, which is divided up across the three years. This is undoubtedly one of the most profound passages anywhere in the Bible – the only extended account we have of Jesus relating to his Father in prayer. The theme of waiting is implicit in that Jesus is 'waiting' for his impending death, and his prayer – both for the disciples and, in the latter verses, for all believers – is that in all the difficulties and crises of life they will not be removed from the world but 'protected from the evil one'. Waiting times can be frustrating and uncertain, but sometimes God wants us to learn to use them to grow in faith so that we're ready for the next part of the journey. The suggested hymns reflect both the depth of the Gospel readings and the triumph and celebration of the Ascension.

Hymns

TRADITIONAL

- *Forth in the peace of Christ we go (187)*
- *God is love, let heaven adore him (217)*
- *God moves in a mysterious way (222)*
- *Let all the world (382)*
- *Lift high the cross (394)*
- *The head that once was crowned with thorns (644)*

CONTEMPORARY

- *Come on and celebrate (125)*
- *God forgave my sin (212)*
- *God is our strength from days of old (220)*
- *I, the Lord of sea and sky (332)*
- *O, Heaven is in my heart (499)*
- *Will you come and follow me (752)*

CHANT

- *Adoramus te, Domine (921)*

CHILDREN'S SONG

- *Hallelu, hallelu (814)*

Readings

Year A   Acts 1:6-14; 1 Peter 4:12-14, 5:6-11; John 17:1-11

Year B   Acts 1:15-17, 21-26; 1 John 5:9-13; John 17:6-19

Year C   Acts 16:16-34; Revelation 22:12-14, 16-17, 20-21; John 17:20-26

Confession

Father of all, we confess
that we have not always
put our lives in your hands.
For looking to our own strength
instead of trusting you wholeheartedly,
Lord, forgive and restore us.
For looking to this passing world
instead of living for eternity,
Lord, forgive and restore us.
For looking for instant pleasure
instead of waiting on you,
Lord, forgive and restore us.
**Give us a keener awareness of your love
and a deeper faith in your promises, we pray,
through Jesus Christ, your Son, our Lord.
Amen.**

Absolution

Almighty God, our loving Father,
whose mercy extends to all who trust in him,

forgive all *your* sins and wrongdoing,
and give *you* a wider vision of his purposes,
for the sake of his Son,
our Saviour Jesus Christ. Amen.

Prayer

Father God, Creator and Sustainer of all,
we offer you our thanksgiving and requests
as we bow before you, saying:
Lord, receive our prayer,
and answer as you know best.

Father God, we pray for this hurting,
broken world;
many suffer the results of inhumanity
and cruelty,
and many carry the heavy burden of bigotry
and abuse.
We share your sadness and ask you to bless
the victims and those who seek to aid them . . .
Lord receive our prayer,
and answer as you know best.

Father God, we pray for the troubled,
discouraged Church;
many are disconsolate about the future,
while others are defensive of past glories.
We share your concern for those
who do not know you,
and ask you to move us
from moaning to mission . . .
Lord, receive our prayer,
and answer as you know best.

Father God, we pray for our community,
and those who shape it;
with its flaws and weaknesses
may it yet become
a glimpse of your kingdom here on earth.
We share your compassion for the vulnerable
and weak,
and ask you to bless our witness and service . . .
Lord, receive our prayer,
and answer as you know best.

Father God, we pray for ourselves;
be with us in busy times and waiting times,
encourage us by your presence,
and uphold us with your love.
Lord, receive our prayer,

and answer as you know best,
through your Son
Jesus Christ our Lord. Amen.

All-age address

Waiting isn't the most popular pastime in society today! We resent waiting for buses and trains, or attention in the bank and post office, and expect whatever we want instantly. Children in particular find waiting difficult – no doubt they always have, but their expectations have been fuelled by the media. The disciples had to wait for the gift of the Holy Spirit, and then they recognised that he wasn't a product designed to make them feel better about themselves or their situation, but was the power of God in their lives to equip them to serve him. The New Testament gives us no encouragement to use the Spirit primarily for our own benefit.

This talk picks up the theme of 'waiting' to emphasise that all God's work is his initiative, and we fit in with his timescale. The points can be reinforced either with cartoon-style pictures or by using volunteers briefed in advance.

1) *Waiting can be frustrating*. We all hate waiting for the bus or train, particularly if it's late or the weather's bad. A picture of a bus queue with umbrellas up, or a real one made up of the volunteers will illustrate this neatly. We aren't comfortable in the cold and wet, and we want to get to our destination as soon as possible. If the bus is late it's even worse! The disciples probably felt frustrated. They knew Jesus had promised the Holy Spirit but couldn't have known when or how they'd receive it. As Christians we all feel this way at times, but we have to learn that God will act in his time – if he'd sent the Spirit a few days earlier there might have been far fewer people in Jerusalem to hear the good news.

2) *Waiting can be exciting*. We all like to have an event or occasion to look forward to – a birthday party, family get-together, holiday or special outing. A picture of people preparing for an event is very effective, as are your volunteers doing the same. Often we'll get out our best clothes or buy a new

outfit, choose food which is reserved for special treats, or make travelling arrangements. None of this is quite as good as the event itself, but by being properly prepared we enjoy it more when it comes. The disciples used their time of waiting in prayer, and in times of waiting we can make ourselves more ready for what God has in store next by reading the Bible and praying.

3) *Waiting can be productive.* We all know how slowly the time seems to go when we're anticipating something special. Sometimes we say, 'I can't wait for it to happen'. As a result the time in between can seem wasted and futile. Here you could have a picture of people twiddling their thumbs, or get your volunteers to do the same. But in the meantime there's plenty to be getting on with. God won't give us everything all at once. He knows it wouldn't be good for us and it isn't part of his will for the human race. But he gives us all we need to serve him now, in our present circumstances. As we do this (even though we might wish for something more exciting to happen), our faith grows and we become ready to serve him in other ways later on.

PENTECOST SUNDAY

In liturgical terms Pentecost is the most important festival of the Church's Year after Easter and Christmas. Unlike Mothering Sunday and Harvest Festival, it's probably seen more as an 'in-house' celebration for keen churchgoers – among those who aren't, many may well never have heard of it. Those in the know might describe it as the Church's birthday, which on one level is reasonable. Certainly those who were gathered with the apostles when the Holy Spirit descended came together as the earliest grouping of believers, and thereafter the Christian Church spread rapidly throughout the Middle East before taking root in Europe, Africa and Asia. From those earliest days in Jerusalem, believers have met for worship and fellowship right across the world, forming the largest institution the world has ever seen, transcending barriers of race and culture as no other has done. If the Christian faith seems a marginal influence on western society today, it has had a major impact in other parts of the world, such as South Africa, while in South Korea, Nigeria, Sudan and Uganda the Church has grown several times over in the most difficult circumstances.

All of which started from the twelve disciples, uneducated and unsure of themselves, and the 120 believers gathered on the Day of Pentecost – not the most obvious human resource to bring together to launch a world-transforming religion! But in God's economy there are only people made in his image, not human resources, and his wisdom takes precedence over human reasoning. So what overcame these folk, and what difference did it make? Luke tries to answer the first of these, but whatever happened in that room, the power unleashed has proved unstoppable, perhaps most of all in the face of concerted efforts to stop it. The second could be answered by Christians ever since then, who have experienced the transforming power of the Holy Spirit and gone on to share it and live it in amazing ways.

So it's much more than a 'birthday' or anniversary we celebrate at Pentecost, though a special cake to go with the after-church coffee usually goes down well! Another way of celebrating is to ask for contributions to a 'birthday present' which could be sent to a church with a particular need in another part of the world – mission agencies are always happy to help with suggestions for a suitable project. But the main focus of the celebration is the reality of the Holy Spirit in the lives of all Christians. As far as the Common Worship lectionary is concerned, the Pentecost reading from Acts 2 can be read instead of either the Old or the New Testament reading, both of which are provided. There is also an alternative Year A Gospel reading from John 7.

Hymns

TRADITIONAL

- *Breathe on me, breath of God (84)*
- *Come down, O love divine (114)*
- *Come, Holy Ghost, our souls inspire (117)*
- *Gracious Spirit, Holy Ghost (245)*
- *O breath of life (476)*
- *O thou, who camest from above (541)*

CONTEMPORARY

- *All over the world (20)*
- *Filled with the Spirit's power (170)*
- *Jesus is Lord (352)*
- *Spirit of the living God (614/615)*
- *There's a spirit in the air (661)*
- *The Spirit lives to set us free (666)*

CHANT

- *Veni, Sancte spiritus (948)*

CHILDREN'S SONG

- *When the spirit of the Lord (912)*

Readings

Year A   Numbers 11:24-30*; 1 Corinthians 12:3b-13*; John 20:19-23†

Year B   Ezekiel 37:1-14*; Romans 8:22-27*; John 15:26-27, 16:4b-15

Year C   Genesis 11:1-9*; Romans 8:14-17*; John 14:8-17

* or Acts 2:1-21
† or John 7:37-39

Confession

Spirit of Jesus,
you came upon the disciples
as though in wind and flame,
filling them with your power and authority.
We confess that our lives show little evidence
of your power at work in us,
and our witness little sign of your authority.
Forgive us, we pray,
and fill us anew with the power of your Spirit,
that our tongues may declare your glory
and our lives reveal your love,
for the sake of our Saviour Jesus Christ. Amen.

Absolution

Almighty God,
whose Spirit comes upon all
who are open to him,
grant *you* forgiveness for all *your* sins,
peace in *your* hearts
and strength to live for him
day by day,
through Jesus Christ our Lord. Amen.

Prayer

God our Father, you came upon the disciples
as flame and wind,
filling them with your Holy Spirit;
Come to us now, and bless us;
Fill us with your Spirit of love.

We thank you for the power of your Spirit,
strengthening us to work for you in the world.
We ask you to help us as we serve you . . .
Come to us now, and bless us;
Fill us with your powerful Spirit.

We thank you for the wisdom of your Spirit,
helping us to understand better your will for us.
We ask you to inform us as we serve you . . .
Come to us now, and bless us;
Fill us with your wise Spirit.

We thank you for the peace of your Spirit,
making us confident of your love.
We ask you to inspire us as we bring your
peace to the world . . .
Come to us now, and bless us;
Fill us with your peaceful Spirit.

We thank you for the gifts of your Spirit,
equipping us for the work you have called us to.
We ask you to enable us
as we strive for your kingdom . . .
Come to us now, and bless us;
Fill us with your generous Spirit.

We thank you for the healing of your Spirit,
which brings relief from the burdens of
suffering.
We ask you to make us sensitive
in caring for those in need . . .
Come to us now, and bless us;
Fill us with your compassionate Spirit.

We thank you for the fruits of your Spirit,
which demonstrate your transforming love.
We ask you to make our lives fruitful
in your service . . .
Come to us now, and bless us;
**Fill us with your Spirit of unity
and make us one in heart and mind
to serve you in Christ our Lord. Amen.**

All-age address

For many people the Holy Spirit is a rather
alien concept, perhaps associated vaguely
with media reports of emotional excesses and
extreme fundamentalist views. Some may
even have heard tales (possibly apocryphal) of
individuals suffering severe emotional damage through their involvement in a 'charismatic' group. Inevitably there will be a wide
variety of personal reactions to such things,
and an all-age address definitely isn't the
place to tackle them, but it's vital to ensure
that the baby isn't thrown out with the bath
water. The aim of this address, therefore, is to
explain simply what it means to be filled with
the Spirit, and how his power can flow
through us. The only visual aids you'll need to
find in advance are a pair of gloves and a
length of electrical flex.

1) Start with a recap on the run-up to Pentecost.
   The believers were all together praying
   about what might happen next, and waiting for God to reveal himself to them. What
   they experienced was immensely powerful,
   though Luke takes care to describe what

happened as 'a sound like a violent wind' and 'what seemed to be tongues of fire'. The event may have been impossible to describe, but the effect was crystal clear – the disciples were filled with the Holy Spirit. At this point take up the pair of gloves. One glance indicates they've been well designed to fit someone's hand, but on their own they flop about and are useless. Only when they're filled with the right-sized hand do they become useful. Similarly, God has made us for himself, but we can't be used in his service until we're filled with his presence and love, which is what he designed us for. Just as a hand is needed to make sense of a glove, so we need the Holy Spirit to make sense of our lives and give them a purpose.

2) Now move on to the cable. This shouldn't have any plugs or sockets attached and ideally the bare wires should be visible. The sole purpose of electrical flex is to enable a current to be transferred from a power source to operate an appliance. It has no use until one end is plugged into an electricity supply so that power can flow through. But it also needs to flow into something that runs on electricity; otherwise it's extremely dangerous (you could produce a radio, electric kettle or similar article to illustrate this). The Holy Spirit is the power of God in our lives, but like the cable we're simply channels for it to flow through. We need to be connected not only to God, the source of all power, but also to his work here on earth, if we're to be useful to him. Conclude by stressing that the Holy Spirit is the third person of the Trinity, rather than an abstract force, and that his role is to draw us into and keep us in our heavenly Father's love, so that we're enabled and equipped to serve him.

3) An additional but effective illustration is to hold up an uninflated balloon. After the glove somebody's guaranteed to make the connection! When the balloon has been inflated and tied, let it go randomly. A filled balloon isn't the easiest thing to control. Nor is the Holy Spirit under our control. As he fills us so we move as he directs –

unpredictable, even risky at times, but infinitely rewarding as we follow him by faith.

TRINITY SUNDAY AND ORDINARY TIME

We now enter a long spell of Ordinary Time, which officially starts on the day after Pentecost Sunday. But with Trinity Sunday following on immediately, the second Sunday after Pentecost becomes the first to be kept as part of Ordinary Time, though Common Worship reverts to the Book of Common Prayer's description of it as the First Sunday After Trinity. In the Common Worship lectionary Ordinary Time ends at All Saints' Day, so there are 22 Sundays after Trinity (Propers 4-25), finishing on the last Sunday in October (or 24 October when 31 October falls on a Sunday and is kept as All Saints' Day) – Proper 25 is always used on last Sunday after Trinity, which means the earlier Sundays (Propers 4-7) are omitted in those years when Easter arrives in mid- or late April. In addition, however, you'll need to remember that while the readings always relate to the *date*, the collect and post-communion prayer will be those for whichever *Sunday after Trinity* it is. For the Principal Service, the New Testament and Gospel readings continue to follow their sequences, but with the Old Testament there is the option either of semi-continuous readings, or of passages reflecting the Gospel – both are included here, the former always listed first.

TRINITY SUNDAY

Trinity Sunday comes between Pentecost and the long stretch of Ordinary Time that lasts until All Saintstide. It is a principal Feast Day in its own right, though not strictly part of any season. Everyone agrees that the doctrine of the Holy Trinity is essential to the Christian faith – God as three distinct persons, yet at the same time one entity. Unfortunately no concept in the Christian faith is harder to grasp, let alone explain! We simply have to accept that our human minds are finite, and unable to explain everything in rational terms.

The actual term 'Trinity' isn't used in the Bible (being coined a century later, though several passages refer to all three persons of the Trinity in close proximity), but for the early Christians the necessity soon arose to define the limits of Christian belief, and to counter any false or misleading teaching about God or Jesus. We can understand fully why they wanted to defend the faith in rational terms, but ultimately God is beyond explaining – if he fitted neatly into our mental constructs he wouldn't be much of a God at all! It's therefore important not to confuse the congregation with theories and speculation about something which in the final analysis is incomprehensible. It is far preferable to stress the value of developing a well-balanced and secure faith which can stand firm in times of doubt or adversity, and to underline the perfect inter-relationships within the Trinity which should be reflected in the life of the Church.

Hymns

TRADITIONAL

- *Bright the vision that delighted (86)*
- *Father, Lord of all creation (163)*
- *Father of heaven, whose love profound (165)*
- *Firmly I believe and truly (174)*
- *Holy, holy, holy, Lord God almighty (286)*
- *I bind unto myself this day (302)*

CONTEMPORARY

- *Father, we love you (167)*
- *Holy, holy (284)*
- *Holy, holy, holy is the Lord (285)*
- *Lord, the light of your love (419)*
- *There is a Redeemer (658)*
- *We believe in God the Father (711)*

CHANT

- *Sanctum nomen Domini (940)*

CHILDREN'S SONG

- *Have we made our God too small? (815)*

Readings

Year A   Isaiah 40:12-17, 27-31; 2 Corinthians 13:11-13; Matthew 28:16-20

Year B   Isaiah 6:1-8; Romans 8:12-17; John 3:1-17

Year C   Proverbs 8:1-4, 22-31; Romans 5:1-5; John 16:12-15

Confession

Lord God almighty, enthroned in heaven,
you are high and exalted,
perfect in love and purity.
We confess that we are unclean
in thought, word and deed,
and not worthy to stand in your presence.
We are sorry and ashamed,
and ask you to forgive our wrongdoing.
Take away our guilt, we pray,
and make us fit to do your will,
through your Son, Jesus Christ our Lord. Amen.

Absolution

Almighty God,
who forgives all who turn to him
in repentance and faith,
have mercy on *you*,
pardon and cleanse *you* of all *your* sins,
and send *you* out to proclaim his glory,
for the sake of his Son,
Jesus Christ our Lord. Amen.

Prayer

We come to you, Almighty God,
three persons yet one,
bowing in awe before your majesty,

but accepting your invitation
to bring before you our prayers and requests.
Merciful Lord,
hear us and answer us.

Eternal Father, reigning in glory
over all things,
the world is covered by despair and degradation
instead of being filled with your glory.
War and violence lead to innocent suffering;
crime and conflict result in fear;
greed and selfishness despoil your Creation.
We pray for governments and world leaders . . .
Merciful Lord,
hear us and answer us.

Loving Jesus, dying to redeem humankind,
and rising in victory over evil and death,
the Church is weakened by disunity and apathy.
Divisions have destroyed credibility;
silence has impeded effective witness.
We pray for Christian leaders
and communicators . . .
Merciful Lord,
hear us and answer us.

Life-giving Spirit, reassuring
and strengthening in times of need,
our friends and loved ones need comfort
and healing.
Some feel stressed and anxious;
others are unwell or upset;
We pray for all those known to us,
that your love will surround them . . .
Merciful Lord,
hear us and answer us.

Holy God, source of all life,
we pray for those we love but see no longer,
and ask you to comfort all
who have been bereaved . . .
Merciful Lord,
hear us and answer us.
May we live and work together in unity,
and so reflect your love and glory
to the world around,
through Jesus Christ our Lord. Amen.

All-age address

The ideal visual aid for this address is a camera tripod, preferably with an inexpensive camera attached. If you're worried about the safety of the equipment, make sure you put down a blanket or gym mat so that it receives a soft landing if it falls.

1) Start by extending just one leg of the tripod. It'll be self-evident that this doesn't provide any stability at all. If our Christian faith has only one leg, we'll find it too isn't likely to stand up. If we only believe in God the Father, he remains distant and remote in heaven, uninterested in what's happening down here on earth, or unable to influence it; if we believe only in Jesus, he's a good, even remarkable man, but no more than that; if all we believe in is the Holy Spirit, we end up with a few personal experiences but no solid reality.

2) Now extend a second leg of the tripod. It might be a bit of an improvement, but it's still not able to hold the camera steady. If we omit God the Father, we lose all sense of God's greatness and glory; if we leave out Jesus, we can't relate God to our life on earth; if we leave out the Holy Spirit, we're left with a purely cerebral belief that has little effect on our lives.

3) We need all three legs of the tripod to be in use before we can safely leave the camera on it, but with three legs it will remain firm even in quite difficult circumstances (which you could demonstrate by adjusting it to cope with a step or other obstacle). Our faith needs God the Father, the Son and the Holy Spirit if it's to stand firm, especially when things aren't so easy. Just as all three legs work together to hold the camera in place, so the three persons of the Trinity work in complete harmony. As Christians we're called to reflect that unity of love and purpose in our daily living.

PROPER 4

Sunday between 29 May and 4 June inclusive
(if after Trinity Sunday)

This Sunday's readings will only be used when Easter falls towards the end of March. Year A's passage from Matthew concludes the Sermon on the Mount, Year B's from Mark contains an account of Jesus' disputes with the authorities over the Sabbath, while Year C's from Luke tells of the Roman centurion's faith. As the Gospel readings are of necessity very varied during Ordinary Time, an outline address is provided for Years A and C, while for Year B, the outline for Proper 3 would be equally relevant.

Hymns

TRADITIONAL

- *Be thou my guardian and my guide (69)*
- *Glorious things of thee are spoken (205)*
- *Immortal love, for ever full (315)*
- *Jesus shall reign, where'er the sun (359)*
- *O God, our help in ages past (494)*
- *We pray thee, heavenly Father (720)*

CONTEMPORARY

- *Be still and know (66)*
- *Father God, gentle Father God (158)*
- *God is our strength and refuge (219)*
- *Jubilate, ev'rybody (371)*
- *My Jesus, my Saviour (461)*
- *You are beautiful beyond description (760)*

CHANT

- *O Lord, my heart is not proud (939)*

CHILDREN'S SONG

- *Don't build your house on the sandy land (790)*

Readings

Year A Genesis 6:9-22, 7:24, 8:14-19 or
Deuteronomy 11:18-21, 26-28;
Romans 1:16-17, 3:22b-28 (29-31);
Matthew 7:21-29

Year B 1 Samuel 3:1-10 (11-20) or
Deuteronomy 5:12-15;
2 Corinthians 4:5-12; Mark 2:23-3:6

Year C 1 Kings 18:20-21, (22-29), 30-39 or
1 Kings 8:22-23, 41-43; Galatians 1:1-12;
Luke 7:1-10

Confession

Holy God, we come to you in repentance
and sorrow,
recognising our sins and failings,
conscious that we need your forgiveness.
Our thoughts have been far from you;
our words have not been governed by you;
our actions have not been under your control.
We are sorry, and humbly seek your pardon.
In your mercy cleanse our lives,
take away our sin, and redirect us
to live your way,
through your Son, our Saviour Jesus Christ,
Amen.

Absolution

God, whose mercy and grace are without limit,
hear the cry of *your* heart,
pardon and deliver *you* from all *your* sin,
and guide *you* through this life
to the eternal joys of the life to come,
through his Son Jesus Christ our Lord. Amen.

Prayer

We come to God as our Sovereign,
praying for his will to be done
and saying: Lord, hear us and answer,
as we pray in your name.

We think of the world
and the many threats and pressures it faces,
from greed, corruption and exploitation.
We pray for victims of natural disaster,
inhuman cruelty and man-made tragedy . . .
Give courage to those who dedicate their lives
to the relief of suffering,
and perseverance to overcome obstacles.
Lord, hear us and answer,
as we pray in your name.

We think of the leaders of the world,
as they grapple with disturbing issues
raised by human rights, scientific research
and information technology.
We pray for those who make decisions
and enact laws . . .
Give them wisdom to know what is right,
and courage to practise it.
Lord, hear us and answer,
as we pray in your name.

We think of our local community,
its schools and healthcare facilities,
workplaces and institutions.
We pray for those who live or work around
us . . .
Give comfort to the suffering, protect the weak,
encourage the downhearted, and strengthen us
as we live for you day by day.
Lord, hear us and answer,
as we pray in your name.

We think of the Church, national and local,
and its worship, witness and service.
We pray for church leaders,
members of synods and committees,
and those engaged in public ministry,
or currently training for it . . .
Give all Christian people a commitment
to proclaiming your gospel
and serving you as one.
Lord, hear us and answer,
as we pray in your name.

We think of those suffering
as a result of ill-health, grief, or worry.
We pray especially for . . .
Give them reassurance that they are
in your loving hands,
and confidence that you are with them
in every situation.
Lord, hear us and answer,
as we pray in your name.

We think of our own lives this week,
the things we will do, the people we will meet,
the places in which we will find ourselves.
Exciting or mundane, joyful or sad,
may your unfailing love fill every moment.
Lord hear us and answer,
as we pray in your name,
Jesus Christ our Lord, Amen.

All-age address 1

This first outline is based on Jesus' parable of the wise and foolish builders, and makes the point that the principles of constructing a building also apply to the Christian life. It needs a fair amount of preparation, plus a willingness to think bigger than usual and take a few risks! You'll need a reasonably large sandpit, several large jugs of water, a bucket and spade, and some bricks (real, as opposed to the children's toy version). A number of volunteers are needed to help with the demonstration; age is irrelevant but younger members will probably be more enthusiastic.

1) First, ask two assistants to make a sand castle using the bucket and spade. As they do this, compliment the quality of their work. When it's finished, ask two more to pour a jug or two of water over it, as violently as possible. It won't take long for it to start washing away. Either consult the congregation about the problem or point out yourself that good foundations and durable materials are a prerequisite of a building that will last. Our faith won't survive either, unless we base it on Jesus Christ and on the spiritual things that last for ever, rather than the material goods of this world.

2) Now ask the volunteers to construct a wall in the sandpit with the bricks (maybe a dozen or so), and again pour water over them. You'll certainly wash away any grains of sand, but the bricks won't move. They aren't especially beautiful in themselves but when they're put together with other bricks to make a house, the finished product can look very smart and impressive – and it'll last! Jesus wants his hearers to understand that our faith must endure all the storms and stresses of this life, made of 'material' that will last (that is, putting his words into practice), and put together in a coherent pattern. Spiritual maturity is seen in a faith and a Church that can weather difficulties and opposition and stand firm.

All-age address 2

This outline looks at the question of faith from the perspective of Luke's account of the healing of the centurion's servant. Considerable distress has sometimes been caused by the suggestion that such healing is invariably and directly linked to the amount of faith on display, but, while Jesus commends the centurion for his faith, this is more to show up the lack of faith among the Jews than to indicate the circumstances under which he's willing to heal. There are several effective ways to illustrate faith.

1) Invite a volunteer to come and sit on a chair. The mere fact of the invitation may arouse suspicions as to whether it's safe or not, but an element of trust is necessary when sitting on any chair! Admittedly, this isn't entirely a matter of faith as visual evidence and past experience help us decide if a particular chair is reliable, but make the point that however much we talk about it, faith is seen in the act of sitting down. The centurion knew of Jesus' reputation, and may even have discussed it with his friends, but Jesus knew his faith was real by his action in sending a message to him.

2) Another test of faith is to ask a volunteer to fall over and trust that they will be caught – the most effective method is to ask four other volunteers in advance to link hands in a circle and catch the person in the middle as they fall and return them to an upright position, so that the process can be repeated. Children are far more trusting than adults at this exercise! Stress that the element of faith is far more real now, but that the more the one in the middle is caught by the others, the more trust will be built up. The more we put our trust in God, the more we'll discover he's completely faithful and never lets us down. That's how our faith is strengthened.

3) Offer a pound coin (or however much you think appropriate) to anyone in the congregation who's willing to come and take it from you. Amazingly, most people will think there's a catch in it somewhere, except younger children, whose parents may well try instead to restrain them at this point. The worst-case scenario is half the congregation queuing up for it, so make sure you know your limit! Faith in this case means taking someone at their word, believing they'll keep their promise, and receiving what they're offering. The centurion believed Jesus meant what he said, that he would keep his word, and so he acted on it. As a result the thing he most wanted happened – his favourite servant was healed.

PROPER 5

Sunday between 5 and 11 June inclusive
(if after Trinity Sunday)

From now until the end of October the Gospel readings run in sequence, and while each Gospel is not read in its entirety (not necessary when accounts common to two, or all three of them are taken into account), the coverage is fairly comprehensive. Year A's passage from Matthew is in two parts – the story of the calling of Matthew and the healing of a woman with a haemorrhage and of a young girl who had just died. In Year B the passage from Mark consists of the dispute over Jesus' authority to cast out demons, while Year C's Gospel from Luke recounts the raising of a widow's son.

Hymns

TRADITIONAL

- *Come ye faithful (131)*
- *Immortal love, for ever full (315)*
- *Jesu, all holy (341)*
- *Jesus calls us: o'er the tumult (347)*
- *Lord of all hopefulness (413)*
- *There's a wideness in God's mercy (662)*

CONTEMPORARY

- *I will bless the Lord (335)*
- *Only by grace (528)*
- *Thanks for the fellowship (632)*
- *The Kingdom of God (646)*
- *When God almighty came to earth (733)*
- *Will you come and follow me (752)*

CHANT

- *The Lord is my light (944)*

CHILDREN'S SONG

- *Step by step (885)*

Readings

Year A   Genesis 12:1-9 or Hosea 5:15-6:6;
Romans 4:13-25; Matthew 9:9-13, 18-26

Year B   1 Samuel 8:4-11, (12-15), 16-20,
(11:14-15) or Genesis 3:8-15;
2 Corinthians 4:13-5:1; Mark 3:20-35

Year C   1 Kings 17:8-16 or 17-24;
Galatians 1:11-24; Luke 7:11-17

Confession

Lord of all,
in your holy presence we kneel in penitence,
knowing that our lips are impure,
our hands unclean,
our hearts unfit to come near you.
We are sorry and ashamed
of our wrongdoing,
and ask you to forgive our waywardness
and self-centredness.
Have mercy on us,
wash away all our sins,
and by your grace make us worthy
to stand before you and serve your kingdom,
through Jesus Christ our Saviour.
Amen.

Absolution

Almighty God,
whose power can heal the sick
and raise the dead
have mercy on *you*,
forgive all *your* sins,
heal *your* backsliding,
and raise *you* to a new and eternal life,
through his Son Jesus Christ, our risen Lord.
Amen.

Prayer

God calls us to hear his voice
and respond to his love
as we bring him our prayers
for the Church, the world and those in need,
saying:
Lord, hear us in your mercy,
and answer us in your love.

Lord, your Church is under threat
from persecution and apathy outside,
disunity and confusion within.
Give courage to all Christians who face suffering

or death for their faith . . .
Bind together all who own Christ as Lord,
and motivate us to work for your kingdom,
Lord, hear us in your mercy,
and answer us in your love.

Lord, this world is in turmoil,
and insecurity rules our lives.
Hostility and conflict are ever-present;
poverty and economic chaos degrade lives;
corruption brings leadership into disrepute.
Give wisdom to governments
to rule wisely and justly . . .
Empower all who struggle for peace and justice,
and give hope to those
whose struggle seems in vain.
Lord, hear us in your mercy,
and answer us in your love.

Lord, many need the touch of your loving hand;
the elderly and infirm,
the jobless and homeless,
the physically and mentally ill,
the grieving and the despairing . . .
Bring them relief from their troubles
and healing from their pain,
and through those who care about them
show them the depth of your compassion.
Lord, hear us in your mercy,
and answer us in your love.

Lord, we too need you day by day,
in work and leisure, in community and solitude,
in waking and sleeping.
Stay with us as friend and go with us as guide,
that we may live in your strength
and rest in your love.
Lord, hear us in your mercy,
and answer us in your love,
for the sake of your Kingdom. Amen.

All-age address 1

The issue of life after death was somewhat controversial in Jesus' time, and viewed by Jewish traditionalists as a trendy, even dangerous new idea, which enabled Paul to make effective use of a split among his opponents (Acts 23:7-8). The accounts of his resuscitation of the dead in two of these gospel readings must have caused quite some consternation among the religious authorities. It might be argued that the little girl had only just died (not much consolation when there's no casualty unit or emergency treatment available!) but the widow's son had evidently been dead long enough for the funeral to be in progress. Contemporary society tries to shy away from death, or failing that to talk about it *ad nauseam*, but the nationwide reaction to the death of the Princess of Wales indicated the extent of the problem for many people. It would be tempting to argue that it isn't a suitable topic for all-age worship, but in the context of resurrection and new life it's fundamental to the Christian faith. Here are three ways to illustrate a Christian understanding of death and new life:

1) Take a pot-plant which looks dead in winter (a fuchsia is an excellent example) and point out that only a few weeks previously it looked brown and dead, with no sign of life. It's certainly true that last year's flowers, leaves and branches have died, so that this year's growth truly is new life, which wouldn't be possible unless the old had died. As Christians we recognise that our bodies, the visible sign that we're alive, inevitably deteriorate and die. However, in Christ, who defeated death by his resurrection, we are restored to the eternal life for which our heavenly Father created us, and which sin destroyed. Our old earthly life has to finish so that we can enter into the far better one which lies ahead.

2) Obtain a couple of house sale leaflets from an estate agent and as you display them or read a few details out, ask who's moved house recently. Explain that major changes like this in our lives can often feel like a bereavement (leaving a school or job are similar experiences). However, if we don't 'die' to our old life in that house or school, we can't start another one in a new house or at university. Christians believe that even while we remain on this earth we have a foretaste of what that new life after death will be like, when we can enjoy God's presence for ever and be what he made us to be.

3) Finally bring out a baby's training beaker, a child's plastic drinking glass, a chunky mug and a bone china cup. Show that there's a development here, from a small child learning to drink without spills, to a child learning to drink from a normal mug that won't break if it's dropped, to the sort of mug that adorns most university and college rooms. Finally bring out the best bone china crockery. As each stage of growing up to adulthood is reached, so the signs of the previous phase are left behind – we don't expect grown-ups to use plastic training beakers, though no doubt they once did! In moving on to each new stage of life we 'die' to the old with its immaturity and more limited scope. As Christians we die to our old life with its sins, weaknesses and limitations so that we can move on to something better.

Jesus' miracles were a picture of how through the death and resurrection of Jesus we can receive new life, which enables us to die to the old. In him, as those around him realised very well, a whole new perspective on life and death was being opened up.

All-age address 2

The passage from Mark, describing how the Pharisees accused Jesus of casting out demons through Beelzebub, is one of the hardest in all the Gospels to understand. We no longer think readily in such terms, but underlying their criticism is one which everyone will understand – what gives Jesus the authority to do and say what he does? The last thing the religious leaders wanted was for him to be recognised as acting solely on God's authority. So they accused him instead of invoking the powers of darkness to exorcise demons and evil spirits, a quite ludicrous argument, as Jesus quickly demonstrated. For this address you'll need just a few symbols of authority, such as a police officer's cap or helmet, a passport, an ID tag permitting access to a building, a pantomime crown or tiara and a doctor's white coat and stethoscope.

1) Police officers are employed to ensure the rest of us obey the laws of the country, and to help people who are in difficulty or danger. If we see a blue light flashing we know we must stop or drive a bit slower; if the police have sealed an area off we aren't allowed to go there. Most people don't argue with police officers for very long. But their authority comes from the law itself, and they themselves are subject to it.

2) A passport is important to enable us to travel in other countries. Show the message from Her Majesty in the front cover to the rulers of other nations. When we go to those places we do so with that authority in our passport.

3) An ID tag provides authorisation to be in a particular place, usually from the owner, because we have the right to be there or have to be as part of our work.

4) A doctor's coat and stethoscope shows that this person is skilled, trained and authorised to handle certain drugs, prescribe courses of treatment or even to carry out surgery. Before they can function as doctors they must pass exams and be accepted by the medical authorities as able to do their work to the necessary standards.

5) A crown is the ultimate symbol of authority, as all the other examples derive their authority from someone or something else. But where does a monarch get authority from? No earthly ruler can govern without authority from God (quite different from self-appointed power). Jesus is King of kings, yet he was quite clear that everything he did was in obedience to his heavenly Father. The religious leadership of his day refused to recognise this, and this refusal led them to making absurd and blasphemous suggestions which meant they were turning their backs on God in order to protect their own reputation. In so doing they were showing everyone that Jesus' authority was greater because it came straight from his Father.

PROPER 6

Sunday between 12 and 18 June inclusive
(if after Trinity Sunday)

As the Gospel readings settle into their sequential pattern it may seem as though significant chunks are being omitted. Even allowing for the Infancy and Passion narratives, Matthew and Luke are too long to fit into twenty-five weeks of readings, while some material is common to two, or all three synoptic gospels. In the Gospel for Year A Matthew tells of Jesus' need for more co-workers, and the sending out of the disciples; Year B sees Mark describing two parables of the kingdom, while in Year C Luke recounts Jesus' anointing by a sinful woman, and adds a few verses about the women who followed Jesus.

Hymns

TRADITIONAL

- *All people that on earth do dwell (21)*
- *In full and glad surrender (322)*
- *Love divine, all loves excelling (428)*
- *My faith looks up to thee (453)*
- *Praise, O praise our God and King (566)*
- *The Church's one foundation (636)*

CONTEMPORARY

- *Alleluia, alleluia, give thanks (8)*
- *Come on and celebrate (125)*
- *God forgave my sin (212)*
- *I am a new creation (298)*
- *I danced in the morning (305)*
- *We are his people (708)*

CHANT

- *Adoramus te, Domine Deus (922)*

CHILDREN'S SONG

- *Put your trust (882)*

Readings

Year A   Genesis 18:1-15 (21:1-7) or
          Exodus 19:2-8a; Romans 5:1-8;
          Matthew 9:35-10:8 (9-23)

Year B   1 Samuel 15:34-16:13 or
          Ezekiel 17:22-24; 2 Corinthians 5:6-10
          (11-13) 14-17; Mark 4:26-34
Year C   1 Kings 21:1-10 (11-14) 15-21a or
          2 Samuel 11:26-12:10, 13-15;
          Galatians 2:15-21; Luke 7:36-8:3

Confession

Lord God, our Creator,
we come to you acknowledging our sinfulness
and seeking your forgiveness, saying,
Lord, have mercy on us;
cleanse us and make us whole.

We repent of unwise or unkind words
we have spoken,
causing hurt and anger.
Lord, have mercy on us;
cleanse us and make us whole.

We repent of selfish or thoughtless actions
we have committed,
causing needless misery and irritation.
Lord, have mercy on us;
cleanse us and make us whole.

We repent of unfair or judgemental
attitudes we hold,
causing us to speak unfairly and act unjustly.
Lord, have mercy on us;
cleanse us and make us whole.

We repent of all that falls short
of your standards,
asking you to forgive all our sins
and give us strength to live for your glory.
Lord, have mercy on us;
cleanse us and make us whole,
through Jesus Christ our Lord. Amen.

Absolution

God our Father,
who loves all he has created,
grant *you* pardon and deliverance
from all *your* sins,
peace in *your* hearts,
and the joy of new life
through Christ our Lord. Amen.

Prayer

As members of God's kingdom
we come to Jesus with our prayers, saying:
Lord, may your kingdom grow;
reign in our hearts, we pray.

Bless and guide your people
throughout the world,
ill-treated, marginalised or accepted . . .
Give strength to the suffering,
encouragement to the downhearted,
and unite us all in your love . . .
Lord, may your kingdom grow;
reign in your Church we pray.

Bless and guide the church in this community
as we seek to address the issues around . . .
Give courage to overcome past divisions,
leave aside less important issues
and join together in your name,
so that we can bring your good news
to the world.
Lord, may your kingdom grow;
reign in our church, we pray.

Bless and guide the governments of the world
facing the challenges of deprivation and want,
disputes and bitterness . . .
Give them discernment to make good decisions,
boldness to confront corruption and vice,
and wisdom to act for the good of all.
Lord, may your kingdom grow;
reign in our world, we pray.

Bless and guide our families and friends,
in particular those going through dark times
or facing tough decisions . . .
Give them comfort and peace in their trials,
healing of body and mind,
and confidence that you are alongside,
bringing them the hope of eternal life.
Lord, may your kingdom grow;
reign in their lives, we pray.

Bless and guide us at school or at work,
among family and friends,
and in our neighbourhood;
give us commitment to live for you
and proclaim your love wherever we are.
Lord, may your kingdom grow;
reign in our hearts

and help us live for your glory,
**in the name of our Saviour Jesus Christ.
Amen.**

All-age address 1

This outline is based on the sending out of the disciples, making use of the fact that most people are familiar with receiving orders to fulfil particular tasks or objectives. You'll need to prepare five envelopes with instructions inside, covering the following points: 1) there's work to be done and too few people to do it; 2) the order carries authority for it to be fulfilled; 3) it must be carried out single-mindedly; 4) it won't be easy and there'll be opposition; 5) there needs to be a report back. Given the importance of social concern in Christian mission, a task based on this is suggested, though if you collect money make sure people know exactly which good cause it will go to. In the interests of time it's preferable for this to be completed after the service, with a report back at the next suitable opportunity. The outline is based around this idea; different circumstances may require it to be adapted.

1) Prime two 'volunteers' before the service (if possible children or teenagers), and, having called them out, emphasise the importance of their 'unique skills of persuasion and charm'! Ask them to open the first envelope, which will underline this point, saying that there's plenty of money in people's wallets and purses, but no one else to make a collection for the charity in question. As a pair they must help and support each other in their work. Jesus also sent the disciples out to do his work because there was no one else willing to do it, and Luke tells us he sent them in pairs, to learn how to work co-operatively.

2) The next envelope should contain a signed authorisation from the vicar or most senior minister present, entitling these two people to make a collection on behalf of the church for the chosen charity. As Jesus' followers we don't engage in ministry for lack of anything better to do, nor because we think it's a good idea. All Christian ministry comes

under God's authority, and only if we do it in his name will it be worthwhile.

3) The third envelope should say that the volunteers must concentrate on this and nothing else, taking nothing with them except their own commitment and their authorisation. Jesus knew the disciples would be distracted very easily, so he didn't allow them to take any spare clothes or cash, or even food – they were to fulfil their task single-mindedly and trust God to supply all their needs.

4) The fourth envelope should contain a 'health warning' – this task won't be easy. Not everyone will be so willing to make a donation, and some might even be rude when they're asked. Jesus didn't want his disciples to be under any illusions either about the arduous nature of the work, nor about the likely response in some places. We shouldn't be naive or unrealistic, but Christian ministry isn't based on fulfilling certain 'success criteria'. Rather we're called to faithful proclamation of the good news and loving service to those in need.

5) The final envelope holds the date for feedback on how the work has gone. Luke tells us that the disciples returned joyfully to tell all that had happened. British reserve notwithstanding, we shouldn't be afraid to declare where and how we've seen God at work in the world, and share our own joy at the way his kingdom is growing.

All-age address 2

The second outline is based on Jesus' kingdom parables in Mark 4 (though it serves those in Matthew 13 equally well). The specific illustration here is of growth in the natural world, but it focuses more generally on the nature of God's kingdom. It's assumed that at least some of the congregation will have experienced a foreign business trip or holiday. Beforehand you'll need to find or borrow a passport, some leftover foreign coins, a red warning triangle, a phrase-book and if possible a history of a country you're familiar with.

Begin by asking if anyone's been abroad recently, and follow this up with a question about what makes being abroad different from living in the British Isles. You may find it helpful to write up the suggested differences on an OHP slide or flip-chart. The suggestions you get will certainly include:

1) *People may speak a different language.* Produce the phrase-book and read out a couple of amusing or striking phrases in the language concerned. While it may not matter for a short trip, if we're to engage with those people on a regular or serious level we must learn to speak their language. In God's kingdom there's a quite different 'language' to the one in this world; words like 'materialism', 'racism', 'abuse' and 'selfishness' don't exist. If we're part of God's kingdom we'll learn words like 'caring', 'compassion', 'integrity' and 'love' instead. If you find a suitable history book, use it to explain that even countries which speak our language have a different culture and way of looking at life. The basic attitudes of God's kingdom are the opposite of much that we find elsewhere in the world.

2) *There's a different currency.* Here you can display the coins, saying where they're from to forestall the obvious mental distraction. Explain too that things may be more or less expensive in other countries. God's kingdom has values quite distinct from those in this world – in fact it usually turns them upside down, as Jesus often demonstrated.

3) *There are different laws* – the red warning triangle is a useful and simple example. UK law doesn't yet require one to be carried, whereas many other countries do. God's laws are clearly described in the Bible, and they're quite different to human rules and regulations, based on following the liberating way of Christ, rather than restricting what we can do and threatening punishment (you may want to refer to the latter part of Galatians 5).

4) *There's a different authority* – which is where the passport comes into its own. When we

travel in another country we must obey its laws, but we carry the authority of the Queen to be there. As members of God's kingdom he is our final authority – all human authority comes from him, and it wouldn't be possible to legislate for or against his law of love. Jesus sets us the example of complete obedience to his Father's will, and we must follow his lead, which means complying with civil laws unless they're contrary to his commandments.

All-age address 3

Few people would argue that Luke shows a remarkable empathy with women throughout his Gospel, surely reflecting Jesus' own attitude and approach. From our twenty-first-century perspective it's easy to forget how radical this was for its day – the disciples' reaction to Jesus talking at the well with a Samaritan woman suggests this would have been considered at best improper. However, gender isn't the main concern of the primary account here. Instead Luke contrasts the attitude of a woman regarded as a sinner with that of Simon, the self-righteous Pharisee, to show his readers that a forgiven sinner responds to God's love on a far deeper level than one who barely understands the need for forgiveness. To highlight this contrast use an OHP slide divided into two columns, one for each characteristic – not difficult on a computer. If you're able to draw or have access to a good cartoonist, you could do this on a large sheet of paper or card with pictures rather than words.

1) The two words here are 'affectionate' and 'detached'. The woman showed how she felt about Jesus by weeping and kissing his feet, while Simon hadn't even offered him the greeting of a kiss. Sinful she may have been, but the woman responded to Jesus' love and wasn't bothered what anyone else thought, even if Simon and the other guests were more concerned about him being 'contaminated' by the touch of a sinner.

2) The next two words might be 'generous' and 'mean'. The woman was willing to use an expensive jar of perfume to wash Jesus' feet, whereas Simon hadn't even extended him the courtesy of water to clean them up when he'd arrived. The perfume may have been a symbol of her past life, but now it's dedicated to Jesus.

3) The next words are 'accepting' and 'disapproving'. The woman showed her total acceptance of Jesus by pouring the perfume over him, unlike Simon, who showed no willingness even to pour olive oil (which was much less expensive) on his guest's head, a sign of recognition and welcome.

4) The final words could be 'forgiven' and 'self-righteous'. The woman recognised her need of forgiveness, but Simon and his friends seemed not to have the slightest idea that they might need God to forgive them.

Simon didn't even fulfil what was expected of a host. The woman gave the best she knew to Jesus in response to his love and forgiveness. The more we recognise how much we've been forgiven, the easier it is to express our love for him and commitment to following his ways. The Pharisees' problem was that they looked down their noses at the sinners with whom Jesus associated, and quite failed to see that in God's eyes they too needed to be forgiven. The woman, whatever her past, went home forgiven because she'd demonstrated her faith in Jesus by her action.

PROPER 7

Sunday between 19 and 25 June inclusive
(if after Trinity Sunday)

Year B 1 Samuel 17:(1a, 4-11, 19-23) 32-49 or
17:57-18:5, 10-16 or Job 38:1-11;
2 Corinthians 6:1-13; Mark 4:35-41
Year C 1 Kings 19:1-4 (5-7) 8-15a or
Isaiah 65:1-9; Galatians 3:23-29;
Luke 8:26-39

This is the last of the four Propers which may be omitted, though unless Easter falls fairly late in April it will usually be included. Matthew continues in Year A with last week's Gospel reading, as Jesus tells the disciples the cost of following him; Mark in Year B has the account of Jesus calming the storm, and in Year C Luke describes the healing of an uncontrollable demoniac. Outline addresses are suggested for Years A and B. The Year C Gospel is less easy for younger members of the congregation to comprehend, but the points from Year B about Jesus' lordship can be used with suitable adaptation.

Confession

Lord Jesus,
full of compassion and mercy,
you receive gladly all who come to you
in penitence and faith.
We are truly sorry
that we have fallen short of your standards,
and have lived according to human wisdom
instead of putting our trust in you.
Forgive our sins, we ask you,
and help us put the past behind us
so that we may walk with you
in newness of life,
for your name's sake. Amen.

Hymns

TRADITIONAL

- *All my hope on God is founded (19)*
- *As pants the hart (44)*
- *Eternal Father, strong to save (153)*
- *Jesu, priceless treasure (344)*
- *Lead us, heavenly Father lead us (379)*
- *Praise, my soul, the king of heaven (565)*

Absolution

God our Father,
the unchanging and all-merciful Lord,
have mercy on *you*,
forgive all *your* sins
and take away *your* guilt
for the sake of his Son,
our Saviour Jesus Christ. Amen.

CONTEMPORARY

- *As the deer pants for the water (45)*
- *Christ is alive! (96)*
- *Father, I place into your hands (162)*
- *Give thanks with a grateful heart (202)*
- *Listen to me Yahweh (402)*
- *Now let us from this table rise (472)*

CHANT

- *Calm me, Lord (924)*

Prayer

We stand in the presence of our risen Lord
with many burdens and concerns.
As we offer them to him we pray:
Jesus, stand among us,
in your risen power.

CHILDREN'S SONG

- *'Cheep' said the sparrow (783)*

Readings

Year A Genesis 21:8-21 or Jeremiah 20:7-13;
Romans 6:1b-11; Matthew 10:24-39

Touch with your healing hand, Lord Jesus,
the broken places of our world:
city streets inhabited by homeless children,
shanty towns concealing gross poverty,
communities wearied by violence and insecurity,
countries torn apart by war and famine . . .
Open our eyes to their pain
and help us respond with compassion.
Jesus, stand among us,
in your risen power.

Touch with your gentle Spirit, Lord Jesus,
our confused and divided church:
Christians separated by age-old barriers,
time spent on fruitless discussion
rather than proclaiming your good news,
and witnessing to your transforming love . . .
Open our minds to the riches of your Kingdom,
help us to learn of you from one another,
and to serve you with one heart and mind.
Jesus, stand among us,
in your risen power.

Touch with your loving presence, Lord Jesus,
those whose lives are darkened
by the shadow of suffering:
illness of body or mind,
breakdown of relationships,
the loneliness of bereavement or rejection . . .
Open our hearts to comfort and help them,
and our hands to ease their burden.
Jesus, stand among us,
in your risen power.

Touch with your risen power, Lord Jesus,
our daily lives:
our relationships with those we love,
our routine contacts and phone calls,
our times of activity and business,
our times of relaxation and quiet . . .
Keep our hearts and lives open
to receive your blessing,
our hands and hearts to share your love,
and our eyes fixed on you,
the pioneer and perfecter of our faith.
Jesus, stand among us,
in your risen power,
and fill our hearts with hope and joy,
for your name's sake. Amen.

All-age address 1

Jesus' words about the cost of discipleship are as tough and uncompromising as any he uttered – the idea that Christianity is an escape-route from the reality of normal life would have cut no ice with him! The aim of this address is to demonstrate how anything that's truly worthwhile will cost us not only in cash terms, but also in time and energy, maybe even changing the way we think and act. Preparation is straightforward, requiring only the simplest of props.

1) If you don't own one yourself, obtain a copy of the latest hit CD – it should be easy enough to find a teenager who's bought it already and is willing to loan it for the service. Holding it up for all to see, ask if anyone else has got theirs yet. No doubt some will say they have, but others may say they can't afford it, or are saving up pocket-money. The point is unmissable – nothing comes free. The artists and technical staff have to be paid, the raw materials paid for, distribution and storage costs covered – and, after all that, everyone involved wants to make a profit. So we have to work or save up to pay for it.

2) Now display a holiday brochure, ideally for somewhere exotic or expensive. Ask if anyone's visited this place, and point out that most of us don't have sufficient funds just to go and pay for the holiday. In fact for most of us it would be the trip of a lifetime, and we'd have to work very hard for a long time to be able to afford it. But, if we did so, we'd probably regard the effort, time and cost involved as well worthwhile.

3) Finally, show a degree or diploma certificate, and find out if anyone has something similar. Point out that while we might have to pay for tuition fees, money can't buy a successful result. That only comes from working and giving up our time and energy to this one objective, perhaps even overcoming the objections of others; only when we see the certificate do we realise that it was all worth it.

Conclude by explaining how Jesus was making similar points to those who wanted to follow him. The Christian life isn't a hobby for people who like that kind of thing, or who need something to occupy their time. It will cost those who follow the way of Jesus in time, effort and commitment – and probably money too! The most important and valuable things in life don't come cheaply or easily. It cost Jesus everything to win for us forgiveness and new life, and as his disciples we must expect our way to be tough at times. It's in coming through the difficulties and hardships that we recognise the effort and pain was worth enduring.

All-age address 2

Many people have sought power over the course of human history, but the extreme measures they've taken to try and hold on to it strongly suggest a deep-seated fear of losing control. No one has exerted a more powerful influence on history than Jesus Christ, but he never made any attempt even to gain a position of power, let alone hang on to it. His contemporaries were astonished at his control, but he seemed not to need to manipulate people or situations to his own advantage. The story of the calming of the sea is a good example. This outline looks briefly at human pictures of power, contrasting them with the way Jesus exercised it.

1) Begin by displaying a weather map or forecast, ideally with a good variety of different conditions on it – hot and sunny, rainy and windy, cold and frosty. Say that meteorologists are becoming increasingly good at predicting the weather, but they can't actually control it. No doubt farmers, sporting figures and holidaymakers would be delighted if they could! Possessing information doesn't automatically imply control over a situation. Maybe Jesus knew a storm was brewing; maybe he recommended that everyone take wet weather gear. But what stunned the disciples was his lordship over the elements, a demonstration that the Creator God had become part of his own creation.

2) Now exhibit a photograph, or better still a collage of photos, of various well-known political figures, asking for their identities. All politicians want us to believe they can get the country under control, sort out international crises and make us all millionaires! Once they're elected, however, the story is usually rather different. Some become interested only in their own image, some find they simply can't cope under the pressure, while others distort the truth in order to remain popular. Jesus, here as elsewhere, is in full command of the situation, even though he appears to be totally unaware of it! He shows no signs of stress, no concern for image or popularity, and retains his integrity.

3) The final illustration should be a photo of a great human achievement which involved conquering fear – a round-the-world sailing voyage would be an ideal example. Those who take part in such adventures have to learn to overcome their fears if they're to succeed in their aim. Few things are more intractable or harder to bring under control than deep-seated fears, but Jesus here wipes out the disciples' terror, chiding them for their lack of faith in him. Within a few seconds their only fear is of his awesome power.

Conclude by emphasising that all creation is under God's control, that no situation is beyond his scope, and that his perfect love will remove even our deepest fears. The same points can be made, with slightly different applications, to Luke's account of the healing of the demoniac.

PROPER 8

Sunday between 26 June and 2 July inclusive

The summer holiday season isn't far away now. In schools most exams will be over and the term coming to an end, and at work many people will be organising themselves to take a week or two's break, while seaside resorts and tourist locations will be gearing themselves up for the peak season. Many worshippers will be looking forward to a few weeks of less frenetic activity, and if your church is in a holiday area you may have many extra visitors who will be looking for relaxation and refreshment. But the challenge of the Gospel isn't reduced! The reading from Matthew 10 for Year A finishes a long section on discipleship, while in Year B we read Mark's familiar story combining an unexpected healing with the raising from death of a young girl. Year C's reading from Luke returns to the cost of following Jesus, for which a suitable address outline can be found for Proper 7.

Hymns

TRADITIONAL

- *All praise to thee (22)*
- *Amazing Grace (29)*
- *Lift up your hearts (395)*
- *New every morning is the love (467)*
- *O Lord my God (511)*
- *The God of Abraham praise (642)*

CONTEMPORARY

- *Abba Father (1)*
- *All that I am (23)*
- *Cry 'Freedom' (138)*
- *Follow me (176)*
- *Love is the only law (430)*
- *Moses, I know you're the man (451)*

CHANT

- *Exaude nos, Domine (927)*

CHILDREN'S SONG

- *Come on, let's get up and go (788)*

Readings

Year A Genesis 22:1-14 or Jeremiah 28:5-9; Romans 6:12-23; Matthew 10:40-42

Year B 2 Samuel 1:1, 17-27 or Wisdom of Solomon 1:13-15, 2:23-24 or Lamentations 3:23-33; 2 Corinthians 8:7-15; Mark 5:21-43

Year C 2 Kings 2:1-2, 6-14 or 1 Kings 19:15-16, 19-21; Galatians 5:1, 13-25; Luke 9:51-62

Confession

Loving Father,
you call us to be free,
but we have misused the freedom you give.
We have indulged our selfish desires
instead of serving one another;
we have criticised and condemned
instead of encouraging;
we have become arrogant and proud
instead of serving humbly.
We are sorry and ashamed,
and repent of all we have done wrong.
Forgive us, we pray,
and renew us by your Spirit,
that our lives may bear fruit for your glory,
through our Saviour, Jesus Christ. Amen.

Absolution

God our Maker,
whose very nature is love,
have mercy on *you*,
forgive all *your* sins,
and give *you* grace to walk with him
in step with his Spirit,
through Jesus Christ our Lord. Amen.

Prayer

We call to the Lord
who lifts us from the depths,
offering him our prayers
for the Church and the world and saying:
Hear us, O Lord, and be merciful;
Lord, be our help.

We call to you, our Father,
praying for your worldwide Church,
facing opposition or persecution,

struggling against apathy and cynicism,
or coping with severely limited resources . . .
Bless and guide Christian leaders
of all traditions,
in national roles or local congregations,
and inspire us with all Christian people
to spread your good news
throughout the world.
Hear us, O Lord, and be merciful;
Lord, be our help.

We call to you, Lord Jesus,
praying for our whole earth,
with its environmental degradation,
international tensions,
rank injustice and desperate poverty . . .
Give wisdom to government leaders
and agencies,
business directors and media controllers,
that they may walk the paths
of truth and peace,
and give courage to all Christian people
to uphold your standards.
Hear us, O Lord, and be merciful;
Lord, be our help.

We call to you, Holy Spirit,
praying for anyone we know
who is enduring illness of body or mind,
caring for infirm or elderly loved ones,
or facing difficult decisions . . .
Give them strength
to endure their time of testing,
and confidence to believe
that all things work together for good
to those who love God.
Hear us, O Lord, and be merciful;
Lord, be our help.

We call to you, blessed Trinity,
praying that our faith may be rooted
in your word,
and visible in our lives day by day.
As we know your saving grace in our hearts,
may our lips and our lives declare your praises.
Hear us, O Lord, and be merciful;
**Lord, be our help now,
and our joy for evermore. Amen.**

All-age address 1

Although the last three verses of Matthew 10 are
brief, they're profound enough to warrant an

address outline in their own right. This one
focuses on possible responses to Jesus and the
disciples he sends out in his name. The only
props needed are suitable magazine adverts,
articles, headlines or pictures, and a cup of cold
water.

1) Find an advert or two with a clear message
(and large enough to be visible), and either
paste them on to separate pieces of card or
form them into a collage. Ask for suggestions
about what the message might be – adver-
tisers are rarely very subtle! Point out that
just as they want us to understand what
they're saying, so God wants us to be clear
about his message too. That's why he sent
the prophets, though many refused to listen
to them. Nor were Jesus' contemporaries
always willing to hear him explain what
God was saying. Jesus says here that listening
to God's message through his servants is
just as important as giving it.

2) Now select a few headlines or brief words
extolling someone who's behaved cour-
ageously or commendably. Having sought
views about what was praiseworthy in these,
point out that the media frequently emphasise bad news, even making cynical comments about 'do-gooders'. This is in marked
contrast to Jesus' words, which indicate how
highly God values those who accept and
encourage righteousness and justice.

3) Jesus' own illustration of a cup of cold water
is simple, clear and easy to produce, though
it needs expanding for our culture. It may
seem rather paltry to us, but what matters is
the public gesture of support for those who
speak God's words and do his works. In
receiving and accepting them we're opening
ourselves to our heavenly Father and accepting him too. You might conclude by seeking
support (with money and prayer) for a
Christian worker in difficult circumstances.

All-age address 2

Mark's account of the raising of Jairus' daughter
is also one of his longest, mainly because on his
way to the house Jesus was delayed both by the

crowds who wanted to see him and by a very persistent woman. Having described the healing of the demoniac, a man beyond his own or anyone else's ability to control, Mark now introduces us to a young girl on her death-bed, and a middle-aged woman the doctors had given up on. According to the understanding of those times, at least, no one could do any more for them. He also contrasts the faith of the girl's father and the woman with the disinterest and scorn of those around. This outline looks at the way Jesus goes about ministering to them, using the mnemonic WHOLE, either as a computer-generated OHP slide or flip-chart diagram.

1) Although he's engaged in teaching people when Jairus comes to him, Jesus responds immediately to the request, no doubt comforting the distraught father as they head towards his home. As a synagogue leader Jairus may have risked opposition from other religious folk for approaching Jesus like this, but although it's the only hope left he clearly believes Jesus can heal his daughter. Uncover or bring out the words *'Went Immediately'*.

2) Unfortunately the crowds slow them down, and as they press their way through, the woman, also believing Jesus to be the one person who can heal her, touches his cloak. The disciples think he's over-reacting – a lot of people would have bumped into him – but Jesus knows this is quite different, a deliberate act of faith, so he stops to find out who it is. He stops what he's doing, if only for a few moments, to care for the person in need. The words here read *'Healed Immediately'*.

3) The unexpected hold-ups mean Jesus still hasn't reached the child, and by now it's too late. Jairus' friends come out telling him to stop wasting Jesus' time because the child's already dead – possibly from an infection such as meningitis, which takes hold rapidly. But Jesus won't be put off, and he simply encourages Jairus to hang on to his faith as they head for the house. When they arrive the mourners are in full flow, and when Jesus claims the girl is just asleep (a euphemism for death) they laugh and jeer. Here reveal the words *'Overcame Doubt'*.

4) Jesus sends everyone else out of the house, apart from the girl's parents and the three disciples. Once the atmosphere is calmed down he takes them into her room, and holding her hand he tells her to get up. To their amazement she does just that! Jesus didn't want to make a spectacle of the whole thing so he kept this part of his ministry very private, not least out of consideration for both parents and daughter. The words to display now are *'Left Doubt Outside'*.

5) Jesus omits the theology lecture at this point and deals with the most urgent matter – the girl needs food, maybe because she's not eaten for a while. He also makes the firm request that they say nothing about what's happened, possibly because he knew that otherwise they'd be inundated with attention. This gives the opportunity for the final words, *'Encouraged to Live Normally'*. Even after such an astonishing miracle it wouldn't have been healthy for this little family to think of themselves as something set apart or different. By continuing to live their daily lives fully they'd automatically be testifying to the power of God to make people whole again.

PROPER 9

Sunday between 3 and 9 July inclusive

As we move on through the gospels, we come now in Year A to two passages from Matthew 11 in which the religious leaders' view of Jesus is contrasted with the true perspective. Year B consists of Mark's account of the twelve being sent out, which is paralleled by the more detailed version in Luke 10 for Year C – both of these can make use of the outline suggested for Year A of Proper 6.

Hymns

TRADITIONAL

- *All ye who seek a comfort sure (26)*
- *Happy are they, they that love God (262)*
- *Help us to help each other, Lord (275)*
- *I heard the voice of Jesus say (310)*
- *Thy hand, O God, has guided (689)*
- *When I survey the wondrous cross (738)*

CONTEMPORARY

- *An army of ordinary people (31)*
- *From the sun's rising (197)*
- *God's Spirit is in my heart (231)*
- *Great is the Lord and most worthy of praise (248)*
- *I danced in the morning (305)*
- *Love is his word (429)*

CHANT

- *Laudate Dominum (933)*

CHILDREN'S SONG

- *Out into the great wide world we go (873)*

Readings

Year A   Genesis 24:34-38, 42-49, 58-67 or
          Zechariah 9:9-12; Romans 7:15-25a;
          Matthew 11:16-19, 25-30
Year B   2 Samuel 5:1-5, 9-10 or Ezekiel 2:1-5;
          2 Corinthians 12:2-10; Mark 6:1-13
Year C   2 Kings 5:1-14 or Isaiah 66:10-14;
          Galatians 6:(1-6) 7-16;
          Luke 10:1-11, 16-20

Confession

Acknowledging our sinfulness
and trusting in our Saviour,
we confess our sins, saying,
Show us your mercy, O Lord,
and bring us your salvation.

You command us to put no other god
in a higher place than you,
but we fail to make your kingdom
our top priority.
Show us your mercy, O Lord,
and bring us your salvation.

You command us to love you
with all our heart, soul, mind and strength,
but our time and energy
is taken up with our own concerns.
Show us your mercy, O Lord,
and bring us your salvation.

You command us to love our neighbours
as ourselves,
but we are blind to the needs and interests
of those around.
Show us your mercy, O Lord,
and bring us your salvation.

Forgive our failures and wrongdoing,
and give us strength to serve you
with commitment and joy.
Show us your mercy, O Lord,
**and bring us your salvation,
now and in eternity,
through Jesus Christ our Lord. Amen.**

Absolution

Almighty God,
who saves completely those who call upon him,
have mercy on *you*,
pardon *you* for every kind of wrong,
and lead *you* out from darkness
to walk in the light of the Lord,
both now and for ever,
through Christ our Lord. Amen.

Prayer

We enter with joy and thanksgiving
the presence of the Lord who sends us out,
offering our prayers to him and saying:

Lord, as we hear your call,
we will go where you lead.

You send us out into the world to bring healing
and the good news of your kingdom.
We pray for the places where suffering and pain
are an everyday experience for many,
where lives are clouded by inequality
and injustice . . .
Bless all who bring the light of your love
into the darkness of evil.
Lord, as we hear your call,
we will go where you lead.

You send us into the world together,
to learn to work together as partners
in the Gospel.
We pray for the Church,
for a spirit of co-operation and mutual support
and an end to barriers of suspicion
and isolationism . . .
Bless all Christian ministers, lay and ordained,
as they lead your people
in announcing the good news.
Lord, as we hear your call,
we will go where you lead.

You send us to the sick and dying,
the despairing and brokenhearted,
to minister your healing touch,
and bring consolation to the comfortless.
We pray for any known to us . . .
Bless all who suffer, and reassure them
of the good news of your risen presence.
Lord, as we hear your call,
we will go where you lead.

You send us out in your name,
not promising that the path will be easy
but assuring us that your grace
is sufficient for all our needs.
Lord, as we hear your call,
**we will go where you lead,
knowing that you are with us
throughout our earthly journey,
and then for evermore,
through Jesus Christ our Lord. Amen.**

All-age address

Most of us will say from time to time, 'Whatever I do, it's wrong!', usually implying that we're in a situation where we'll be criticised or condemned, whichever course of action we take. There may be an underlying assumption that those criticising would be determined to find fault under any circumstances. This was certainly true in Jesus' case. Many of his contemporaries had condemned John the Baptist for 'not eating or drinking', but now they were writing Jesus off precisely because he did eat and drink – they'd have refused to see any good in him, no matter what he did. Jesus contrasts this with the attitude of 'little children' a bit later in the chapter. 'Little children' clearly implies more than infants or under-11s, referring less to an age-group than to a frame of mind, adopted by people who may not regard themselves as clever or educated, but who are more open to what God is showing them. This outline therefore looks at ways of learning and perceiving the truth.

1) Those who learn most are those who realise they still have much to learn. Start by asking if anyone's learning French (German or Spanish might also be possible) and if someone owns up to studying it, say for GCSE or A-level, ask them to speak a few words. Praise them for their linguistic skills, then produce a French dictionary and ask if they know it from cover to cover. The answer's guaranteed to be 'No', even if the compiler's in the congregation! Go on to say that even if someone knew every single word in the French language, they might not know how to write or speak it idiomatically. That requires a comprehensive knowledge of France and its different regions, its history, its culture and so on. Most of us don't know that much about our own country, still less another! Make the point that it would take a pretty daft person to claim they had nothing left to learn. The same's true of the Christian faith – the more we know about God, the Bible and the Christian life, the more we recognise how much we still have to learn.

2) Now ask if anyone's been to France or another country, or even lived there – if possible get them to describe a few of the differences between there and your present location. Emphasise that knowing *about* that country

isn't the same as knowing it personally. Even personal knowledge grows throughout our lives, as any happily married couple will attest. Jesus' contemporaries thought they knew everything about God, but as Jesus pointed out on a number of occasions, they didn't know him for themselves. Only in this personal relationship can we experience his gentleness and humility, his rest when we feel burdened.

3) Finally, half-fill a glass with water and ask someone to describe it. They'll almost certainly say 'half-empty' or 'half-full'. Then ask two people on opposite sides of the church to say whether it's on their left or right. Of course, both are telling the truth – as they see it! As human beings our perceptions are limited, and we only see things from one point of view. The truth is far greater than we can ever comprehend ourselves, and if the Spirit is to guide us into all truth we must be open to learning and growing as Christians, accepting our limitations and allowing God to teach us his ways.

PROPER 10

Sunday between 10 and 16 July inclusive

This Sunday's readings are all particularly well known. The parable of the Sower and its 'explanation' from Matthew 13 forms Year A's gospel reading; in Year B we have Mark's account of the beheading of John the Baptist; and from Luke 10 in Year C comes arguably the most familiar of all the parables, the Good Samaritan. It's never easy to tackle a very well-known parable, not only to find a rewarding slant on it when Jesus' succinctness speaks for itself, but also because there are unspoken assumptions around about 'what it really means'. The story of John the Baptist's demise is equally famous, though some may feel its subject-matter isn't entirely suitable for an all-age congregation. On the other hand we should be wary of 'picking and choosing' what we want to read from the Bible, and there's plenty to learn from this sorry sequence of events, without dwelling on its more sordid and gory aspects.

Hymns

TRADITIONAL

- *And can it be (32)*
- *Glory be to Jesus (206)*
- *God is working his purpose out (221)*
- *King of glory, King of peace (375)*
- *Now, my tongue, the mystery telling (473)*
- *The Lord will come and not be slow (655)*

CONTEMPORARY

- *Fill your hearts with joy and gladness (172)*
- *Jesus, Jesus, holy and anointed one (353)*
- *Lord, we know that we have failed you (423)*
- *Meekness and majesty (448)*
- *When I needed a neighbour (736)*
- *You shall go out with joy (766)*

CHANT

- *Wait for the Lord (949)*

CHILDREN'S SONG

- *Farmer, farmer, why do you plough? (796)*

Readings

Year A   Genesis 25:19-34 or Isaiah 55:10-13; Romans 8:1-11; Matthew 13:1-9, 18-23

Year B   2 Samuel 6:1-5, 12b-19 or Amos 7:7-15; Ephesians 1:3-14; Mark 6:14-29

Year C   Amos 7:7-17 or Deuteronomy 30:9-14; Colossians 1:1-14; Luke 10:25-37

Confession

God our Father, you have commanded us
to love you more than anything else,
and our neighbours as ourselves.
We confess that we are too preoccupied
with the concerns of this world,
and fail to give you the highest place in our lives;
that we think more of our own interests,
and fail to account for the needs of others.
Have mercy on us, we pray,
forgive our self-centred ways,
and increase our commitment to your kingdom,
for the sake of your Son,
Jesus Christ our Lord. Amen.

Absolution

Our heavenly Father,
whose care for his children never ceases,
grant *you* pardon for the wrong *you* have done
and the good *you* have not done,
deliver *you* from self-concern,
and grant *you* joy in sharing his love,
through Christ our Lord. Amen.

Prayer

Together we pray
that the fruits of God's kingdom
may be seen in our lives and in this world
as we say,
Lord, may the seed you sow
bear fruit for your glory.

We ask that the soil of your Church
be productive so that seeds of truth
and righteousness
may grow there for your glory.
Where your people face ill-treatment,
may courage prevail;
where they face corruption,

may truth and integrity overcome;
where they face disinterest,
may your hope and joy triumph.
Lord, may the seed you sow
bear fruit for your glory.

We ask that the soil of society be fruitful
so that seeds of peace and justice
may flourish and prosper.
Where there is violence and conflict,
establish harmony;
where there is poverty and hardship,
transform them with your riches;
where there is despair or misery,
dispel them with your eternal hope.
Lord, may the seed you sow
bear fruit for your glory.

We ask that the barren soil of suffering and pain
be turned into places of growth.
Where there is illness or depression,
give your healing;
where there is loneliness or grief,
give your comfort;
where there is fear or anxiety,
give your encouragement.
Especially we pray for . . .
Lord, may the seed you sow
bear fruit for your glory.

We ask that our own lives may be good soil,
yielding a harvest of goodness and love
for your kingdom.
Lord, may the seed you sow
bear fruit for your glory,
as we hear and respond to your word,
through Jesus Christ our Lord. Amen.

All-age address 1

Jesus' parables are so wonderfully concise, structured and illustrated that any attempt to explain or elaborate them can easily rob them of their power and impact. It's usually best to let them speak for themselves, perhaps with the help of simple visual aids to reinforce the point he's making. The parable of the sower needs nothing more than this, and the only preparation necessary is to gather the relevant items beforehand – a packet of seeds and four large flowerpots: one containing some old rocks or rubble, another with more rocks and rubble lightly covered with soil, one filled with soil and plenty of weeds, and the last one simply holding soil.

1) Take the packet of seeds and read out the instructions which will recommend planting in good clean soil for best results. Open it and display the first flowerpot, asking as you do so whether it will be of any use for these seeds. You should very rapidly get the answer that nothing could grow in it, and any seed that lands on it will be food for birds. Jesus made this same point, and likened it to the people who heard what he said, but immediately forgot about it and carried on as they were before. We still use the expression 'to fall on stony ground' to describe what happens when our words go unheeded. If we fail to listen carefully when God speaks to us, our lives will be like that, completely lifeless, with no personal or spiritual growth.

2) Now bring out the second flowerpot, show it to the congregation, and sprinkle a few seeds on it, again asking what will happen to them. 'Something might grow if you're lucky' is the sort of reply you'll receive. And it might, but not for long or very well. There's enough soil for growth to start but it's too shallow for anything to last, especially in either bad or hot weather. Jesus likened this to people who hear and respond to him, but give up as soon as the going gets tough. Our faith needs to be deeply rooted in him if it's to survive and grow.

3) The third flowerpot is held up for inspection at this point, and again you throw a few seeds on it, in among the weeds, asking how well these might grow. Point out the quantity of soil now available, but add that as long as it's full of weeds they'll strangle the life out of any new plant. Jesus used this to describe those who hear and respond but find their faith choked out by the concerns of everyday life. We need to deal with these distractions by seeing them in their true perspective if our faith is to grow and mature.

4) The final pot should meet with everyone's approval for planting seeds! This soil will

be productive because it's clean, rich and deep enough for plants to grow and develop. Conclude by saying that if we're to grow as Christians and become mature in our faith, we need to sort out the parts of our lives which are stony, shallow or weed-ridden. Sometimes we hear God's voice but it makes no impression at all; sometimes we start to respond but it soon seems too hard and we give up; sometimes we mean to respond to him, but become distracted by concerns here and now. Jesus wants us to be fruitful for him, like the good soil, so that our lives demonstrate the good news of his love and care, and so that our trust in him becomes deeper as we go through life.

All-age address 2

It's said that there have been more Christian martyrs in the twentieth century than in the previous nineteen since the time of Christ. There's no reason to doubt this statistic, though few Christians in western society will have first-hand experience of facing ill-treatment or even death for their faith. The worst we're likely to endure is ridicule or 'cold-shouldering'. This outline develops the idea of suffering for one's faith from the story of John the Baptist.

1) Gather together a few symbols of punishment – a cane or strap, a detention book from school, handcuffs, etc. Alternatively, produce them on an OHP transparency, and as you reveal them, ask what sort of offence these might punish (e.g. being cheeky to parents, failing to do homework, stealing). However, care should be taken if referring to smacking or caning, as some may be offended by the suggestion that this is a suitable way to reprimand bad behaviour – even though no value judgement is being made, you should consider how best to express this. Point out that there is a whole range of punishments designed to reflect the severity of an offence, from a ticking off to imprisonment. But we all recognise the injustice of someone receiving a punishment when they've done no wrong. That's what had happened to John

the Baptist. He'd been imprisoned for questioning King Herod's personal life and pointing out it's shortcomings.

2) Now say that John had suffered for two reasons – he'd stood up for the right way to behave, and confronted someone powerful who was disobeying God's law. Herod himself was intrigued by John, but his new wife was infuriated, and wanted him dead. Herod was a weak man, and in a vulnerable moment he allowed himself to be manipulated into executing John. Explain that while we probably won't be imprisoned for our faith we may suffer in other ways. If you can create them, clip-art-based OHPs to illustrate these will help make the points:

   a) we may well be laughed at (for going to church, for turning away from wrong);

   b) we may lose friends (especially if they feel threatened by our faith);

   c) we may miss out on promotion or other opportunities because we won't behave dishonestly or tread on other people;

   d) we may feel very vulnerable, especially with those who have authority over us.

John must have known what might happen to him for speaking out but he was courageous enough not to give in to fear and compromise himself. Many Christians have suffered similarly since then. The deeper our faith is, the stronger we'll be when such a time of testing comes our way.

All-age address 3

So familiar is the story of the Good Samaritan that the term is often used to refer to any act of kindness out of the ordinary. What we've lost is the sense of just how radical Jesus' words were to his contemporaries, since Samaritans and Jews were as far apart then, socially and religiously, as Jews and Palestinians today. The lawyer who asked the question thought he'd found a clever way to trap Jesus, but he soon found himself on the back foot, and tried to escape by asking for a definition of 'neighbour' – maybe he regretted it later!

This outline is built around Jesus' redefinition of who our neighbour is, and his challenge to some of our deeply held prejudices. It needs a couple of willing volunteers to act as victims – you might also like to mention a recent televised experiment on a busy street, in which a well-dressed female 'victim' was offered help within a couple of minutes, while a scruffy-looking male 'victim' was ignored for well over half an hour, and then assisted by a gentleman of the road!

1) The first person staggers into the church with torn clothes, tousled hair and, if possible, 'wounds' (created by make-up or face-paint – a friendly make-up artist in amateur dramatics might be willing to help) and collapses, in full view of the congregation. There may be a general reaction of surprise at this, so first ask who'd be willing to help the victim – one or two may well offer. Follow this up with a question about whether they'd still be willing to do so if they knew the man was a terrorist, or an AIDS victim, or perhaps someone they'd fallen out with and weren't speaking to. Point out that it's easy to make a good impression when the circumstances are right, but even easier to make an excuse not to get our hands dirty, as the priest and the lawyer did in Jesus' parable. This man needed immediate practical help, and he received it, not from those who'd have been expected to demonstrate God's love but from a Samaritan, who they'd have despised. Being a neighbour means interrupting what we're doing, however important it may seem, to help someone in need, rather than trying to justify our non-involvement.

2) The second volunteer comes in dressed as a tramp, shaking an old cap with a few coins in it. Again ask how many would be willing to help this person (though it may be advisable to add that money isn't necessarily the best help, as it might be used for harmful purposes). It's easy to be judgemental about such people, but Jesus doesn't allow for that. The Samaritan doesn't ask about the victim's cultural or educational background, his religious beliefs, or even his personal circumstances. Our excuses are usually ways of disguising these man-made barriers, but in God's kingdom they have no place. The lawyer who asked the question found it thrown back at him – which one is the true neighbour? The answer was clear enough, as was Jesus' reply, 'Go and do likewise'.

PROPER 11

Sunday between 17 and 23 July inclusive

The Parable of the Weeds forms the extract from Matthew's Gospel in Year A, continuing the kingdom parables from chapter 13. Year B gives us two extracts from Mark 6, which form the start of his account of the feeding of the five thousand and its sequel, while in Year C we have Luke's brief narrative of a homely scene chez Martha and Mary. A suitable outline address for both these latter two can be found at Proper 1, contrasting the need to be active for God's kingdom with the need for rest and refreshment, growing and learning.

Hymns

TRADITIONAL

- *At the name of Jesus (54)*
- *Bread of heaven, on thee we feed (82)*
- *Come, risen Lord, and deign to be our guest (126)*
- *The King of love my shepherd is (649)*
- *The Lord my pasture shall prepare (653)*
- *Ye watchers and ye holy ones (758)*

CONTEMPORARY

- *Abba Father (1)*
- *Alleluia (x8) (7)*
- *By your side (90)*
- *Father God, gentle Father God (158)*
- *Gather around, for the table is spread (199)*
- *Jesus, stand among us, at the meeting of our lives (361)*

CHANT

- *You are the centre (951)*

CHILDREN'S SONG

- *As Jacob with travel (775)*

Readings

Year A Genesis 28:10-19a or Isaiah 44:6-8; Romans 8:12-25; Matthew 13:24-30, 36-43

Year B 2 Samuel 7:1-14a or Jeremiah 23:1-6; Ephesians 2:11-22; Mark 6:30-34, 53-56

Year C Amos 8:1-12 or Genesis 18:1-10a; Colossians 1:15-28; Luke 10:38-42

Confession

Father of all,
we confess to you our sin and wrongdoing,
and ask your forgiveness
for the times when we have failed you.
For allowing the pressures of everyday life
to crowd you out,
for giving in to temptation's subtle voice,
and for not responding to your loving call,
pardon and deliver us, we pray.
Give us strength to resist
the easy path to destruction,
and to follow the route of Christ
which leads to life eternal,
in whose name we ask this. Amen.

Absolution

Almighty God,
the source of all life and love,
have mercy on *you*,
forgive all *your* sins and failings,
and by his Spirit enable *you*
to overcome evil and live for him,
through our Saviour Jesus Christ. Amen.

Prayer

We come to our heavenly Father,
finding it difficult
to put our deepest thoughts into words,
but knowing his Spirit will help us.
Lord, hear the cry of our hearts,
and show us how to pray.

Lord, events in the world often disturb us;
cruelty and neglect wreck many lives;
dishonesty and greed disfigure public life;
suffering and hardship go unnoticed
and untouched.
By your Spirit guide those who have authority . . .
We ask you to give hope
to the vulnerable and needy.
Lord, hear the cry of our hearts,
and show us how to pray.

Lord, conflicts and discord in the Church
upset us;
disagreements turn into rifts;
human differences become barriers;
fellowship and unity splinter apart.
By your Spirit guide Christian leaders
and ministers . . .

We ask you to give joy and oneness
to your people.
Lord, hear the cry of our hearts,
and show us how to pray.

Lord, pain and suffering among our loved ones
distresses us;
we share in their sadness and anxiety,
and pray for those whose lives are diminished
by illness, immobility, anxiety or desolation.
By your Spirit comfort and heal those we are
concerned for . . .
We ask bring them through their troubles
into your peace and joy.
Lord, hear the cry of our hearts,
and show us how to pray.

Be with us in pleasure and perplexity,
and lead us in the way of eternal life,
rejoicing in the hope you set before us
and living confidently for your glory.
Lord, hear the cry of our hearts,
and show us how to pray,
as we live day by day
in your Spirit's power,
through Jesus Christ our Lord. Amen.

All-age address

The parable of the wheat and the tares raises
the thorny issue of God being our judge, a
concept our society doesn't find easy to
accept. Yet at the same time judgementalism
is rife, as the media demonstrate endlessly.
However, it's important to avoid the trap of
suggesting that God shares our judgements
and makes all the same choices as we do. So
this outline looks at the sort of choices we
make, how we make them, and how God's
judgements differ from that. Some preparation
is necessary so that those who volunteer are
able to make their choices, but this can be as
basic or elaborate as time and circumstances
allow. As always, care is needed if the illustration isn't to overrun the points it's reinforcing.

1) Offer a selection of three types of confec-
tionery – for example, a toffee, a chocolate
and a wine gum – and ask someone to come
up and choose one. When they've done so,
ask them why they made that particular
choice. Taste, colour and texture will all
play a part, as might childhood memories,
but the grounds given will be personal and

entirely arbitrary – on another occasion the
same person might well choose differently!
Stress that, unlike us, God doesn't judge us
in a subjective or arbitrary way.

2) Next hold up three ties of very different
colours and design, and ask another volunteer to come and select one. Although this
will also be somewhat random, another
criterion comes into play, namely the circumstances in which the tie will be used – a
funeral, a wedding, a business meeting, a
party perhaps. Explain that God doesn't
judge people according to whether they suit
his purposes, and write off those who don't.

3) Find three reasonably large pictures of well-
known footballers (the sport isn't important,
but football probably has the broadest range
of appeal), and paste them on to card (you
may find your local team has publicity shots
they'll let you have). As you exhibit them,
ask which one should be playing for England
(Wales, Scotland, Ireland, or whatever team
is relevant locally). No doubt you'll get a
variety of views offered, all based on some
kind of reasoning – one person may think a
strong defender is necessary, to prevent
goals being given away, another will prefer a
midfielder who can win the ball, or a striker
who can score a lot of goals. However, God
doesn't judge us according to our ability.
Instead he chooses us and gives us the gifts
we need to serve and obey him, and the
strength to live by faith.

4) Finally, bring out three wedding photos,
asking as you do so why these people chose
each other. It's unlikely that anyone would
choose a life partner on the basis of their
ability, or because they fit a particular
purpose, yet neither would they say their
decision was arbitrary. The overriding factor
in choosing a spouse is love. Conclude by
emphasising that God chooses us, too,
because he loves us. Jesus' parable contrasts
the servants' attitude with the owner's. They
wanted to root out the weeds immediately
(just as we like immediate judgements), but
the owner tells them to wait until the harvest
is finally ready to be gathered; otherwise
they'll risk destroying some of the wheat as
well. We can't make judgements on God's
behalf, but we can be sure that, unlike ours,
his will always be fair.

PROPER 12

Sunday between 24 and 30 July inclusive

On this Sunday, the Year A reading from Matthew concludes the kingdom parables from chapter 13, while Year C gives us Luke's account of the Lord's Prayer and Jesus' teaching on prayer. However, Year B diverts us for a few weeks into John's gospel, with a sequence of readings from chapter 6. The first of these covers the feeding of the five thousand, picking up from the section omitted last week from Mark 6.

Hymns

TRADITIONAL

- *Lord of our life (417)*
- *Lord, teach us how to pray aright (418)*
- *Now is eternal life (470)*
- *Onward Christian pilgrims (531)*
- *Thy Kingdom come! (690)*
- *We love the place, O God (718)*

CONTEMPORARY

- *Alleluia: praise God (11)*
- *Let us praise God together (388)*
- *Make me a channel of your peace (437)*
- *Seek ye first (590)*
- *Who can sound the depths of sorrow (747)*
- *You are beautiful (760)*

CHANT

- *O Lord, hear my prayer (938)*

CHILDREN'S SONG

- *Break the bread and pour the wine (780)*

Readings

Year A Genesis 29:15-28 or 1 Kings 3:5-12;
Romans 8:26-39;
Matthew 13:31-33, 44-52
Year B 2 Samuel 11:1-15 or 2 Kings 4:42-44;
Ephesians 3:14-21; John 6:1-21
Year C Hosea 1:2-10 or Genesis 18:20-32;
Colossians 2:6-15 (16-19); Luke 11:1-13

Confession

We reach out to the Lord our God,
who is merciful and forgiving,
even though we have rebelled
against him, saying,
we turn to you in repentance;
Lord, pardon and restore us.

For pursuing our own ends,
instead of obeying your will,
we turn to you in repentance;
Lord, pardon and restore us.

For seeking human acclaim,
instead of waiting for your 'Well done!',
we turn to you in repentance;
Lord, pardon and restore us.

For putting our faith in this passing world,
instead of trusting your eternal love,
we turn to you in repentance;
Lord, pardon and restore us.

For behaving as though you did not matter,
instead of owning you as our King,
we turn to you in repentance;
**Lord, pardon and restore us,
and make us fit for your service
through Christ our Saviour. Amen.**

Absolution

God, who is slow to anger and swift to bless,
forgive all *your* sins and wrongdoing,
give *you* strength to obey him,
and fill *you* with the joy of his eternal kingdom,
through Jesus Christ our Lord. Amen.

Prayer

We come with confidence to God our Father,
praying as he teaches us
for his kingdom to come and his will to be done.
Lord, we ask this in your name;
hear us as we pray in faith.

May your will be done in the world around us,
desolated by our unwillingness
to act as good stewards of its riches.
Help us all to care for your creation . . .
and to work for all to share equally

in what your goodness has provided.
Lord, we ask this in your name;
hear us as we pray in faith.

May your will be done through governments,
leading the nations of the world
in times of crisis and change,
in peace or conflict, prosperity or adversity.
Help them to work for the common good . . .
to resist the temptations of power
and to promote justice and equality
for all people.
Lord, we ask this in your name;
hear us as we pray in faith.

May your will be done in our local community
through councillors and care organisations.
Help schools to nurture children in your ways;
social workers to offer new directions;
surgeries and hospitals to give relief and healing;
hospices and care homes to bring comfort
and hope to those nearing the end of their
lives . . .
Lord, we ask this in your name;
hear us as we pray in faith.

May your will be done in the lives of those
who need your comfort and healing . . .
Help them to know you share their troubles,
and bear their burdens.
Pierce the dark clouds of their present difficulties
with the light of your eternal presence.
Lord, we ask this in your name;
hear us as we pray in faith.

May your will be done through us
as we worship and serve you.
Help us to be channels of your peace
to bring your light into the darkness
of our world.
Lord, we ask this in your name;
**hear us as we pray in faith
for the sake of your Son,
our Lord Jesus Christ. Amen.**

All-age address 1

So far the Gospel readings from Matthew 13 have covered just two parables – the sower and the weeds. Today's verses cover another five! However, they're very brief, with just one (the net) returning to the theme of judgement, and the others focusing more on growth, impact and value. At first a mustard seed, a lump of yeast and a hidden pearl seem to have little in common, but in Jesus' parables all start off insignificant or hidden; only later are they seen to increase beyond imagining in scope, effect and value. The props for this outline are basic and should prove easy to obtain.

1) Take a fairly small seed (preferably one that can be seen only at close quarters) and place it in an unmarked envelope prior to the service. As you start, take it out and ask if someone can identify it. One or two might think it's a speck of dust, others will guess correctly that it'll grow into something if planted – an expert gardener might even identify it correctly! At a suitable point, tell the congregation what the seed will grow into when it's planted. It may not be at all obvious now, but it contains all that's necessary in the right growing conditions to become a geranium, lettuce or whatever you've chosen. The seed of God's kingdom will also grow so that, while it may seem very insignificant now, in due course it will come to dominate everything else.

2) Instead of putting live yeast into bread dough (rather messy as part of the liturgy!) a simpler way of conveying Jesus' second point is to make a cup of tea or coffee, and ask someone to add milk and sugar. Then suggest they drink it without either – which they'll immediately say is impossible. Like the yeast in Jesus' parable, the sugar and milk permeate the whole drink and change its taste permanently. God's kingdom may seem as small as those grains of sugar or a dash of milk, but one day it will indelibly transform the whole world.

3) The final picture is of something valuable but hidden, so that its value is only recognised by a few. Try to find something of moderate value which has been stored in the loft for some years, or discovered in a junk shop, without anyone realising its true worth – an old piece of jewellery or piece of porcelain might fit the bill (an old Dinky car is also an excellent example as its value is less

immediately obvious). You could ask the congregation to suggest how much the article is worth, but then add that it's not for sale because it's valuable to you. We treasure our own special possessions but Jesus wants his followers to put an even higher value on his kingdom, so that we'd be willing to give up almost anything else to obtain it. Conclude by reiterating Jesus' final point, that the kingdom's treasures are both old and new, to be found both in the wisdom of the past and the insights of the present.

All-age address 2

The narrative of the feeding of the five thousand, in John's gospel at least, has a distinctly Eucharistic flavour which is brought out more fully towards the end of this chapter. This outline therefore concentrates more on the miracle itself and the importance of being fed spiritually as well as physically. A variety of foods will need to be brought in to illustrate the parallels.

1) Carbohydrates are well illustrated by a bread roll, potato or bowl of cereal. Most folk are now well clued up about dietary matters (not least children from their school lessons), so it should be easy to extract the information that such foods are vital as a source of energy and warmth.

2) Proteins could be represented by milk or an egg, and somebody is likely to know that they're particularly useful for promoting the body's healing function (as well as providing more energy and heat!).

3) Eggs also exemplify the fats (as do cheese, butter, etc.). They too produce energy and warmth, but also help particular organs to work correctly, such as kidneys and eyes.

4) Vitamins can also be found in dairy products, though an orange or banana is a more familiar source. Everybody knows they're necessary to maintain the body in good working order, and to assist in the production of antibodies which fight disease.

5) Minerals such as calcium, found in dairy produce and green vegetables, are vital for healthy bones and teeth, while iron (in eggs, green vegetables and wholemeal bread) is essential for the blood.

6) Roughage is found in most vegetables and fruits (as well as cereals and certain types of bread), and is vital if the appetite is to be satisfied.

Don't allow this to degenerate into a science lesson – the point is that we all need a diet which contains these good things if we're to be healthy and well. Parallel each of these with the spiritual nourishment we need if we're to be truly whole. God's word gives strength and vitality of spirit to those who receive it; it promotes healing and wholeness; it's as essential to our daily living and health as good food; it satisfies us in the way nothing else can. No one would ever suggest we eat anything other than a healthy diet. As Christians we must give our spiritual diet an equally high priority.

All-age address 3

Jesus' teaching on prayer has never been equalled for its depth and richness, nor for its utter simplicity. Any attempt to be too elaborate or glib in handling the subject is bound to miss the target, so this outline aims simply to open up the significance for ourselves of Jesus' words to his disciples – that if they ask they will receive, if they seek they will find, if they knock there'll be a reply. Preparation involves making three cards, each written on both sides. The first has 'Ask' with 'Receive' on its reverse; the second has 'Seek' backed by 'Find'; the third has 'Knock' on one side and 'Open' on the other.

1) Start by asking what various members of the congregation would like as a birthday present (warning that you're not making any promises!). Some will make very modest demands, but others will be hoping for a new bicycle, computer, clothes, even a car. Point out that while asking for something is legitimate, there's no obligation on the donor to provide it! Ask a volunteer to hold

up the 'Ask' card at this point. Children will ask for all sorts of gifts, but for most families there isn't enough money to buy everything that's asked for, and wise parents or guardians recognise that, however much money they may have, it would be bad for children to be given whatever they want. Jesus certainly wasn't suggesting that his heavenly Father would give us absolutely anything – we'd all like more money, or a bigger house, but would soon become selfish and materialistic if God only answered prayers like those. Instead, Jesus wants us to keep on praying for things God wants, for his kingdom to come and for his will to be done, not least through us. Turn the card round now, and stress that if we pray like this we'll always receive an answer from God, even if it isn't the one we thought we'd get.

2) Display the 'Seek' card next, and ask if anyone's lost anything recently – the chances are that you'll hear about keys, credit cards, umbrellas or handbags! It's likely that someone will be willing to say how they tried to find the lost article. Maybe they turned the house out, returned to where they'd been earlier, or even phoned the police. If we lose something valuable we'll go to any lengths to find it again. God's kingdom's like that – (reverse the card as you make this point). The more effort we put into seeking his will, the more blessing we'll find in doing it.

3) Finally have someone hold up the 'Knock' card. Ask who enjoys visiting friends, and then whether their friends are always in when they call. If we know someone's in the house, especially if they've invited us, we'll carry on knocking at the door (in a polite British way, of course!) until the door is opened. Now reverse the card, saying finally that if we're faithful in our praying, God will open the door of opportunity at exactly the right time for us. It won't be an opportunity to serve our own ends, but to build God's kingdom and serve him.

PROPER 13

Sunday between 31 July and 6 August inclusive

For Year A Matthew's Gospel provides us this week with his account of the feeding of the 5000, while in Year B, Mark continues to be replaced by chapter 6 of John's Gospel. As we continue with Luke in Year C he records Jesus' parable of the Rich Fool, a passage which resonates deeply with our own times. A suitable outline address for Year A can be found under Proper 12.

Hymns

TRADITIONAL

- *Alleluia, sing to Jesus (12)*
- *Bread of heaven, on thee we feed (82)*
- *Guide me, O thou great Redeemer (252)*
- *He who would valiant be (281)*
- *Put thou thy trust in God (576)*
- *Take my life and let it be (625)*

CONTEMPORARY

- *Bread is blessed and broken (81)*
- *Have mercy on us, O Lord (269)*
- *Gather around, for the table is spread (199)*
- *My Lord, what love is this (462)*
- *Thanks for the fellowship (632)*
- *There's a quiet understanding (659)*

CHANT

- *You are the centre (951)*

CHILDREN'S SONG

- *Jesus is greater (847)*

Readings

Year A   Genesis 32:22-31 or Isaiah 55:1-5; Romans 9:1-5; Matthew 14:13-21

Year B   2 Samuel 11:26-12:13a or Exodus 16:2-4, 9-15; Ephesians 4:1-16; John 6:24-35

Year C   Hosea 11:1-11 or Ecclesiastes 1:2, 12-14; 2:18-23; Colossians 3:1-11; Luke 12:13-21

Confession

We kneel before you, Creator God, repenting of our many failures. We have used your world to accumulate wealth rather than build your kingdom; we have put personal comfort above meeting the needs of others; we have lived according to human wisdom rather than by faith in you. Have mercy on us, we pray, forgive our self-centredness, and by your Spirit help us to store up treasure in heaven, through Jesus Christ our Lord. Amen.

Absolution

Almighty God, who has made all things for our enjoyment, grant *you* forgiveness for all *your* sins, strength to live a new life by faith in him, and fix *your* eyes on the things which are above, through Christ our Lord. Amen.

Prayer

Our heavenly Father, who created the vastness of the universe, knows our needs and the inexpressible prayers of our hearts, which we bring to him now, saying, Lord, we call on you; **hear and answer our prayer.**

Hear us as we pray for the church and those who lead it, locally and nationally . . . Bless and guide the ministry of evangelists and mission workers, pastors and teachers, prophets and preachers, that they may build up the body of Christ . . . May we work together to bring others into your kingdom. Lord, we call on you; **hear and answer our prayer.**

Hear us as we pray for this world and those you have given influence over it . . . Guide bankers and economists to work honestly and fairly, guide the police and lawyers to strive for justice,

guide politicians and activists
to seek peace . . .
May we work together
for the standards of your kingdom.
Lord, we call on you;
hear and answer our prayer.

Hear us as we pray for the needy and deprived:
for those without home or family to belong to,
those vulnerable and open to abuse
by the powerful,
those lacking the most basic resources
for living . . .
Guide carers, healers and aid-workers
to show your compassion . . .
May we join in mutual care for the needy.
Lord, we call on you;
hear and answer our prayer.

Hear us as we pray for loved ones
and neighbours,
those passing through the dark shadows
of suffering in mind or body . . .
Guide them in times of distress
with your healing hand,
and hide them in the shadow of your wings.
Lord, we call on you;
hear and answer our prayer.

Hear us as we pray for ourselves,
that our steps may keep to your path
as we walk with you by faith.
Lord, we call on you;
hear and answer our prayers,
for the sake of your Son,
Jesus Christ our Lord. Amen.

All-age address 1

For something which forms a staple part of our diet, bread comes in an incredible variety of forms. Apart from the sliced loaves which come in packets, we can buy cottage or whole-meal loaves, bloomers or baguettes, split tins or ciabatti, rye bread, pittas, nans . . . and as well as being tasty they make a very attractive illustration for an all-age talk! This outline develops the idea of Jesus as the Bread of Life, using the real thing to help us understand something of what he meant. A few examples of different types of bread are needed (including

one or two of foreign origin), and, if possible, a lump of bread dough, some yeast, and 'one you prepared earlier'. You may find an enthusiastic baker among the congregation to help you with this, but bear in mind that it is slightly messy and requires an apron to ensure clothes aren't spoiled. If you normally wear robes, you may feel they're not the most suitable attire!

1) First bring out the dough and either ask for a volunteer to come and knead it or do so yourself. At the same time, ask why bread is so important in our diet. There are several possible responses to this, the first of which is likely to be 'It's good for us'. Bread contains many elements which promote good health, though it's not necessary to list them. Just as bread forms the basis of our diet, so we also need Jesus to be our spiritual diet. Listening to him, following him, growing in him, are all essential to our spiritual health.

2) The next response may well be 'You can use it for anything'. Bread is very adaptable, can be used in a variety of ways and blends well with most other tastes. There's no situation in life in which Jesus doesn't fit, because all life has its origin in him. His presence transforms even the bleakest of outlooks.

3) Another possible response is 'It fills you up' – you may get this from mothers who have to feed hungry offspring! A couple of rounds of sandwiches doesn't leave a lot of room for anything else. Just as bread can satisfy our physical hunger, so Jesus, the Bread of Life, satisfies our spiritual hunger or longing. As we feed on him day by day we find that we need nothing else.

4) If you're using dough and yeast, bring out the yeast at this point and explain that the bread won't rise without it. Add some yeast and ask why it isn't rising, then explain that the yeast needs time to work through the whole lump of dough. The same is true of our spiritual life – it doesn't just suddenly happen but, like the yeast, God's love gradually affects the whole way we think and live, which you can demonstrate by bringing out a baked loaf that's ready to eat.

5) Finally display a few different kinds of bread from across the world, at the same time emphasising that Jesus is the Bread of Life for all people, whatever their colour, race, education, age or gender.

All-age address 2

Jesus wasn't one to pull his punches, and throughout the Gospels he regularly challenged the assumptions of the day, not least in practical matters such as money. This parable was his response to a rather tedious question from someone who wanted to prove he was in the right in a dispute with his brother over a legacy. Jesus refused to be drawn into taking sides, but he also got under his questioner's skin by confronting his need to increase his wealth. The parable of the rich man who thought he'd got it made is a chilling indictment of this mentality – in this world's terms he appeared successful and well-heeled, but in God's eyes he was a short-sighted fool who was prepared to mortgage his eternal future for what proved to be very short-term gain. We too live in a society which confuses making the most of each moment as a gift from God with living for the moment, as though there were no future. This outline aims to address, as Jesus did, the prevailing short-term materialistic philosophy by which many people live, and requires just a few simple preparations plus a couple of forewarned volunteers.

1) Find an old print or painting which is of little or no value and describe it as though you were an expert on the Antiques Roadshow. Make it clear that you've found this in the loft and you're convinced it's a priceless old master which will make you a fortune! You could even say how you'd use the hundreds of thousands of pounds it must be worth. Then go to your first volunteer, who poses as an art expert and explains that the most he could offer you for it is £2.46. Express your disappointment, but go on to indicate that even if it had been worth a vast sum, you wouldn't have been any happier. In fact, many of those who've won huge sums on the Lottery have become miserable as a result. Jesus wanted the man to realise that while we need money to live, if it takes over our life we'll become discontented and unhappy.

2) Prepare a piece of paper on which is written 'Share Certificate' and '1,000,000'. If it looks authentic so much the better, though nobody will be fooled. Tell everyone that your investments have paid off and you've got a million shares, so you're going to a stockbroker to cash them. Your second volunteer acts this role, and tells you that the companies you've invested in have gone bankrupt, so the shares are worthless. After a brief show of disappointment explain that during the Black Monday share crash of 1987 many people who thought they'd got rich quickly suddenly discovered they had nothing. The wealth of this world is very short-lived, and can't bring any lasting satisfaction. Jesus wanted his hearers to understand that the best investment they could ever make was in God's kingdom. The gains aren't immediate or spectacular, but they last for ever.

3) Jesus finishes his parable with the rich man's death. All his wealth will go to someone else and he'll soon be forgotten, because he was interested only in feathering his own nest. By making God's kingdom our priority we get the 'treasures' of this world in their proper perspective, to be enjoyed, but above all used for God's glory and to bring his love and care to others, especially those in need. All of us have to die and then answer to God for what we did with our lives. Since we don't know when that will be, how important it is to be prepared for it now.

PROPER 14

Sunday between 7 and 13 August inclusive

We continue in Matthew 14 in Year A with his account of Jesus walking on water, to which the writer adds how Peter attempted to emulate this – the outline suggested in Proper 7 for Year C could be utilised for this, with a brief addition added here to tackle Peter's failure to walk on the lake. In Year B we have a third extract from Jesus' Bread of Life discourse in John 6, and in Year C Luke's Gospel continues in chapter 12 with more of Jesus' teaching about wealth and 'investing our treasure' in heaven, including the parable of the servants who were ready for their master's return.

Hymns

TRADITIONAL

- *Dear Lord and Father of mankind (144)*
- *Eternal Father, strong to save (153)*
- *Oft in danger, oft in woe (487)*
- *The Lord will come, and not be slow (655)*
- *Through all the changing scenes of life (686)*
- *To thee, O Lord, our hearts we raise (696)*

CONTEMPORARY

- *Come on and celebrate (125)*
- *I am the Bread of Life (299)*
- *I will bless the Lord (335)*
- *Light of the minds that know him (397)*
- *Listen, let your heart keep seeking (401)*
- *Tell his praise in song and story (630)*

CHANT

- *Eat this bread (926)*

CHILDREN'S SONG

- *Put your trust (882)*

Readings

Year A   Genesis 37:1-4, 12-28 or
          1 Kings 19:9-18; Romans 10:5-15;
          Matthew 14:22-33
Year B   2 Samuel 18:5-9, 15, 31-33 or
          1 Kings 19:4-8; Ephesians 4:25-5:2;
          John 6:35, 41-51
Year C   Isaiah 1:1, 10-20 or Genesis 15:1-6;
          Hebrews 11:1-3, 8-16; Luke 12:32-40

Confession

We turn back to the Lord,
from whose paths we have strayed, saying,
In your mercy, O Lord,
redeem us and help us.

You created our hands for loving service,
but we have used them to grasp and snatch.
In your mercy, O Lord,
redeem us and help us.

You created our lips to sing your praise
and tell your good news,
but we have used them to criticise and scorn.
In your mercy, O Lord,
redeem us and help us.

You created our minds to think of your glory,
but we have dwelt only on this passing world.
In your mercy, O Lord,
redeem us and help us.

You created our hearts to respond to your love
and share it with others,
but we have considered only our own interests.
In your mercy, O Lord,
redeem us and help us.
to live the new life
in Jesus Christ our Lord. Amen.

Absolution

Almighty God,
who created *you* in his own image,
forgive *your* waywardness and sinfulness,
pardon *your* wrongdoing,
and restore *you* to himself through his Son,
Jesus Christ our Lord. Amen.

Prayer

With confidence and quiet hearts,
we approach our heavenly Father
with our prayers and thanksgiving, saying:
Lord, our hope is in you;
with you there is unfailing love.

We bring you our concerns
for the many hurting places of our world,
where hunger and starvation dominate,
and hatred or conflict deprive people
of freedom . . .
We pray for those whose pain is continuous;
the homeless, addicts, alcoholics,
the isolated, and victims of abuse . . .

May the distress in our hearts
become practical action
to share your love with them.
Lord, our hope is in you;
with you there is unfailing love.

We bring you our prayers for the Church;
for local fellowship and ecumenical groups,
for Christian leaders, both local and national,
and for young people throughout the world . . .
We pray for all projects and initiatives
which bring your people together,
and demonstrate the good news of Jesus
to those who do not know it . . .
May we work with one purpose and vision.
Lord, our hope is in you;
with you there is unfailing love.

We bring you our loved ones and friends,
and those in our community
who are burdened with care or suffering . . .
We pray for hospitals,
for medical and nursing staff,
for psychiatrists and counsellors,
who work to bring relief and healing . . .
May we extend your healing touch to the sick.
Lord, our hope is in you;
with you there is unfailing love.

We bring you those who have died
in the faith of Christ . . .
We pray for their loved ones enduring
the lonely grief of bereavement,
and ask you to bless and comfort them . . .
May we be challenged by the example
of those who have gone before us.
Lord, our hope is in you;
with you there is unfailing love.

Heavenly Father we bring you ourselves,
weak and fallible as we are,
praying for the strength and guidance
of the Holy Spirit
to help us live for you.
Lord, our hope is in you;
with you there is unfailing love,
seen in your Son Jesus Christ,
through whom we offer these prayers. Amen.

All-age address 1

The second outline address for Proper 7 (based on Mark's account of Jesus calming the storm) is equally applicable to Matthew's account.

However, Matthew adds the extra dimension of Peter's attempt to walk on the water, so you might prefer to use this adaptation of the third point.

Start by showing the picture of a round-the-world voyage (or some similar achievement) and talk briefly about the natural fear the participants must have had, and how they prepared thoroughly for every possible risk and eventuality. Peter wasn't trying to achieve something he'd been working up to for most of his life. He wanted Jesus to prove who he really was by giving him the courage to walk on the water. But his fear got the better of his faith, and Jesus had to catch hold of him as he started to sink in the wind-driven waves. We'd probably all share Peter's terror in this situation, but the power of Jesus can overcome even our deepest human fears if we allow him to be Lord of our lives as well as Lord of creation.

All-age address 2

The more extended discourses and passages of John's Gospel require rather more thought if they're to be translated effectively and meaningfully into an all-age worship address. In this section of chapter 6 Jesus' statement that he is the Bread of Life has irritated the religious leadership, who cope with it by belittling his background and trying to make him merely human. All they could see was the carpenter's son from Nazareth, so they were blind to the bigger picture. This outline is simple, but a little preparation is necessary. Take a couple of full-page pictures from the ever-useful Sunday colour supplements (or any other source, provided the picture is at least A4 size and easily recognised). One should be of a well-known person (ideally a pop star, TV or sporting personality who children will relate to); the other could be of a well-known place (Nelson's Column, Tower Bridge, the Eiffel Tower, or anywhere else the congregation will identify straightaway). Paste them on to card and cut them into five or six irregular-shaped pieces.

1) Take the first picture (it doesn't matter which) and show the congregation one piece of it. Ask if anyone knows who or where it is – hopefully any guesses will be wrong at this stage! Add a piece at a time, stopping to ask if anyone's worked it out. Sooner or later it

will become obvious. Explain that at first we often don't recognise things because we only see one part of the picture. That was the religious leaders' problem. All they saw was a carpenter's son, and they got it wrong because they wouldn't look any further.

2) Now go through the same process with the second picture. This time explain that the people of Jesus' time didn't know all that we now do, and they hadn't yet recognised the connection between the manna in the wilderness (a story they'd have all learned as children) and Jesus who said he was the bread who came down from heaven. Only later did the early Christians recognise what he really meant as they celebrated the 'Lord's Supper' as Jesus had commanded them. They knew who Jesus was, and slowly their eyes were opened to see how the whole of his life made sense in the light of their scriptures, the Old Testament. Conclude by emphasising how easy it is for all of us to reduce Jesus down to one small part of the picture and ignore everything else. Stress the importance of us having open eyes so that we see the 'big picture', and understand Jesus not just in terms of the whole Bible, essential though that is, but in the context of our own lives too, and the lives of other people.

All-age address 3

Jesus often spoke of the need for his followers to be ready – something we thought about at Advent. The passage from Luke's Gospel combines the parable of the reliable servants who were ready for their master's return with the action required of us to ensure that we're similarly ready. A suitable outline address is the second all-age address for Advent Sunday, but the following outline is an adaptation of that. It needs a couple of primed volunteers and a few props – dusters and some furniture polish, some flowers in a vase, and some token dinner-party food (e.g. a bottle of wine, a few 'nibbles' and maybe a couple of glasses). You could also use a table and chairs as the 'set' for a room, though this isn't necessary.

1) Your volunteers are hosts expecting some guests, although there's some uncertainty about their arrival time. Indicate that they want to be properly ready whenever this should be, so they're making preparations. The first volunteer is busy with the duster and polish, and when you ask what they're up to, they should explain that 'the place is a tip', and in need of a clean and tidy-up. If we invite guests to our home we want it to look clean and presentable, rather than dusty, grubby, and littered with old newspapers or sweet wrappers. If we're to be ready for Jesus, our master, our lives need to be cleaned up, and the clutter and mess sorted out. That's not something we can do by ourselves, so we need his strength and forgiveness to enable us to deal with it.

2) The second volunteer starts to arrange the glasses and brings out the wine and nibbles (or whatever's appropriate to your community). When you ask why they're doing this, they say that it's much easier to pay attention to guests if you've made the necessary preparations in advance. Jesus' parable is about a wedding feast, but he goes even further by saying that if the master comes home to find his servants so well prepared, even in the middle of the night, he'll be willing to wait at table for them! Our friends would find it very strange if they arrived in response to our invitation only to find that no food had been prepared. Jesus expects us to be prepared for his return with a 'banquet' of obedience to him, and care for others.

3) One of the volunteers now brings out the vase of flowers, saying that it will help make the place more welcoming. It's not something you have to do, but an extra touch that makes guests feel more welcomed and cared for. Jesus wants us to be ready, not by grudgingly doing what he says but by welcoming him gladly into our lives.

4) Finally, get the volunteers to sit down and 'nod off' for a moment. As soon as their eyes are shut two more volunteers arrive unannounced as the guests. Oh dear! God doesn't want us to make domestic preparations, but when he arrives he wants to see us active in his service, by caring for those in need rather than indulging our material desires, and sharing his love with others. That's the way to be truly ready for him, and to hear him say, 'Well done'.

PROPER 15

Sunday between 14 and 20 August inclusive

As we continue through the middle of the holiday season Matthew's Gospel reading in Year A tells of the faith of the Canaanite woman, while in Year B the readings from chapter 6 of John's Gospel continue with Jesus explaining that those who eat of his flesh and drink of his blood will have eternal life – a suitable outline address for this can be found at Maundy Thursday, when we give thanks for the institution of the Lord's Supper. The Year C Gospel from Luke 12 is also quite daunting in the context of all-age worship, and the focus here is on 'interpreting the times'.

Hymns

TRADITIONAL

- *Author of life divine (56)*
- *Awake, awake: fling off the night (57)*
- *Give us the wings of faith to rise (204)*
- *God of mercy, God of grace (227)*
- *My God, and is thy table spread (456)*
- *Thee we adore, O hidden Saviour, thee (640)*

CONTEMPORARY

- *Broken for me, broken for you (87)*
- *Here is bread (277)*
- *Lord, we come to ask your healing (422)*
- *O Lord, all the world belongs to you (509)*
- *Taste and see the goodness of the Lord (628)*
- *The table's set, Lord (668)*

CHANT

- *Eat this bread (926)*

CHILDREN'S SONG

- *Break the bread and pour the wine (780)*

Readings

Year A   Genesis 45:1-15 or Isaiah 56:1, 6-8;
Romans 11:1-2a, 29-32;
Matthew 15:(10-20) 21-28

Year B   1 Kings 2:10-12; 3:3-14 or
Proverbs 9:1-6; Ephesians 5:15-20;
John 6:51-58

Year C   Isaiah 5:1-7 or Jeremiah 23:23-29;
Hebrews 11:29-12:2; Luke 12:49-56

Confession

Lord God, full of mercy and compassion,
we confess to you our sin and failure.
Our mouths have not always
proclaimed your praise;
our feet have not always been swift
to follow where you lead;
our hearts are often unprepared
for you to come and dwell.
We are truly sorry and ask you to forgive us.
Make us clean we pray,
and by your Spirit strengthen us
to live in the way which pleases you,
to the glory of your name. Amen.

Absolution

God our Father,
who welcomes all who turn to him
in penitence and faith,
have mercy on *you*,
pardon and deliver *you* from all wrongdoing,
and lead *you* out from darkness
into the light of his eternal glory. Amen.

Prayer

Remembering that our heavenly Father
is faithful and just,
we bring him our requests and cares,
knowing he will keep his promise
to hear and answer us.
Lord, you are gracious and compassionate;
remember your promise for ever.

Hear us as we pray for the Christian Church,
spread across the world yet one in your love:
for bishops, clergy and leaders;
for teachers and pastors,
missionaries and evangelists;
for local congregations . . .
May your people overcome divisions of culture,
and work as one for your kingdom.
Lord, you are gracious and compassionate;
remember your promise for ever.

Hear us as we pray for the world we live in,
damaged by greed and self-will,
yet still reflecting your love:
for politicians and diplomats
working in international relations;
for journalists and broadcasters
conveying information and opinion;
for financiers and economists
handling vast sums of money . . .
May those with great responsibility
use it wisely, for the good of all.
Lord, you are gracious and compassionate;
remember your promise for ever.

Hear us as we pray for the hurting and needy,
bearing their burden yet forgotten by society:
for the homeless and destitute;
for the exploited and downtrodden;
for the fearful and lonely;
for those we know and care for . . .
May your arms of love surround them,
your hand reach out to them,
and your voice reassure them
as you guide them through their trials.
Lord, you are gracious and compassionate;
remember your promise of mercy.

Hear us as we commit ourselves to your care
and trust you for all that lies ahead.
May we rejoice in your presence
and go forward in your strength
until we reach the prize
of your calling in Christ Jesus.
Lord, you are gracious and compassionate;
**remember your promise of mercy
in Jesus our Saviour,
now and for evermore. Amen.**

All-age address 1

The account of Jesus healing a Canaanite (or Syro-Phoenician) woman's daughter will be familiar to many regular worshippers from the Prayer of Humble Access. In asking Jesus to heal her daughter, she knew she was acting out of turn, at least from the Jews' point of view, but she was willing to believe that this might not be a problem for Jesus. Even though he tested her faith initially, it was strong enough to stand firm, and Jesus willingly healed the child. The Jews believed strongly that God favoured them above the Gentiles, so the true significance of this miracle wasn't lost on the writers of Matthew and Mark. Some preparation is needed in the form of four large cardboard boxes (ideally of the size used by removal firms for packing), one long side of each being covered with plain white paper. One word is written on each of these: 'race', 'class', 'gender', 'culture'. Fold the bottom and top flaps inside, and start with a forewarned volunteer who stands still while the boxes are lowered over his head, each one resting on the previous one. These are the barriers which people erect between each other, and which the healing power of Jesus destroys.

1) 'Race' should be on the top box. The woman from Syrian Phoenicia was of Greek origin according to Mark, and for Jews she was racially inferior as a Gentile. Racial bigotry is particularly hard to overcome as it relates to all kinds of deep-seated fears and assumptions about something no one has any control over. The woman herself recognised how she would be perceived by the Jews, but Jesus shows that the insulting term 'dogs' is not how he sees those of other races. At this point take away the box to reveal a bit of the volunteer. Jesus treated people as equal, regardless of their racial background – we should do likewise.

2) Next should come the 'gender' box. We're fortunate to live at a time when women are accepted on the same level as men more than ever before – it's hard for us to imagine how difficult life was for a woman in Jesus' time. This woman had to overcome all the typical male prejudices of the day in order to claim Jesus' attention, and even the disciples were rather patronising. Maybe Jesus teased her gently (her reply possibly suggests she realised that), but she wasn't going to give up just because she was female. Now remove the second box, emphasising that women are just as valuable in God's sight as men.

3) 'Class' comes next, and if we feel we do reasonably well on 'race' and 'gender' issues, the British have a strong class system which is hard to budge because it's so ingrained. This woman clearly recognised

that her race and sex left her at a disadvantage in Jewish society, or put her in 'a lower class'. Many factors affect how we view class – education, accent, family background, financial status – but none of them mattered to Jesus. Unlike us he never pigeon-holed people, but accepted everyone on their own merits. Indeed, he was far more accepting of people like this woman than of the self-righteous religious hypocrites who flaunted their social status. As you say this, remove the box, leaving just one.

4) The fourth box is marked 'culture', and perhaps contains a mixture of elements – race, religious belief, artistic expression . . . However, it's sometimes a barrier and we use it to stereotype people who see things a bit differently to ourselves. Jesus does the opposite, taking each person for who they are.

In performing this miracle Jesus is challenging all kinds of contemporary conventions, but he commends the woman's faith in a way which we see on only one other occasion in the Gospels (the Centurion whose servant was healed). She may be different in some ways but like him her faith puts most of Israel to shame. As you remove the last box, conclude by saying that God doesn't put people in boxes and build barriers around them. As Christians the love of Christ within us should help to break all of these down wherever we encounter them.

All-age address 2

Jesus' words in the passage from Luke have been much misunderstood and misrepresented – he's clearly describing the consequences of his mission, not its purpose. Since he never advocated conflict or violence, and commended the peacemakers, Jesus can't be encouraging his followers to turn on their own families. But it's quite possible that within his own family there were potentially destructive tensions over his ministry, and this was certainly true for many of his followers. Therefore he wants them to interpret the 'signs of the times'. Since they could do it in simple matters such as forecasting the weather, surely they're also capable of interpreting correctly the events of his ministry. This outline aims to help show how God can be seen at work in the world and in our lives by looking at the way we draw conclusions from everyday events.

1) There are few areas of life which are more subject to media speculation and interpretation than sport. Football tends to be the most widely acknowledged sport in most areas, though if cricket, rugby, motor racing or something else makes more sense in your community then use that. Whichever sport you choose, pundits will be assessing the chances and merits of both teams and individuals, and the possible results of league and cup competitions. You may well find your local club is willing to let you have a team photo or something similar to use as a visual aid. It's hardly an exact science though. Past and present form may be a guide, key players may be injured, and weather conditions may be a factor, but there'll always be some guesswork. That's not true of God. He doesn't leave us guessing about what might happen next but guides us forward day by day as we trust him to lead us in the right paths.

2) At the same time the British also love speculating about the weather! It's a basic conversation starter, and we spend a great deal of time commenting on present conditions or anticipating those in store. Either photocopy an outline map of the country and mark it with words such as 'windy', 'sunny and warm', 'rainy' or 'icy', or display a wall map, indicating what sort of weather each area will enjoy. Nowadays we can be very accurate in forecasting the weather, thanks to satellites and scientific advances. Jesus' contemporaries didn't have that advantage, though they were able to make reasonable attempts at predicting the weather. Sadly they didn't apply the same principles to God, and refused to recognise that he had sent his Son to be the promised Messiah. We don't know everything about God just because we're Christians, but we can be sure that he'll keep his promises and guide us in the right paths.

3) Finally bring out an item of little value (for example, an old cup and saucer, or an ornament) and ask for opinions as to whether its value will increase with time – some answers will be more serious than others! While we know that certain things have become more valuable over a number of years, human estimations of their worth will fluctuate unpredictably. The religious leaders of Jesus' day seemed concerned only with fickle and temporary human values and were quite incapable of seeing in him things that related to eternity. The only values we can be sure of are the ones which last for ever, which is why Jesus tells us to make sure our treasure is stored up in heaven.

PROPER 16

Sunday between 21 and 27 August inclusive

As we read on through Matthew's Gospel in Year A, we reach Peter's confession of Christ at Caesarea Philippi, while Year B sees the conclusion of the brief excursion into John 6. Year C brings us Luke's retelling of the healing of a crippled woman on the Sabbath, and the subsequent clash with the Jewish authorities.

Hymns

TRADITIONAL

- *Be thou my vision (70)*
- *Bread of the world in mercy broken (83)*
- *I'm not ashamed to own my Lord (316)*
- *Lord Christ, who on thy heart (407)*
- *Praise my soul, the King of heaven (565)*
- *Soldiers of Christ, arise (606)*

CONTEMPORARY

- *Alleluia, alleluia, give thanks (8)*
- *From the very depths of darkness (198)*
- *I danced in the morning (305)*
- *Jesus, the broken bread (363)*
- *Lamb of God, Holy One (377)*
- *You are the King of Glory (762)*

CHANT

- *Bless the Lord, my soul (923)*

CHILDREN'S SONG

- *Jesus is special (848)*

Readings

Year A   Exodus 1:8-2:10 or Isaiah 51:1-6;
Romans 12:1-8; Matthew 16:13-20
Year B   1 Kings 8:(1, 6, 10-11) 22-30, 41-43 or
Joshua 24:1-2a, 14-18;
Ephesians 6:10-20; John 6:56-69
Year C   Jeremiah 1:4-10 or Isaiah 58:9b-14;
Hebrews 12:18-29; Luke 13:10-17

Confession

Merciful God, our loving Father,
we acknowledge our sins before you
with penitent hearts.
We have not always offered ourselves to you
as living sacrifices;
our lives are not always transformed
by a renewed mind;
we have not always used the gifts of the Spirit
to build up one another in the Body of Christ.
We ask you to forgive us
through your Son Jesus Christ,
so that we may not be conformed
to this world,
but instead live to your praise and glory.
Amen.

Absolution

God our Father,
from whom comes every good and perfect gift,
grant *you* pardon for all
that has been unworthy of him,
forgive all *your* sin,
and renew *you* in mind,
transforming *you* into his likeness
for the sake of his Son,
Jesus Christ our Lord. Amen.

Prayer

As we bring the burden of our prayers to God,
who satisfies and renews us, we say:
Lord, you work justice for the oppressed;
make your ways known to all people.

We bring you those oppressed
by the circumstances of their lives:
street children in the world's great cities;
inhabitants of refugee camps;
casualties of civil war or harsh government;
victims of crime and abuse . . .
Reassure and comfort them in their misery,
and open the hearts of the wealthy
to be generous and compassionate.
Lord, you work justice for the oppressed;
make your ways known to all people.

We bring you those oppressed
by the consequences of their own behaviour:

drug addicts, alcoholics,
prisoners, young offenders,
and those whose lives do not conform . . .
Meet them at their point of deepest need,
and heal them of all harmful influences
or past hurt.
Lord, you work justice for the oppressed;
make your ways known to all people.

We bring you those oppressed
by illness or handicap:
the hospital-bound and housebound
the frail and infirm elderly, the chronically sick,
the depressed or mentally disturbed . . .
May they know your peace and encouragement,
and your healing love at work in their lives.
Lord, you work justice for the oppressed;
make your ways known to all people.

We bring you the Church of which we are part,
called to proclaim your message
of release for those in captivity . . .
Open our eyes to recognise those
who are enslaved,
our lips to announce the good news
of freedom through Jesus Christ,
and our hearts to respond
with your compassion.
Lord, you work justice for the oppressed;
make your ways known to all people,
that the whole earth may sing your praise
and rejoice in your love,
through our Saviour Jesus Christ. Amen.

All-age address 1

The passage from Matthew 16 in which Peter confesses Jesus to be the promised Messiah can be well served by the address outline for the Sunday Next Before Lent, based on the Transfiguration. However, the vital point here is not just Peter's recognition of Jesus, but his acknowledgement of who he is, and his response. For this address you need to add a simple extra point about how we might react to someone well known or important if we met them. For example you could ask for, or make, suggestions about the right way to respond to a request from the headteacher, the managing director, the prime minister or the Archbishop of Canterbury. You may need to ignore disrespectful answers, but in general

terms if one of those asked us to do something, we'd be very likely to comply with the request! Conclude by saying that just as Peter fulfilled his commission from his Master, so, as we respond in faith to Christ and his calling, he will give us the strength to carry it out.

All-age address 2

The cost of following Jesus isn't the most popular subject for any sermon, but in an age of glossy, high-powered marketing and sales techniques it's an essential aspect of the Gospel to proclaim. In marketing or recruitment terms Jesus' refusal to shirk the realities of the Gospel would be fairly disastrous! However, it's both untrue to the Gospel and dangerously misleading to imply that a decision to follow Christ will provide an escape route from all known problems and lead to a trouble-free life. The following simple outline aims to present both the reality and the joys of the life of faith. It uses five simple cartoon-style drawings either on a computer-generated OHP acetate or a flip-chart, although if you had an experienced climber in your congregation they would probably have greater impact – not many congregations are likely to have such access, however.

1) The first picture is of a steep mountain, with two small climber figures looking up and pointing to it. Start out by saying that anyone wanting to reach the summit will need to think carefully about how tough it'll be to get there. There's no point tackling it if they haven't thought about the challenge it presents, and how they'll meet it.

2) The second picture is of our two climbers preparing their mountaineering gear – boots, rope and a pickaxe, for example. They obviously realise it's more than a stroll in the country! Jesus never promised that the Christian life would be as simple and undemanding as a gentle ramble – on the contrary, he was quite clear that at times it would be as tough as mountain climbing. However, he also promised that his Holy Spirit would give all the strength and resources needed to meet the demands of following him.

3) The third picture is of the two climbers climbing a steep slope with their rucksacks on their backs – some indication of exertion and fatigue would underline the point. Mountaineers have to carry their own equipment, and it sometimes feels very heavy! Jesus said that 'carrying our cross' is an essential part of the life of faith, and there'll be times when we feel like giving up or trying another way. Perseverance is a vital aspect of discipleship.

4) The fourth picture is of one climber lying down, holding his leg in pain, while the other one is helping him. On our Christian journey there'll also be times when we fall or get hurt. Jesus has promised that he will be there alongside us, to heal, pick us up and dust us down, and set us on our way again.

5) The final picture is of the two climbers on top of the mountain, with a flag flying and big smiles on their faces. After all the exertion and bruises they've made it, and they're enjoying the wonderful view and the fact that they're on the summit! The enjoyment is greater because they've struggled to get there. The Christian life isn't easy, but if we keep going in God's strength we know that one day we'll have the joy of seeing him ourselves and being with him for ever.

All-age address 3

Luke's account of Jesus healing a crippled woman on the Sabbath is focused primarily on the subsequent dispute with the authorities. Having lots of detailed rules suited them well as it kept them in control, but where those rules worked against the welfare of those in need, or against the true worship of God, Jesus was more than willing to disregard them. The outline address for Proper 3 is equally applicable to this passage. However, you'll need to include a few words of explanation about the Sabbath rules, and why the leader of the synagogue was cross with both Jesus and those who'd come for healing. More important still, emphasise that Jesus' priority was to make the woman whole, breaking the power of evil over her and bringing glory to God – what better thing to do on the Sabbath! As Christians, our primary rule must be the 'law of love', and all other laws must keep in line with that, however important they may seem.

PROPER 17

Sunday between 28 August and 3 September inclusive

In Year A this week Matthew recalls Jesus teaching the disciples that he must die, and telling them about the cost of following him – suitable outline addresses for this can be found either under Proper 7 (Address 1) or Proper 16 (Address 1). In Year B we return to Mark in chapter 7, and hear Jesus teaching the people about what's clean and unclean in God's sight. Luke in Year C quotes Jesus' teaching on status and service.

Hymns

TRADITIONAL

- *Be still, my soul (68)*
- *Dearest Jesu, we are here (143)*
- *Fight the good fight (169)*
- *Strengthen for service, Lord (619)*
- *Take up thy cross, the Saviour said (626)*
- *Thine arm, O Lord, in days of old (671)*

CONTEMPORARY

- *Be still, for the presence of the Lord (67)*
- *Follow me (176)*
- *Great indeed are your works, O Lord (247)*
- *Moses, I know you're the man (451)*
- *From heaven you came (195)*
- *One more step along the world I go (525)*

CHANT

- *Silent, surrendered (941)*

CHILDREN'S SONG

- *Step by step (885)*

Readings

Year A   Exodus 3:1-15 or Jeremiah 15:15-21; Romans 12:9-21; Matthew 16:21-28

Year B   Song of Solomon 2:8-13 or Deuteronomy 4:1-2, 6-9; James 1:17-27; Mark 7:1-8, 14-15, 21-23

Year C   Jeremiah 2:4-13 or Proverbs 25:6-7 or Ecclesiasticus 10:12-18; Hebrews 13:1-8, 15-16; Luke 14:1, 7-14

Confession

Hear us, God of our salvation,
as we cry to you for mercy;
Lord, forgive and help us.
We have pursued status for ourselves
instead of the welfare of others;
Lord, forgive and help us.
We have cultivated public status
instead of private devotion;
Lord, forgive and help us.
We have followed the wide and comfortable road
instead of the rugged path that leads to you.
Lord, forgive and help us.
Have mercy on us, we pray,
cleanse us from all that defiles,
and set our feet in the way of eternal life,
through our Lord Jesus Christ. Amen.

Absolution

God, who saves and heals
all who repent and turn from evil,
have mercy on *you*, forgive all *your* sins,
and strengthen *you* to obey his will,
through Jesus Christ our Lord. Amen.

Prayer

We turn to our Father God,
from whom comes every good and perfect gift,
offering our thanks and prayers and saying,
Lord, as your word comes to us,
help us to be hearers and doers.

Your word tells us not to discriminate
or show favouritism.
We pray for the marginalised and exploited,
victims of injustice and greed,
the downtrodden and ignored,
left without resources or hope . . .
Help us to stand alongside them,
showing mercy and sharing your love.
Lord, your word comes to us,
help us to be hearers and doers.

Your word tells us that faith
must be accompanied by action.
We pray for those who go in Christ's name
to bring aid and relief and set captives free,
to reach out to the poor and unwanted . . .

Help us to show our faith is real
through acts of practical care and generosity.
Lord, as your word comes to us,
help us to be hearers and doers.

Your word tells us that true faith
is seen in care for the suffering and defenceless.
We pray for those in distress through illness,
bereavement, anxiety or personal crisis . . .
Help us to befriend the friendless,
support the weak, and comfort the hurting.
Lord, as your word comes to us,
help us to be hearers and doers.

Your word tells us that we are justified
by faith and action together.
We pray for our own church fellowship
as part of the worldwide Body of Christ,
that in word and deed we may show
the reality of what we believe . . .
Help us to encourage rather than criticise;
to be generous rather than condemn;
to share the mind of Christ,
counting the wellbeing of our neighbour
above our own.
Lord, as your word comes to us,
help us to be hearers and doers,
secure in our faith and bold to do your will,
through Jesus Christ our Lord. Amen.

All-age address 1

So many of the conflicts which arose between
Jesus and the religious leaders were to do with
keeping rules. The argument over clean and
unclean foods was no exception, and, as usual,
Jesus' opponents had completely missed the
point. Eating certain foods doesn't make us
unclean, nor does abstaining from them mean
that we're clean! No doubt the teachers of the
law were ritually clean, and proud of it, but
they failed to understand that their attitudes
and intransigence made them unclean in God's
eyes. This outline aims to make that distinction,
and to do so requires careful preparation in
advance. You'll need a little washing powder,
detergent and a bar of soap, plus a piece of
fabric which is no longer needed (an old T-shirt,
for example), and a plate heavily stained by
food. A volunteer with grubby hands is your
final visual aid, and for each of these a bowl of

hot water is necessary (best brought in by
another volunteer at the appropriate time). If
you prefer not to get wet yourself, you'll need
another volunteer to do the washing.

1) Take the detergent and extol the virtues of
its cleansing properties before producing
the dirty plate. Having asked for opinions
about whether the stains can be removed,
place it in the first bowl of water and add
some detergent. It may need to soak for a
while but eventually a bit of scrubbing
should make it usable again. This is surface
dirt, which washes off quite easily. The
Pharisees treated sin as a disobedience to
their rules, which could be dealt with by
keeping to the prescribed rituals, but this
was a superficial and inadequate view.

2) Beforehand rub the T-shirt well in garden
soil, so that it becomes a nasty shade of grey.
Do a quick commercial for the soap-powder
before holding up the soiled garment, and
then dip it in the second bowl, adding a
little soap powder and rubbing vigorously.
It should be possible to make a visible
difference fairly quickly. Point out that in
this case the dirt is much more ingrained. Sin
is deeply ingrained into our lives, making
us unclean. Jesus came to deal not just
with visible sins, but with the deeply held
attitudes which often underlie them.

3) Now your unwashed volunteer comes
forward, and you show the congregation
his hands, eliciting noises of disgust. Offer
the bar of soap and the third bowl, again
expounding its qualities. This is also surface
dirt, and should come off fairly easily. Explain
that the Pharisees could only see the surface.
Your volunteer's hands may be clean, but if
he or she had a cold or virus, soap would
be of no use whatever – to treat it internally
they'd need antibiotics or Lemsip!

Conclude by saying that Jesus challenged the
superficiality of his opponents – the real
problem wasn't what could be seen (the food
they ate) but what lay beneath the surface
(wrong thoughts leading to wrong behaviour).
God doesn't accept us because we keep to
certain rituals. When we recognise and repent

of our sins, he forgives us and cleans us up from within through the death of Jesus.

All-age address 2

Status is usually a major ingredient in any group of people – pecking orders and status symbols were as influential in Jesus' day as in ours. Having been invited to a meal with a prominent Pharisee he observed how many of the guests sought an honoured place at table – a major status symbol in that culture. This could clearly lead to social embarrassment or humiliation, but Jesus also contrasts this with status in God's kingdom. Each society inevitably has its own. Different social levels, based on a variety of factors, are unavoidable, and all attempts to make everyone equal have come unstuck. The Gospel goes far beyond imposing a new social structure, which would soon create its own new distinctions – it over-turns all our human aspirations. For this simple outline a few recognisable status symbols are all that's needed (pictures pasted on card or model replicas will be easier to obtain than the real thing!).

1) First, show a picture or small model of a Ferrari. A large, fast car is often a symbol of status based on power. The owner obviously has plenty of cash, but wants to demonstrate more than that. Somehow, we wouldn't feel like arguing with the owner of such a vehicle! Human beings are very tempted to exercise power over each other, but status in God's Kingdom is based on humility.

2) Next, show a picture of a Rolex watch (assuming you don't own one!). Here's a symbol of extreme 'good taste', a sign of pedigree and class. Whoever owns it is keen on cultural superiority. Our human tendency is to find ways of proving that we're in some way 'a cut above' others, even if those on the wrong end of it may accuse us of 'snobbery'. It's a futile exercise, because no one can really define 'good taste'. Jesus tells his hearers not to spend their money on things to create an impression, but on providing for those who can't repay or give any return.

3) To finish, display a picture of a major social event with elegantly dressed guests, or a symbol (perhaps an elegant invitation card). Some people show off by being seen in the right company and clothes, to show they're socially 'upmarket'. God regards all people as equal, and while social layers may have a limited short-term functional value, they don't reflect God's view of humankind. Instead of promoting self-image, Jesus tells us to take a humbler position, as he did. He was humiliated on the Cross, but now has the most honoured place in God's kingdom. Like him we're to consider the interests and welfare of others before our own, looking for our reward only from our heavenly Father.

PROPER 18

Sunday between 4 and 10 September inclusive

As a new academic year begins, and many folk return from holiday, we approach the end of the readings from each Gospel. In Year A Matthew relates Jesus' teaching on forgiveness, and in Year B we read Mark's account of the healing of the Syro-Phoenician woman's daughter, as well as the healing of a deaf-mute. In Year C Luke in his turn sets out Jesus' teaching on the cost of being a disciple. A suitable outline address for the passage from Mark can be found at Proper 15 (Address 1), while for Luke those from either Proper 7 (Address 1) or Proper 16 (Address 1) can be used.

Hymns

TRADITIONAL

- *All things bright and beautiful (25)*
- *Forgive our sins, as we forgive (180)*
- *New songs of celebration render (468)*
- *O Lord, we long to see your face (514)*
- *Onward, Christian pilgrims (531)*
- *There's a wideness in God's mercy (662)*

CONTEMPORARY

- *Change my heart, O God (92)*
- *Father God, gentle Father God (158)*
- *Love is the only law (430)*
- *Take up your cross, he says (627)*
- *Thanks for the fellowship (632)*
- *There's a quiet understanding (659)*

CHANT

- *Kyrie 1 (Taizé) (958)*

CHILDREN'S SONG

- *Isn't it good (837)*

Readings

Year A   Exodus 12:1-14 or Ezekiel 33:7-11;
         Romans 13:8-14; Matthew 18:15-20
Year B   Proverbs 22:1-2, 8-9, 22-23 or
         Isaiah 35:4-7a;
         James 2:1-10, (11-13), 14-17;
         Mark 7:24-37

Year C   Jeremiah 18:1-11 or
         Deuteronomy 30:15-20;
         Philemon 1-21; Luke 14:25-33

Confession

Lord God, you teach us
that love is the fulfilment of the law,
but we have not obeyed its demands;
Lord, forgive and renew us.

Your law demands
that we do not harm our neighbours
but love them as ourselves.
We are sorry for the damage done
through careless words and selfish actions;
Lord, forgive and renew us.

Your law demands
that we do not covet or steal
anything belonging to our neighbours.
We are sorry for seeking to improve our own lot
and ignoring the need around us;
Lord, forgive and renew us.

Your law demands
that we put aside deeds of darkness
and walk in your light.
We are sorry for trying to disguise our sins,
and thinking we can hide them from you;
Lord, forgive and renew us.

Your law demands
that we obey your new commandment
to love one another.
For living only to ourselves,
and not loving one another or you
with a sincere and true heart,
Lord, forgive and renew us.
Give us grace to clothe ourselves
with the Lord Jesus Christ
and live to his praise and glory,
in whose name we pray. Amen.

Absolution

God, whose law is trustworthy and perfect,
have mercy on *you*, forgive all *your* sins
and bring *you* to newness of life,
that *you* may no longer live to self
but to the glory of our Saviour Jesus Christ.
Amen.

Prayer

Our Father God knows the desires of our hearts,
even when they are too deep to express.
We reach out to him in faith,
bringing our prayers, spoken and unspoken,
saying:
Lord, you are more ready to answer
than we to ask;
hear us as we pray in faith.

We pray for the Church across the world,
worshipping and serving you with us,
especially where it is faithful
under great pressure . . .
By your Spirit, guide all Christian leaders,
teachers and pastors, preachers and evangelists,
that your people may grow in faith and love . . .
Lord, you are more ready to answer
than we to ask;
hear us as we pray in faith.

We pray for the world you call us to serve,
with needs which threaten to overwhelm,
and countless victims of disaster
and inhumanity . . .
By your Spirit, guide our nation
and the leaders of the world,
give them courage to confront evil
and corruption,
and uphold the standards of your kingdom.
Lord, you are more ready to answer
than we to ask;
hear us as we pray in faith.

We pray for our families, friends and loved ones,
naming those in particular need
as a result of illness, grief, loneliness
or confusion . . .
By your Spirit, give them strength
to endure their present distress,
and confidence to believe
you will bring them through
into renewed joy and deepened faith.
Lord, you are more ready to answer
than we to ask;
hear us as we pray in faith.

We pray for our own faith and Christian witness
as we seek to make your love known.
Make us bold to proclaim your good news,
and faithful in following you.

Lord, you are more ready to answer
than we to ask;
**hear us as we pray in faith
and answer us according to your holy will,
through Jesus Christ our Lord. Amen.**

All-age address

This address outline is based on the passage from Matthew 18, emphasising positive and negative relationships rather than legal procedures. By way of preparation you'll need a sheet of A3 paper and a suitably sized picture-frame from an art supplies shop (if you use a photo frame, you'll need to remove the glass). On the sheet of paper write words describing relationships – e.g. 'family', 'friends', 'business partners', 'colleagues', 'acquaintances', 'fellow Christians', etc. – when it's full, secure it to the frame. Next take some smaller sized pieces of paper and write on each a damaging behaviour or attitude – 'jealousy', 'envy', 'conflict', 'rivalry', 'gossip', 'malice', 'hatred', 'resentment', etc. One of these will be wrapped in turn around a tennis ball, which will be thrown at the paper in the frame. Finally, take some identical pieces of paper and write on them words such as 'love', 'kindness', 'patience', 'forgiveness', 'generosity', 'compassion' and 'sensitivity'.

1) Take the first paper and wrap it around the ball, explaining that in the frame are words which describe relationships. Ask a child to throw the paper-covered ball at the sheet in the frame, which will tear easily. After this has happened retrieve the ball and ask the child what's written on it. If the word is 'jealousy', explain how jealousy can destroy relationships. Repeat this process no more than six times, explaining how easily families and friendships are destroyed by such attitudes.

2) When the paper is beyond repair, ask the congregation what sort of things might restore relationships. Armed with a few helpful suggestions, bring out the previously taped together sheets with their 'positive' words, pointing out that these are things which build up our relationships with one another. Then attach it to the frame.

Wind up by referring to Jesus' words. He knew that even when things go wrong, honesty and integrity count for a great deal. Only as a last resort, if the other person continues the disagreement, are we to break off the relationship. But more important than disagreeing is agreeing before God, because God created us to live in relationship. Where we do so harmoniously and constructively he promises to be present, and to answer our prayers, because prayer in that context won't be selfish, but in line with his will.

PROPER 19

Sunday between 11 and 17 September inclusive

This Sunday's Year A gospel reading from Matthew is Jesus' parable of the Unforgiving Servant, while Year B consists of Mark's account of Peter's confession of Christ at Caesarea Philippi, for which a suitable outline address can be found under Proper 16 (All-age Address 1). Year C contains two of Luke's three famous parables about things lost and found again.

Hymns

TRADITIONAL

- *Amazing Grace (29)*
- *Great is thy faithfulness (249)*
- *Hark, my soul, it is the Lord (264)*
- *I will sing the wondrous story (337)*
- *My God, how wonderful you are (457)*
- *Praise, my soul, the King of heaven (565)*

CONTEMPORARY

- *All that I am, all that I do (23)*
- *Have mercy on us, O Lord (269)*
- *I love you, Lord (313)*
- *Jesus, Jesus, holy and anointed one (353)*
- *Meekness and majesty (448)*
- *My Lord, what love is this (462)*

CHANT

- *O Lord, hear my prayer (938)*

CHILDREN'S SONG

- *I have a friend (829)*

Readings

Year A   Exodus 14:19-31 or Genesis 50:15-21;
         Romans 14:1-12; Matthew 18:21-35
Year B   Proverbs 1:20-33 or Isaiah 50:4-9a;
         James 3:1-12; Mark 8:27-38
Year C   Jeremiah 4:11-12, 22-28 or
         Exodus 32:7-14; 1 Timothy 1:12-17;
         Luke 15:1-10

Confession

Gracious Father, whose love never ceases,
we repent of the sins we have committed
against you and each other.
We find trivial faults in others
while ignoring our own sinfulness;
we are critical and ungenerous in judging others
while overlooking our own failings;
we seek your pardon
without forgiving those who have wronged us.
Have mercy on us,
and in receiving your forgiveness,
make us willing to forgive others,
through Christ our Lord. Amen.

Absolution

God, the source of forgiveness and grace,
deliver *you* from all *your* sins,
and in his mercy restore *you* to his service,
that *you* may be freed from the chains of guilt
into the joy of eternal life
in Jesus Christ our Lord. Amen.

Prayer

We take to our Father in heaven,
who knows the deepest thoughts of our hearts,
all our burdens and concerns, saying:
Lord, hear us as we call to you;
accept the prayer of our hearts.

Bless and guide your Church
as it proclaims the good news,
and give wisdom to all who speak
in your name . . .
May their words be wise and sensitive,
rooted in truth, and framed by your love,
so that your people may be built up in unity
and your kingdom extended.
Lord, hear us as we call to you;
accept the prayer of our hearts.

Bless all who use words
to direct the course of this world's affairs,
in business or politics, the media or education . . .
May their words be honest and positive,
founded on integrity,
and fuelled by concern for the needy,
so that justice and peace are spread abroad.

Lord, hear us as we call to you;
accept the prayer of our hearts.

Bless all who use words
to nurture and encourage:
in healthcare, social work and counselling . . .
May their words be kind and supportive,
based on compassion and commitment,
filled with hope and courage.
Lord, hear us as we call to you;
accept the prayer of our hearts.

Bless those who find it impossible
to express their pain and suffering in words,
whether in illness, sadness or crisis . . .
May they know you carrying them
in the darkest times,
understanding their deepest longings
and holding them in your loving arms.
Lord, hear us as we call to you;
accept the prayer of our hearts.

Bless all we do and say,
that our minds may be directed by your love
and our tongues controlled by your peace,
so that in word and action
our lives may bring glory to your name.
Lord, hear us as we call to you;
**accept the prayer of our hearts
for the sake of your Son,
Jesus Christ our Lord. Amen.**

All-age address 1

Few concepts are more difficult to convey in simple terms than forgiveness. In large measure we understand it through experiencing it, and in any cross-section of people there will be a wide range of experiences of being forgiven. Jesus was familiar with this, as his parable of the Unforgiving Servant bears out. Here he challenges a contemporary concept of forgiveness, in which, as Peter rather naively indicates, it had become a cog in the legal machine. Jesus puts the emphasis instead on the love and mercy which alone can bring it about. Contemporary society is equally judgemental and unforgiving of those who are unable or unwilling to conform, so Jesus' teaching is particularly apposite. This outline focuses on three aspects of forgiveness brought out by Jesus – it's based entirely on mercy, it depends on us recognising our need of it, and we can only receive it to the extent that we're prepared to give it to others. It needs three well-briefed volunteers and a few props, and could be set up like the popular TV programme *Watercolour Challenge*.

1) The two volunteers sit at adjacent tables painting a picture. One bumps the other's table fairly violently, spoiling their work of art and knocking the water pot over. The other jumps up and threatens to do likewise. At this point step in and ask whether this response is deserved, or constructive. It's unlikely that many will answer 'Yes' to either question. Explain that while our natural 'sense of justice' wants to see the guilty party experience the suffering they've caused to others, we know that won't improve the situation. The only way forward is for the second person to forgive the first for their clumsiness and to set the record straight, so that the matter is forgotten and their relationship resumed. In Jesus' parable the only solution was for the King voluntarily to forgive the servant his debt and set him free.

2) This time the second volunteer deliberately smears the first's picture, causing indignation and another threat of reprisal. Intervene, asking what the appropriate response to this situation might be. 'Forgiveness' and 'contrition' (or words expressing the same idea) are the terms sought. Smearing the culprit's own picture would do no more than make the victim feel better (or 'avenged'), so however undeserved it may seem, forgiveness has to be the answer. But the guilty one also needs to acknowledge that wrong has been done, and can't be rectified, other than by receiving the freely offered forgiveness. Jesus wants us to understand that our heavenly Father is like this, willing to forgive the worst things we've ever done provided that we recognise our wrongdoing, receive his forgiveness and live as his followers.

3) The final scene involves the third volunteer, also painting at a table adjacent to the other two. The second volunteer again spoils

the first's artwork, and after threatened retribution receives forgiveness. While this is happening the third accidentally makes a slight mark on the second's painting. On discovering this the former culprit, now the victim, threatens to ruin the third's work. Despite entreaties and the comment that the damage is barely visible, the second destroys the third's picture, at which point the first loses his rag and asks you to destroy the second's. Explain that while God is never vindictive, he cannot force us to be forgiven. By definition, forgiveness is a gift of grace; it can't be legislated for. We choose to receive it, and we choose whether to give it. God doesn't 'let us off the hook', but rather 'wipes our slate clean'. We are called, as those forgiven by him, both to model in our lives, and to demonstrate in our relationships, God's forgiveness and grace, not out of a sense of duty, but from a transformed heart.

All-age address 2

Luke gathers together three of Jesus' best-known parables about things which are lost – a sheep, a coin and a son. Since most of us lose things, in some cases fairly regularly, we can identify readily with his points. This outline follows a similar pattern to Luke 15, and needs a few visual aids – a small family pet, such as a hamster or one of the smaller breeds of dog, a 'lost pet' notice, a set of keys (optional), a small piece of jewellery (not valuable!) and a fictitious 'missing person' poster.

1) Start by saying that everyone loses things from time to time – maybe an umbrella, the pen by the telephone, or a letter. Mostly these aren't too important or valuable, and they often turn up later in some unexpected place. Occasionally, something more precious or vital goes astray, and then we send out a full-scale search party and don't stop looking until it's been found. If time allows say that you've lost your keys and can't get back into your home until you've found them. 'Hide' them somewhere to be discovered and quickly returned. Now produce the pet and the notice offering a reward for finding a lost one, and indicate that the

shepherd had a similar relationship with his sheep as we might with our pets. He was willing to go to any lengths to find one that was lost. God was also prepared to do anything to bring us back to himself, too, whatever the cost to him. And he's as happy to receive us back as we would be to find our lost pet alive and well.

2) Now produce the ring (ideally one that looks like an engagement ring), and ask a married or engaged woman how she would feel if she lost her ring – this will only elicit one answer! The woman in Jesus' parable would have had similar emotions about losing her coin, which was probably part of her dowry. We don't know its exact value, but what mattered to her was its association. So she turned the whole house upside down until she found it. Again, there was great joy when she did so. The picture of God's saving activity is the same, but significantly a woman is used here as the example – a radical idea for its day!

3) Finally, hold up the missing person poster, pointing out as you do so that the person isn't lost like a toddler in a supermarket – this person knows his whereabouts but his family and friends don't. He's lost to them. There are many anguished families who wonder about one of their relatives who hasn't been heard of for ages. The father in Jesus' parable had no idea where his son was, or whether he'd ever see him again, but he never gave up hope, and was always on the lookout. When the son finally decided to return, he was still some way from home when his father rushed to greet him and gave him a royal welcome. The son didn't deserve this welcome (as his elder brother soon pointed out) but the past was forgiven and the joy at his return overwhelming. Jesus is making the same point again, but much more poignantly.

Finish by saying that as God's children, we hurt him when we go away from him; there's nothing he won't do to bring us back to where we once were, however bad or daft our actions. His joy is as unlimited as his forgiveness.

PROPER 20

Sunday between 18 and 24 September inclusive

Nearing the end of this long stretch of 'Ordinary Time' we reach Matthew 20 in Year A, and Jesus' parable of the Workers in the Vineyard. Year B's passage from Mark 9 starts with Jesus' prediction of his death and resurrection to his bemused disciples, followed by their arguments about status. In Year C Luke recounts Jesus' most puzzling parable, that of the Shrewd Manager.

Hymns

TRADITIONAL

- *All people that on earth do dwell (21)*
- *Father, hear the prayer we offer (161)*
- *Guide me, O thou great Redeemer (252)*
- *Praise, O praise our God and King (566)*
- *Stand up, stand up for Jesus (617)*
- *Teach me, my God and King (629)*

CONTEMPORARY

- *Cry 'Freedom!' (138)*
- *For I'm building a people of power (181)*
- *From heaven you came (195)*
- *Inspired by love and anger (325)*
- *Let there be love shared among us (386)*
- *Peace is flowing like a river (553)*

CHANT

- *Exaudi nos, Domine (927)*

CHILDREN'S SONG

- *Give me peace, O Lord (802)*

Readings

Year A   Exodus 16:2-15 or Jonah 3:10-4:11;
         Philippians 1:21-30; Matthew 20:1-16
Year B   Proverbs 31:10-31 or Wisdom 1:16-2:1,
         12-22 or Jeremiah 11:18-20;
         James 3:13-4:3, 7-8a; Mark 9:30-37
Year C   Jeremiah 8:18-9:1 or Amos 8:4-7;
         1 Timothy 2:1-7; Luke 16:1-13

Confession

God of grace and glory,
we confess with sorrow
that we have failed to live up to your calling.
We repent of our waywardness
and straying from your path;
our carelessness and lack of concern for others;
our self-will and rejection of your ways.
Forgive all our sin, we pray,
and renew us by your Spirit,
that our hearts may be ruled
by the peace of Christ,
and our lives dedicated to
his glory. Amen.

Absolution

God our Father,
who calls us to follow and serve him,
pardon all *your* sin,
forgive all *your* failures,
and restore *you* to the joy
of being one with him and each other,
through Jesus Christ our Lord. Amen.

Prayer

As those called by God our Father
to work for his kingdom,
we come to pray for the Church and the world,
saying: Master, receive our prayers;
strengthen us to work for you.

We pray for the work of your Church
throughout the world,
where there is poverty and hardship,
where there is despair and fear . . .
May all Christians strive together
for the good of the whole world,
and bring closer your reign of justice and peace.
Master, receive these prayers;
strengthen us to work for you.

We pray for the work of reconciliation
and relief of suffering
which continues in the face of evil
and destruction . . .
May all aid workers and carers
be strengthened and encouraged by your Spirit

as they counter hostility and suspicion
with your love.
Master, receive these prayers;
strengthen us to work for you.

We pray for the work of government and leaders
here and throughout the world . . .
May all politicians and community leaders
acknowledge your ultimate authority
and act justly in the interests of all.
Master, receive these prayers;
strengthen us to work for you.

We pray for those who matter most to us,
our families and friends,
and those whose concerns touch our hearts . . .
We remember those who are ill or infirm,
anxious or grieving . . .
May they feel your healing touch
and the peace of your abiding presence.
Master, receive these prayers;
strengthen us to work for you.

We pray for ourselves, at work and rest,
in thinking and speaking,
and ask that your Holy Spirit
will guide us into your ways and truth.
May your love and joy be seen in all we do.
Master, receive these prayers;
**strengthen us to work for you,
seeking no reward
apart from knowing we do your will,
for the sake of Christ our Lord. Amen.**

All-age address 1

The parable of the Workers in the Vineyard doesn't seem quite to fit in with the Human Rights Act! We regard equal treatment and opportunity for all employees nowadays as a moral imperative. In fact, Jesus based this parable on what was considered normal practice in those days, but his message clearly isn't about fair or unfair employment practices. What he wants his hearers to understand is the way in which the values of the kingdom turn human designs on their heads. The landowner here is scrupulously fair, abiding by the agreements he's made with each worker; more than that, he goes out himself to find and hire them (not something a landowner would normally do). The biggest surprise, however, is his generosity to those he employed last, and his refusal to differentiate between his workers. Unlike us, God doesn't operate on the basis of merit and reward, but on grace and kindness even to those we might regard as undeserving (an uncomfortable message for the legalistic Pharisees). This outline picks up the theme of surprising generosity, and while simple it does require preparatory shopping. You'll need an expensive-looking box of chocolates, a large bar of chocolate, a Mars Bar (or equivalent) and enough small wrapped sweets to give out to most of the congregation. You might also want to prime one or two members in advance.

1) Start by saying how important it is to express thanks to people, and explain that you want to thank certain folk who work very hard for your church. Then take a selection of the small wrapped sweets in a dish and ask a long-serving member of the congregation to choose one as a thank you for all his hard work. Repeat this a few times with, for example, a musician or choir member, a church warden (or senior lay leader), a sidesman or steward, a PCC member, a flower-arranger or a member of the cleaning rota. Finish by stressing that you wanted to to be absolutely fair to everyone.

2) Now move on to point out that we often see things differently. To someone who's done a bit more than they needed to, you might give a Mars Bar; to someone who takes a fair amount of responsibility you might present a large bar of chocolate; and for someone who's really important or hardworking you might go mad and buy a special box of chocolates. With each point produce the relevant item. There's nothing wrong with this kind of generosity, but it works entirely on the basis of rewarding people according to what they've done.

3) God is completely different, and Jesus' parable shows how like the landowner he treats everyone with the same level of generosity. The workers he took on near the

end of the day received exactly the same as those who'd worked all through the day. He wasn't being unfair to them – they were receiving more than fair payment for the day's work, and their complaints were based on jealousy. The Pharisees and Scribes didn't like Jesus' concern for the poor and needy, and felt they should receive better treatment in comparison. But God deals with people on the basis of his love, not on whether they've fulfilled certain obligations. Conclude by explaining that you're going to give everyone a wrapped sweet, not as a reward for services rendered but as a picture of God's love, which is given freely to everyone, regardless of background or achievement.

All-age address 2

Status-seeking is something that's all too familiar in our society, but while people may use different symbols now to indicate their social position, they're not doing anything new. Fighting over a 'pecking order' occurs in almost any group, not least the church, so there's no surprise that it cropped up among the disciples, even though they should have known better if they'd been listening to Jesus' teaching. But he'd heard them, and they must have felt distinctly embarrassed to admit what they'd been arguing over. Jesus used a 'live visual aid' (a small child, regarded then as having no status) to illustrate the attitude of those who are part of God's Kingdom. This outline follows suit, using the idea of the 'balloon debate'. You'll need four well-briefed volunteers who can play an impromptu part in a lively and relaxed way.

1) The first volunteer brings in a certificate of educational achievement (real or fictitious!) and goes on about how important it is for the church to have people who are well-qualified, intelligent, capable of making right decisions, etc. After a moment or two interrupt him and ask whether one or two other gifts might be useful in church, to which he responds that someone needs to look after the money well.

2) The second volunteer appears with a cheque-book and set of accounts, and immediately launches into a speech on the importance of good accounting and wise stewardship. He adds a bit about rich Christians being able to put more money into the church, but you should cut across his self-promotion by asking if other talents might also help the church to move forwards.

3) The third volunteer now brings in a sheaf of music (and possibly a small instrument) and then tells everyone how vital creative and artistic people are to the church, as without them there'd be no beautiful liturgy or music, no drama or artistic work, etc. Before his head gets too big, break into his monologue with the same question – can the church get anywhere just with these talents?

4) Now the final volunteer appears, brandishing cleaning equipment and starts to discourse on the problems the church would have if there weren't ordinary people who roll up their sleeves and get on with the real work. Before the 'too many chiefs and not enough Indians' mentality sets in, the others interrupt and assert their own importance, and an argument is clearly brewing . . .

5) Interrupt all this yourself by 'telling them off' for arguing and showing off, and emphasise the importance of good leadership. Since it's all obviously a drama, conclude at this point by emphasising that the church needs people who are good at thinking, at accounting, at music and at cleaning – they all play a vital part in its life and mission. By far the most important is the servant, not concerned about status or who he's seen with, but instead getting on with serving his master. Jesus showed the disciples a small child, who they'd have totally overlooked in their quarrel, and pointed out that in God's kingdom those who welcomed that child in effect welcomed him too. God cares for the least important in human society as much as he does the influential and significant, and those who follow his ways must do likewise.

All-age address 3

The parable of the Shrewd Manager is one of Jesus' most puzzling utterances, at least at face value, since he seems to be condoning dishonesty and lack of integrity. Few parables have been interpreted in so many different ways, and it isn't entirely obvious, even on closer inspection, exactly what point Jesus is making. The manager in question was probably incompetent rather than dishonest – he's wasted his master's resources rather than stolen them – but he's under no illusion that his job is on the line, so he sets out to make preparations for what life might be like after the books have been audited and he's facing unemployment. It's likely that some of Jesus' hearers were reformed tax-collectors who would have related to this story of a man protecting his own interests, but Jesus would hardly have been commending them to continue with dubious financial practices. The man's personal honesty isn't the central point here. This outline focuses on the issue raised by Jesus of preparing for a new life, and requires a few simple props related to moving house.

1) It's more than likely that someone in the congregation will have moved house in the recent past, and they may be willing to answer a few simple questions about the process. Why did you move? How did you choose where to move to? Were you sad to leave your old home? Did you do much hard work? Have you still got boxes to unpack? Did you settle in quickly in the new home? You could even use a couple of estate agent's leaflets to illustrate this. Explain that the man in Jesus' parable knew he'd have to move. He hadn't done his job well and knew he'd be given the sack. So he thought carefully and decided to make preparations for his new life.

2) Some people find they must move as a result of financial difficulties. This man thought about his financial situation (you could use a cheque book or financial document to illustrate this point). Moving house is expensive, but this man was also faced with losing his income, so he used his remaining work time to ease the economic burden of his employer's clients by reducing their debt repayments (God had forbidden the Jews to charge interest, though it's not clear whether the employer was doing so here). In effect he was buying their favour and friendship.

3) Sometimes people move to a smaller house because of health problems. This employee thought about his health situation, and recognised he was no longer strong enough to do hard physical work, the only alternative open to him apart from the humiliation of begging. He would need the help of others.

4) Sometimes people move to be nearer family or friends, and others know they'll be moving away from their present social circle. This man thought about his social situation and realised at once that he'd need friends in order to survive. His employer commended his shrewdness, if not his integrity, and Jesus uses him to warn his hearers that they too must recognise that their present circumstances will change, one day for ever. Healthy relationships are more important in eternal terms than a healthy bank balance. We must also recognise that we need each other's help in this life.

Conclude by adding that Jesus encourages us to be honest and act with integrity in matters both small and large, and warns us that we can't serve both material possessions and God. Like the Pharisees, we must learn that the values of God's kingdom are totally different from ours.

PROPER 21

Sunday between 25 September
and 1 October inclusive

Numbers 11:4-6, 10-16, 24-29;
James 5:13-20; Mark 9:38-50
Year C   Jeremiah 32:1-3a, 6-15 or
Amos 6:1a, 4-7; 1 Timothy 6:6-19;
Luke 16:19-31

At this time of year many churches will be celebrating Harvest Festival, so in Year C Luke's account of the parable of Dives and Lazarus has a particular significance in terms of using what God has given us in order to care for the poor. In Year B too, Mark reminds us that Jesus often taught people along these lines. In Year A the passage from Matthew starts off with the dispute over Jesus' authority, continuing with the parable of the Two Sons, which shows that actions matter more than words for those who follow Jesus.

Hymns

TRADITIONAL

- *All my hope on God is founded (19)*
- *Happy are they, they that love God (262)*
- *May the mind of Christ my Saviour (447)*
- *O Jesus, I have promised (503)*
- *Praise to the Holiest in the height (572)*
- *To the name of our salvation (698)*

CONTEMPORARY

- *Christ triumphant (104)*
- *God's Spirit is in my heart (231)*
- *He is Lord (274)*
- *Jesus at your name (345)*
- *Jesus, name above all names (355)*
- *King of kings and Lord of lords (376)*

CHANT

- *Wait for the Lord (949)*

CHILDREN'S SONG

- *I want to be a tree that's bearing fruit (842)*

Readings

Year A   Exodus 17:1-17 or Ezekiel 18:1-4,
25-32; Philippians 2:1-13;
Matthew 21:23-32
Year B   Esther 7:1-6, 9-10; 9:20-22 or

Confession

Father God, Creator and Life-giver,
we confess before you and one another
the sin which separates us from you.
We repent of our wrongdoing
in thoughtless words and selfish actions,
in seeking status for ourselves
while neglecting the poor.
We are sorry and ashamed,
and humbly ask your forgiveness.
By your Spirit increase our faith
and strengthen our will,
that we may walk in your ways
of compassion and care,
through Jesus Christ our Lord. Amen.

Absolution

God our Father,
who knows the deepest desires of our hearts,
hear *your* prayer of repentance,
grant *you* pardon and forgiveness
for all *your* sins,
and guide *you* on the path
that leads to eternal life in Jesus Christ our Lord.
Amen.

Prayer

Confident that our heavenly Father hears us
as we pray in faith,
we bring him all that concerns and troubles us,
saying: Lord, you are our refuge and fortress;
receive this prayer of faith.

We hold up to you the poor of this world:
refugees, asylum-seekers,
persecuted minorities,
the downtrodden and forgotten . . .
May they find hope in you when they despair,
courage when they feel fearful,
and joy in your promise
that they are on your heart.

Lord, you are our refuge and fortress;
receive this prayer of faith.

We hold up to you the wealthy and powerful:
financiers and directors,
economists, accountants, and lawyers . . .
May they recognise that all they have
comes from you alone,
using their assets
and discharging their responsibilities
for the relief of those burdened by poverty.
Lord, you are our refuge and our fortress;
receive this prayer of faith.

We hold up to you
the worldwide Christian church –
in freedom or hardship,
in strength or weakness,
in joy or sorrow . . .
May we and all Christians show Christ's love
in words of wisdom and gentleness
and in acts of compassion and mercy.
Lord, you are our refuge and fortress;
receive this prayer of faith.

We hold up to you the suffering and needy,
including those we know . . .
May they feel the touch of your hand,
healing and restoring,
and supporting them in their time of trouble.
Lord, you are our refuge and fortress;
receive this prayer of faith.

We hold up to you our own situations:
decisions to be made,
problems to be faced,
challenges to be accepted . . .
May we live the new life in Christ,
and commit ourselves wholeheartedly
to your kingdom.
Lord, you are our refuge and fortress;
**receive this prayer of faith
in the name of our Saviour Jesus Christ. Amen.**

All-age address 1

The four Gospels all record Jesus' disputes
and conflicts with the religious authorities in
various degrees of detail. Underlying all of
these was their discomfort with the challenge
Jesus presented, and their refusal to recognise
the source of his authority in his heavenly
Father. They could find an answer for everything, and were assiduous in observing the
Law, but it was all just words. The parable of
the two sons sums it up – the first son may
have challenged his father's instruction, but
eventually he did what was required of him,
unlike his brother, who doubtless made an
immediate impression with his apparent
willingness, but never got round to doing
what he said he would. Like that father, God
wants to see his children bearing fruit for him,
not just uttering fine words. This outline aims
to stress that actions speak louder than words,
and requires only a few previously briefed
volunteers and a minimal amount of
preparation, involving three simple written
instructions placed in an envelope and sealed.

1) The first envelope could be given to a
young child. It should contain a simple and
instantly achievable instruction, for example:
'Fetch me a glass of water.' You're unlikely
to get a refusal (unless you organise it first!)
but persuade your volunteer not to go
straightaway, so that you can highlight the
significance of doing as well as saying.
While the errand is being completed, explain
that such instructions are uncomplicated,
and it's easy to say, 'Yes, of course', without
then quite getting round to it.

2) The second envelope is best given to an
adult, and the instruction here should have
wider implications, such as, 'Obey the
Highway Code'. Ask your volunteer whether
or not it's important to adhere to every last
instruction in it, and then find out whether
they actually do so! Explain that these
instructions aren't for the benefit of one
person but to keep all road-users safe.
Unfortunately, we don't always keep to the
Highway Code as we should, whether
through carelessness, over-confidence, or
simple forgetfulness.

3) The third envelope contains an instruction
that no one could hope to fulfil – 'Sort out
the problem of Third World debt', for
example. It doesn't lie within the power of
just one person to achieve such a thing.
Most people will agree that 'something

needs to be done', but that's not the same as doing it. It's easier to discuss than to tackle, and on our own we may feel we can do nothing. However, we all have a responsibility to work together to make a difference.

Round these points off by reiterating Jesus' words. If we obey someone, we recognise their authority, but if we say we'll do so and then fail to, we're also guilty of hypocrisy. This was what Jesus showed up in the religious people's attitude. As James said, we must be doers of the word as well as hearers.

All-age address 2

Jesus' hearers must have been very struck, not to say disconcerted, by his refusal to let them 'sit on the fence'. However, John and some of the other disciples went a bit 'over the top' when they saw someone they didn't know casting out demons in Jesus' name. Jesus' wanted them to realise that anything done in his name would be accepted, regardless of which group the person doing it belonged to. Our actions as well as our words give away whose side we're on. This outline (written in the run-up to the 2002 World Cup) tackles the idea from a football supporter's point of view. (If you find football tedious, it might be possible to use other sports as an example, though none have quite as wide an appeal). Beforehand you'll need to acquire a scarf, baseball cap or shirt in the colours either of your local team and/or one of the top teams – a member of the youth group may well be able to help out.

1) Start by reading out a few of the previous day's scores from a newspaper. It's likely that there'll be some expression of approval at certain results, so follow this up if necessary with a comment such as, 'it's obvious who they support'. Say that many people claim to support a particular team when what they mean is that they follow its results. Their support is simply theoretical and gets no further than pleasure if the team wins.

2) Now ask what evidence there might be of more practical support. Someone will suggest scarves and caps, so produce some at this point, asking for the colours to be identified. Now we can see which side someone's on (dress a volunteer up at this point).

3) Scarves and hats are only superficial. What matters is not looking like a supporter, but actually being one. Ask how you can tell whether someone's a genuine supporter. The probable reaction will be, 'they go to all the matches'. Now the support isn't just in words, or on the surface, but expressed by encouraging and cheering when the players are in action. The most fanatical supporters organise their whole life around the team's activities.

Conclude by developing these points in terms of Jesus' teaching. The man who John didn't recognise was still on his side, and demonstrating this practically by driving out demons. He didn't even need to do that much – Jesus pointed out that even giving someone a cup of cold water in his name is enough. But the support must be more than nice words or superficial gestures. Our lives must be centred around Jesus Christ himself and directed at living for him.

All-age address 3

The parable of Dives and Lazarus deals with rather more than money and charitable giving. Luke includes it at this point because of its obvious connection with the parable of the Shrewd Manager in the preceding verses. What happens to us in the next life depends entirely on the way we live in this one – it's our responsibility to live in accordance with God's will here and now, before it's too late. There's no doubt that Jesus' words were aimed at the wealthy and materialistic Pharisees, whose lifestyle emphasised the difference between themselves and the poor, who they looked down on. By disregarding so blatantly God's instructions about how to treat the poor they were living only for the present, complacently assuming that God would have to accept them. In contrast Luke uses the poor as a picture of the truly pious, who have their place in heaven. The contrast between Dives and Lazarus couldn't be greater, either in this life or the next, which forms the basis of this outline address. Preparation involves no more than finding suitable pictures of people and places 'before and after'.

1) You'll need two pictures of someone who was very famous (either nationally or in the congregation) twenty or thirty years ago, one as they were then and one as they look now (colour supplements and general magazines are always a useful source). Start with the older one and see if anyone recognises who it is. Then show everyone the more recent picture and ask what's changed about the person. Suggestions will probably include grey or maybe less hair, an older looking face, different hairstyle, beard shaved off, etc. Time certainly makes a difference to the way we look, and like it or not, our bodies don't improve with age!

2) Now find pictures of a room or garden before and after redecoration – there are many Ground Force and Changing Rooms-style programmes that everyone will be familiar with, and many magazines run articles along these lines. As before, start off with the earlier picture, and seek suggestions as to what improvements might be made. Then display the later picture, asking whether or not the congregation think it's an improvement. This is a matter of taste, but the decorator/interior designer needs to have a clear idea of what the room will look like when finished.

3) Finally show a picture of a town destroyed by wartime bombing, followed by one after it was rebuilt – good examples are Ypres in Belgium, and Dresden in Germany. Again, the newer version may not appeal to everyone, but the planners needed a clear vision of what they wanted to achieve to give that town a new life after its destruction.

Conclude by pointing out that the way we live now will be determined by what we think the next life will be like. For those who follow the way of Jesus, their clear picture of God's kingdom and rule in their lives will enable them to see that their place in heaven depends not on superficial religiosity or a human idea of 'good taste', but on a life lived in accordance with God's will, and in the service of others, most of all the poor.

PROPER 22

Sunday between 2 and 8 October inclusive

This Sunday's readings aren't the easiest in the Gospels by any means. For Year A we have Jesus' parable of the Tenants, as described by Matthew, and for Year B Mark's account of Jesus' teaching on divorce, and the place of small children in the kingdom. The passage from Luke 17 in Year C consists of two short parables, about faith, and the duties of servants. All-age worship probably isn't the ideal context for a discussion about divorce, given the complexity of the issues it raises and the range of views and experiences likely to be encountered, so the second outline address, dealing with faith, can be used for both the Year B and C gospels. Please note that Common Worship allows for this Sunday to be used as a Dedication Festival where appropriate, though some churches will celebrate this on the last Sunday after Trinity.

Hymns

TRADITIONAL

- *All hail the power of Jesus' name (16)*
- *Be thou my guardian and my guide (69)*
- *It fell upon a summer day (331)*
- *O Lord of every shining constellation (512)*
- *O love, how deep, how broad, how high (516)*
- *We have a gospel to proclaim (716)*

CONTEMPORARY

- *All heaven declares (17)*
- *As the deer pants for the water (45)*
- *I believe in Jesus (301)*
- *Make way, make way (438)*
- *Peace, perfect peace, is the gift (555)*
- *We will lay our burden down (726)*

CHANT

- *The Lord is my light (Rizza) (945)*

CHILDREN'S SONG

- *Each of us is a living stone (793)*

Readings

Year A	Exodus 20:1-4, 7-9, 12-20 or Isaiah 5:1-7; Philippians 3:4b-14; Matthew 21:33-46
Year B	Job 1:1; 2:1-10 or Genesis 2:18-24; Hebrews 1:1-4; 2:5-12; Mark 10:2-16
Year C	Lamentations 1:1-6 or Habakkuk 1:1-4; 2:1-4; 2 Timothy 1:1-14; Luke 17:5-10

Confession

We kneel before our heavenly Father
in penitence for our sins,
yet confident of his forgiveness, saying,
Lord, forgive the sins of your people,
and grant us your salvation.

For living according to human wisdom
rather than in the light of your presence,
Lord, forgive the sins of your people,
and grant us your salvation.

For pursuing our own selfish desires
rather than the paths of righteousness,
Lord, forgive the sins of your people,
and grant us your salvation.

For doing what pleases us
rather than your holy will,
Lord, forgive the sins of your people,
and grant us your salvation.

For seeing only the things of this world
rather than recognising your Son as our Saviour,
Lord, forgive the sins of your people,
and grant us your salvation,
through Jesus Christ our Lord. Amen.

Absolution

God, who turns away no one
who comes to him in repentance and faith,
have mercy on *you*,
pardon and forgive *you* for all your sins,
and bring *you* back to his welcoming presence,
through Christ our Lord. Amen.

Prayer

We come before our merciful God,
conscious of our weak faith
but trusting his promise
to hear us and answer,
saying: Accept the prayer of our heart, Lord,
and answer it in your love.

Merciful God, you know the needs
of the Church
here . . . and throughout the world.
In the weakness of confusion and disunity
may your strength be shown;
in the face of apathy and hostility
may your gospel be proclaimed;
in the bustle of life
may your peace and love be experienced.
Accept the prayer of our heart, Lord,
and answer it in your love.

Merciful God, you know the needs of the world
and its suffering people . . .
victims of natural disaster
or man-made catastrophe,
of political instability or local conflict . . .
In pain and despair
may your compassion be revealed.
Accept the prayer of our heart, Lord,
and answer it in your love.

Merciful God, you know the needs
of our local community . . .
its schools and colleges,
its health centres and places of care,
its businesses and homes,
its unemployed and disaffected members.
In the joy and sorrow of the daily round,
may your good news shine out.
Accept the prayer of our heart, Lord,
and answer it in your love.

Merciful God, you know the needs
of our families and loved ones,
and those of our church family members . . .
In their distress or discomfort,
grief or anxiety,
may the presence of your Spirit, the Comforter,
go alongside them to bring healing and
guidance.
Accept the prayer of our heart, Lord,
and answer it in your love.

Merciful God, you know each of us
and hear our prayers
before we put them into words.
Meet us at our point of need
and take us on to where you have called us.
Accept the prayers of our heart, Lord,
and answer them in your love,
that your will may be done
and your kingdom come,
through Jesus Christ our Lord. Amen.

All-age address 1

Jesus' parable of the Wicked Tenants is a clear anticipation of his impending death at the hands of the Jewish authorities, who understood only too well the point he was making and started to lay plans to curtail his 'subversive' teaching. They had consistently refused to listen to God's voice through the prophets and the Law, using the Scriptures simply to bolster their position in the community and oppress everyone else. In rejecting the Son they were rejecting the Father, and in grave danger of losing their place in the kingdom. Most of today's church-goers wouldn't see themselves as rejecting Jesus, and it's true that 'fashionable' church-going is a thing of the past in many places. However, every Christian needs a reminder that what we claim to be in words we must reflect in our daily lives. This outline address puts the spotlight on why people might reject certain aspects of the Christian faith. It needs some prior preparation.

1) Before the service, dissolve a pinch of mixed herbs with water in a small bowl. Start by asking what sort of foods people dislike and why, and after the usual replies of coconut, almond, Stilton cheese and so on, invite someone to taste your concoction without mentioning its ingredients. Even the smallest amount on a teaspoon will create a grimace! Offer a drink of water to remove the taste and explain that we reject some foods because we don't like their flavour. However, we can't put aside the parts of the Christian faith that we find not to our liking.

2) Brief two volunteers beforehand, the first to abuse the other verbally. The second

responds by walking away and rejecting the offender (ensure that their language remains acceptable!). If people hurt or insult us, our natural response is to shut them out of our circle of friends and reject them. But sometimes we reject people not because they're being rude but because they challenge the way we think or do things. Jesus was never abusive, but his words were challenging and the authorities found it easier to try and get rid of him than to face the challenge.

3) Now show a picture of a Rottweiler or Dobermann (assuming you wouldn't want to bring in a live example!), and ask how people would react if they saw one at close quarters. Many will say they'd get away as quickly as possible from a close encounter of this kind, though you should emphasise that most dogs, even large breeds, are very rarely vicious. Unfortunately, a few well-publicised cases mean that we react negatively in case there is a risk. Fear often provokes rejection. Some of Jesus' contemporaries were afraid of him and of his popularity with the ordinary poor folk, so they rejected him and his words without thinking any further.

Finish by pointing out how easy it is to reject the bits of Jesus' message that make us uncomfortable or worried, in case he makes a difference to the way we live. Not many who come to church are likely to dismiss Jesus out of hand, but what he's looking for are lives which are fruitful for his kingdom. Our faith must be more than good words.

All-age address 2

Faith is a term with a variety of meanings. Some people use it to refer to a religious belief system, others non-religiously to describe a positive or optimistic outlook on life. Many more see those with faith as having some belief in an afterlife while others may go further, thinking of it as a conviction that life has a purpose or even a detailed plan. Christians might speak of 'coming to faith', referring to an initial decision or act of commitment to the Christian faith, but Jesus is talking here about an underlying attitude towards God which fundamentally affects the way Christians live – having come to faith we're then committed to 'living by faith'. This outline address looks at simple life situations which require us to act in faith, and parallels these with Christian faith.

1) There are many actions you can use to demonstrate faith – sitting on a chair is possibly the easiest to stage, but if you're feeling adventurous, ask a child to jump off the pulpit step so that you can catch them, or ask a child to stand in the middle of a ring of four people, and fall confidently knowing it'll be caught. Faith has to contain a large element of trust to be effective.

2) A good example of faith on a wider front is public transport. Produce a timetable for local trains or buses, saying that you'll be travelling this week, and read out a departure time for your destination. Explain that you have sufficient faith to believe the claim of the transport company that they'll be running this service at that time. This may well elicit hoots of derision! Faith also contains an element of belief and confidence – because this has worked successfully in the past it should do so again. Poor experiences soon lead to a lack of faith, as those running the railways discovered. Our faith in God is well-founded on our experience of his goodness and love.

3) Finally, ask your organist or music group leader to change the next hymn (but warn them in advance of your intentions!). Having agreed this, point out that your faith in their ability and willingness was sufficient to believe they'd respond favourably. Clearly, the ultimate test of faith in a relationship is marriage. Likewise, our increasing knowledge of God leads us to trust him as our heavenly Father ever more fully, just as a small child learns to trust its parent.

PROPER 23

Sunday between 9 and 15 October inclusive

This Sunday's gospel readings are all well-known passages. Year A brings us Matthew's recounting of the parable of the Great Wedding Feast, and Year B Mark's description of a rich young man who came to see Jesus. For Year C Luke provides Jesus' miraculous healing of ten lepers, only one of whom returned to give thanks.

Hymns

TRADITIONAL

- *Blessed assurance, Jesus is mine (74)*
- *Have faith in God, my heart (268)*
- *How sweet the name of Jesus sounds (297)*
- *Lord of all hopefulness (413)*
- *Songs of thankfulness and praise (609)*
- *Thy hand, O God, has guided (689)*

CONTEMPORARY

- *Alleluia: praise God (11)*
- *Give thanks with a grateful heart (202)*
- *God is good (214)*
- *God is our strength from days of old (220)*
- *Rejoice in the Lord always (578)*
- *When I feel the touch (734)*

CHANT

- *In the Lord I'll be ever thankful (929)*

CHILDREN'S SONG

- *Thank you, Lord (887)*

Readings

Year A Exodus 32:1-14 or Isaiah 25:1-9; Philippians 4:1-9; Matthew 22:1-14
Year B Job 23:1-9, 16-17 or Amos 5:6-7, 10-15; Hebrews 4:12-16; Mark 10:17-31
Year C Jeremiah 29:1, 4-7 or 2 Kings 5:1-3, 7-15c; 2 Timothy 2:8-15; Luke 17:11-19

Confession

Eternal Father, you graciously invite us
to share in the joy of your kingdom,
but we confess that we have turned our backs
on your generosity,
resisted your kindness,
and chosen to follow our own desires.
Forgive all our sins,
pardon our pride and rebellion,
and restore us to the fellowship of your table,
for the sake of your Son,
our Saviour Jesus Christ. Amen.

Absolution

Our loving God,
who welcomes all who turn to him
in penitence and faith,
have mercy on *you*, forgive all *your* sins
and bring *you* into the eternal joy of the new life
which comes through Jesus Christ,
our risen Lord. Amen.

Prayer

God our Father invites us to his eternal feast,
not because we deserve it
but because he wants us to be present.
We respond to his love and kindness, saying:
Generous God,
make us one with you.

God our Father, you call us and all Christians
to be ambassadors of your kingdom.
Bless and guide your Church,
local and worldwide,
as it worships and serves you . . .
help it to bring your transforming love
to a world in desperate need,
and to live out its unity in Christ our Lord.
Generous God,
make us one in you.

God our Father, there is room in your kingdom
for those on the edges of society:
the homeless and unwanted,
the despairing and downtrodden,
the ignored and ill-treated . . .
Sustain and give hope to those
whose lives are filled with pain and sadness . . .
Generous God,
make us one with them.

God our Father,
there are signs of your kingdom
even in war-torn, distressed places,
where fear and hardship overshadow life . . .
Give comfort to the suffering,
release to the oppressed,
and strength to those who work
to bring relief and peace.
Generous God,
make us one with them.

God our Father, the light of your kingdom
shines in every kind of darkness –
illness of mind or body,
anxiety or distress,
affliction or trial . . .
Reach out with your loving hand
to bring consolation, wholeness and joy.
Generous God,
make us one with them.

God our Father, we pray that in our lives
your kingdom will come and your will be done,
as we serve you in one another
and look forward to your promise of eternal life.
Generous God,
make us one with you,
both now and until that day
when we will rejoice in your presence for ever,
through Jesus, our Lord and Saviour. Amen.

All-age address 1

There's no better demonstration of Jesus' sense of humour than the parable of the great wedding feast. Responding to a particularly pious question from someone decidedly 'holier than thou', he has a field-day with the silly excuses to show up the stupidity of those who, in rejecting him, were rejecting their heavenly Father. The context today may be rather different, but people still make all kinds of excuses for not committing themselves to the way of Christ. Invitations are a good focus for an all-age address, not least because they demand a response. Some advance preparation is needed. Draw up large-scale invitation cards to three different events – a garden party, an important business lunch and a celebrity banquet. The first two should be elaborate and flashy, looking important and glamorous, the third relatively plain. You'll need a volunteer to hold these up for all to see, and you'll also need an invented menu for each, which can be read out. Before you start, show the congregation all three invitations and conduct a quick survey of which event they might go to.

1) The first menu is in French (if possible), so that it sounds pretty impressive until translated into English. A good list of thoroughly unpleasant tastes (dishwater soup, fat and gristle pie, for example) will be guaranteed to provoke a disgusted response! Cap this by suggesting that guests will have to pay £80 a head for the privilege, and underline the quality of the invitation card. Ask the congregation what excuses they could make to avoid going to this – a diplomatic illness or 'back trouble' are likely suggestions, followed maybe by double-booking or a prior engagement. Point out that people often make excuses to avoid something they think will be distasteful or unpleasant.

2) The second 'menu' should be very similar to the first, though emphasise that this is a business lunch, so expenses will be limited and hard work required. Again, find out what excuses people might use to get out of this invitation, while commending the artwork and high-quality production of the invitation itself. Point out that most of us use an excuse to avoid something like this which seems boring and onerous.

3) The final 'menu' should be as mouthwatering as possible, including dishes which will appeal to children such as Big Macs or ice-cream. Add to this by saying that there'll be lots of well-known celebrities there too, and it's all completely free of charge. No one's going to make excuses to turn down this one, even though the invitation itself is a bit plain and uninteresting at first sight.

Finish by saying that many people turn down God's invitation to be part of his kingdom because at first glance it seems less attractive than some other options. So, not realising what they're missing out on, they make their excuses – 'not enough time', 'too much else to do', 'when I'm older', 'I want to spend time with my family'. But, if we look more closely, we realise that for all their immediate appeal, the attractions of this world don't live up to their initial impact and soon become dull or even repulsive. In contrast, the more we experience of God's kingdom, the more we realise it has to offer.

All-age address 2

'The cost of discipleship – only £2.95', read the slogan on the bookstall. If only! Few congregations have exceptionally wealthy members today, but you don't need to be a millionaire to suffer from the same problem as the rich young man who came to Jesus one day. We aren't entirely clear about his motives, but he was genuine enough. Devout and God-fearing, faithful to the Law and sincerely wanting to please God, the biggest obstacle preventing him from following Jesus was that he had too much to lose. Not that Jesus was bothered about wealth *per se*, but he knew that it could engender attitudes which form a barrier to keep God at a safe distance. However much we may complain about being hard up, those same attitudes are just as prevalent now and can have a significant effect on church life. This address outline needs some preparation in order to bring out the blocks which prevent so many people from coming to Jesus and following him. You'll need four boxes of different sizes so they can fit over each other to be removed one at a time, and a small wrapped 'treasure' which will fit into the smallest box.

1) The largest box covers all the others, and on it is written 'Money and possessions'. Like the young man, most of us hang on to what we have, afraid of losing it. This fear is probably the biggest single factor in preventing people from being committed to following Christ. Our society promotes ownership as a cardinal rule of life, but this militates against exercising faith and gives the idea that this life is the only one that matters. It's vital to stress that wrong attitudes to money and possessions aren't the preserve of the really wealthy – however

little we may think we have, we can still allow it to come between us and God.

2) The next box should say 'Time'. After money, the next largest problem for most of us is time, and for the same reason – we never have enough! It can be very demanding to balance all our priorities and give the right amount of time to our work or studies, families or friends, church or social activities. When we feel tired after a day's work, when it feels as though everyone is pressurising us, when we wonder how to fit everything in, God easily gets squeezed out.

3) The third box has the caption 'Other people'. This can be another distraction of major proportions. It may be that one other person (or group of people) becomes more important to us than God, but equally we can become so obsessed with someone who upsets or annoys us that we can't think of anything else. Families can also be unhealthily possessive and demanding. Human relationships are complex, even unfathomable, and can profoundly affect us in all sorts of ways, taking our attention away from our relationship with Christ.

4) The final box says 'Self'. We can spend so much time, energy and even money on ourselves that there's nothing left for anyone or anything else. It's right and proper to attend to health problems or personal relationships and issues, but not to the extent that God is shut out and we're unable to think of anything else. This may be the least obvious obstacle to following the way of Christ, but the hardest to deal with.

At the end you come across the 'treasure' (such as a small gift-wrapped bar of chocolate), and as you do so, point out that the rewards of the Christian life depend on us being willing to remove the obstacles which keep us away from them.

All-age address 3

Saying thank you is something all children learn almost as soon as they can talk. So it's important to recognise that Luke didn't include this incident in order to teach about good manners, but to highlight one man's response to the transforming power of Jesus. The leper who returns to Jesus to give thanks for his healing finds his life transformed, not just because he's been cured of a socially unacceptable disease but even more because his grateful response opens up a new relationship with the Saviour. This outline address, therefore, puts less emphasis on etiquette (though acknowledging the importance of expressing gratitude) than on the relationship which lies behind giving and receiving.

1) Start by offering a member of the congregation a wrapped sweet (Roses chocolates are quite useful as they have been marketed as a way of saying thank you). The response will either be 'No, thank you' or more likely 'Yes, please – thank you'. Thanking someone for their generosity or consideration is an essential part of our relationship with them. If they've given something, however small, it's a sign that they value their relationship with us; our thanks indicates that we also value it.

2) The rest of the address is a simple mnemonic on the word 'thankful'. Each letter is also the initial letter of a word referring to a gift of God for which we should be thankful. A card with each letter and word on it could be held up by a volunteer.

T – Time. Jesus gave the lepers his time and attention, and God has given us the gift of time to use for his glory.

H – Healing. Jesus gave the leper healing from the condition which separated him from other people. He heals us of the things which separate us from each other and God, as well as illness or pain.

A – Answer. Jesus answered their cry for help and mercy. He always answers those who cry to him in distress and sadness.

N – New life. Healing meant a whole new life for the lepers, as they could mix with other people once again. We too have new life in the Spirit through Jesus' death and resurrection.

K – Kindness. The lepers hadn't earned Jesus' act of kindness. God shows us his love and mercy not because we deserve it but because of his kindness.

F – Families and friends. We may not always feel thankful for them, but life would be lonely and frightening on our own. God the Father, Son and Holy Spirit live in relationship, and God created us likewise, to relate to him and to each other.

U – Unlimited joy. Imagine how the lepers must have felt to know they were healed! This isn't superficial jollity but a deep sense of how much God has done, how much we owe him, and how much we want to share that with other people.

L – Love. Jesus' motivation was only ever love. The leper who returned was the one who recognised this and continued the relationship. God's love dwells in our lives and transforms them if we respond to it and allow him to make us more like him.

PROPER 24

Sunday between 16 and 22 October inclusive

Today's reading for Year A from Matthew's Gospel is the well-known passage in which Jesus distinguishes between divine and human authority, and sidesteps a trap set for him by his opponents. Year B's gospel reading from Mark depicts James and John trying to get the best place in heaven, while in Year C Luke retells Jesus' parable of the Persistent Widow.

Hymns

TRADITIONAL

- *Around the throne of God (41)*
- *Come, Holy Ghost, our hearts inspire (117)*
- *Forth in thy name, O Lord, I go (188)*
- *How shall I sing that majesty (296)*
- *Lord, thy word abideth (420)*
- *What a friend we have in Jesus (727)*

CONTEMPORARY

- *Come, wounded healer (130)*
- *Forth in the peace of Christ we go (187)*
- *God of love (226)*
- *Gracious God, in adoration (244)*
- *Jesus is Lord! (352)*
- *Warm as the sun (706)*

CHANT

- *Stay with me (942)*

CHILDREN'S SONG

- *I have a friend (829)*

Readings

Year A   Exodus 33:12-23 or Isaiah 45:1-7;
1 Thessalonians 1:1-10;
Matthew 22:15-22
Year B   Job 38:1-7 (34-41) or Isaiah 53:4-12;
Hebrews 5:1-10; Mark 10:35-45
Year C   Jeremiah 31:27-34 or Genesis 32:22-31;
2 Timothy 3:14-4:5; Luke 18:1-8

Confession

Lord, you are a forgiving God,
slow to anger yet swift to show mercy.

We confess with sorrow
our failure to acknowledge your lordship
over our lives,
our concern with our own well-being,
and our lack of faith.
Pardon all our sins, we ask you,
blot out our offences,
and by your Spirit fit us to be worthy servants
of your kingdom,
through our Saviour Jesus Christ. Amen.

Absolution

Almighty God, whose arms are ever open
to receive those who come to him
in penitence and faith,
have mercy on *you*,
forgive all *your* wrongdoing
and assure *you* of his eternal faithfulness
and goodness,
through Jesus Christ our Lord. Amen.

Prayer

We come before our Father in heaven,
offering him our worship and praise
and laying at his feet the burdens of our heart.
Lord, teach us always to pray,
and never to lose heart.

We think of our brothers and sisters in Christ,
right across the world,
who endure opposition and persecution,
confront evil and corruption,
challenge cynicism and apathy.
We pray for all mission initiatives
and endeavours to share the good news . . .
When we feel disheartened,
give us courage to persevere.
Lord, teach us always to pray,
and never to lose heart.

We think of governments and authorities,
stretched by economic and
community problems,
crime and social divisions,
disaster and famine.
We pray for politicians and civic leaders,
who make laws and decisions . . .
When we feel disillusioned,
give us a vision of your eternal kingdom.
Lord, teach us always to pray,
and never to lose heart.

We think of those whose lives are overshadowed
by illness, disappointment or insecurity,
whose pilgrimage is beset with difficulty . . .
We pray for our families and friends,
and all who need the comfort
of your presence . . .
When we feel dispirited,
renew our zeal and inspire our faith.
Lord, teach us always to pray,
and never to lose heart.

We think of those whose earthly pilgrimage
is ended
and who are now at rest in you . . .
We pray that we may hold their example
before us
and follow them in the narrow way
that leads to eternal life.
Lord, teach us always to pray,
and never to lose heart,
that one day we may rejoice for ever
with them in your kingdom of light,
which we ask in the name of your Son,
our Saviour Jesus Christ. Amen.

All-age address 1

The Gospels contain several instances of Jesus'
opponents trying to snare him into saying
something incriminating, which would give
them an excuse to deal with him. On each
occasion he not only avoided the trap, but did
so with such profound insight that he couldn't
be answered. 'Rendering unto Caesar what
belongs to Caesar' is an expression often used
in a secular context, so familiar is it, though
regrettably less people seem familiar with
rendering to God what is God's. The issue
which underlies Jesus' answer is how to live
as citizens both of this world and of God's
kingdom. It's too complex to tackle in depth in
all-age worship, but this outline aims to provide
a basic understanding both of the tensions
involved and the opportunities available.
It's based on the same principle as the game
'Scruples', and the only preparation needed
is the production of a few 'game cards' with
appropriate questions.

1) The first question is about personal morals.
   'A supermarket cashier gives me £10 too
   much change, but I only realise this when I
   get home. Do I: (a) take it back as soon as
   possible? (b) post it back by return? (c) give
   it to charity since the firm makes big
   profits? (d) keep it?' Two willing members
   of the congregation may be happy to give
   their verdict on this, but finish by asking
   the whole congregation what they think,
   ideally by a show of hands. This issue is
   quite straightforward, and it's not likely
   that (c) or (d) will be supported in a church
   context. Christians are called to be good
   citizens and deal honestly in every aspect
   of their lives.

2) The second question is much more a question of choice. 'I'm thinking about booking
   a summer holiday when an appeal is
   broadcast for famine victims. Should I: (a)
   forget the holiday and give the money I
   would have spent to the charity? (b) book
   the holiday and give an equal amount to
   the charity? (c) book a holiday that costs
   half what I was intending to spend and
   give the rest to charity? (d) decide my
   Christian giving is already organised and
   just book the holiday?' In this case there's
   no easy right or wrong answer as there
   are a number of factors to consider – the
   holiday may be essential for family or
   health reasons; funds may well be limited.
   Christian giving should be an ongoing
   activity rather than a 'knee-jerk' response
   to need. On the other hand, it would be
   wrong as Christians to remain unmoved by
   great human need when we're able to make
   a significant contribution – Jesus was often
   moved by compassion.

3) The third question is more ethical. 'I discover
   that my best friend is addicted to drugs,
   and stealing in order to finance their habit.
   Do I: (a) tell the police at once? (b) warn
   him of the possible consequences? (c) tell
   his parents or a teacher? (d) ignore it and
   assume it's a phase that will pass, and
   anyway it's not my business?' This is a very
   real problem, and even (d) isn't as clear-
   cut as it seems – many youngsters do go
   through difficult phases, and we have no
   automatic right to interfere in the lives of
   others, however much we may disagree with
   their actions. Having said that, it would be
   wrong not to challenge harmful behaviour,
   friends may be unable to control addiction
   on their own, in which case our help may

be invaluable. As Christians we make decisions based on the best interests of everyone concerned, though emphasise that we aren't entitled to become judgemental.

4) The last question is specifically Christian: 'I accept a new job for an organisation, which I then discover expects me to compromise my integrity and faith through deceit and financial irregularity. Do I: (a) resign at once? (b) try to carry on the job without being dishonest? (c) explain my concerns to my superiors and risk dismissal? (d) go along with it because the family comes first and the mortgage has to be paid?' Many Christians are familiar with a scenario like this. No one can dispute that families need to be supported, and as Christians we should be good employees. However, no one has authority to condone wrong-doing, still less to command it, and our Christian witness will be seriously impaired if we close our eyes and consciences to what we know is wrong. Faith can sometimes feel very risky, but making a stand may ultimately do far more for God's kingdom than refusing to accept responsibility.

Conclude by pointing out that as Christians there's not usually a conflict between being citizens and members of the kingdom of God. But when we're faced with the choice of obeying wrong instructions or obeying God, our first duty is to the Lord of lords.

All-age address 2

You can use the second outline address for Proper 20 as the basis for one on this week's Gospel from the following chapter of Mark, but after going through the four status symbols, this time bring on a fifth, a bowl of water and a flannel. This was the status symbol that Jesus used (see John 13:1-15), and, as disciples, this symbol of service should be the only one that defines us.

All-age address 3

It seems odd to our culture that Jesus should speak of a persistent widow – perhaps our minds turn more readily to children who never give up with their demands! – but in those days it was probably the only means she had of obtaining justice. The judge is of equal importance to the parable, self-centred and arrogant. Jesus wants his hearers to understand that if a hard-nosed, unsympathetic magistrate can be swayed by a poor but persistent widow, how much more will our heavenly Father listen to those who cry to him for help. The question of unanswered prayer troubles some people greatly (usually because they didn't get the answer they wanted), but this outline tries to promote an understanding of prayer which goes beyond the 'slot machine' concept.

1) Produce a few 'instant' foods or drinks – coffee, custard, cakes, for example. Point out that we can now go to the supermarket and get instant food which needs little or no preparation. We've become very used to this, and we now find it hard to wait for anything – we want it *now*, and as consumers assume that's our right. God, however, isn't a consumer service provider who's obliged to deal with special orders on the spot. He's our eternal Lord and King, and we can't order him about or drag him down to our own level.

2) Next produce a couple of credit cards, explaining that they enable us to 'have now and pay later'. Older members may still remember having to 'save up' for an item they wanted, but today instant gratification is all too easy – though the consequences later on can be disastrous as the debts mount up. God isn't there to provide whatever we want whenever we want it – the so-called 'prosperity gospel' is a gross distortion of the Gospel of Christ.

3) The widow in the parable was asking for justice rather than self-gratification. God will always hear us when we cry to him in real need, or when we pray for others in need. His answer may not be the one we wanted, but we can be sure it will be the best for us, as God will only ever act in our best interests. To conclude, display a few charity leaflets requesting money and support, and indicate that if our prayers are directed towards these needs, we know God will respond in his love.

PROPER 25

Sunday between 23 and 29 October inclusive

We've now reached the final 'Proper', though your church may use this Sunday to celebrate its Dedication Festival. However, the consecutive Gospel readings continue through to the Sunday before Advent, the Festival of Christ the King. Matthew's Gospel in Year A brings Jesus' words about the greatest commandment, and his status as the Christ, while Mark in Year B has the familiar story of blind Bartimaeus. For Year C we have the short but challenging excerpt from Luke about the Pharisee and the publican.

Hymns

TRADITIONAL

- *At the name of Jesus (54)*
- *From glory to glory advancing (194)*
- *Hail to the Lord's anointed (259)*
- *I know that my Redeemer lives (311)*
- *Love divine, all loves excelling (428)*
- *Through all the changing scenes of life (686)*

CONTEMPORARY

- *God is good (214)*
- *He is exalted (273)*
- *Love is the only law (430)*
- *Open our eyes, Lord (532)*
- *Taste and see the goodness of the Lord (628)*
- *The king is among us (648)*

CHANT

- *In the Lord I'll be ever thankful (929)*

CHILDREN'S SONG

- *I could sing unending songs (823)*

Readings

Year A Deuteronomy 34:1-12 or
Leviticus 19:1-2, 15-18;
1 Thessalonians 2:1-8;
Matthew 22:34-46
Year B Job 42:1-6, 10-17 or Jeremiah 31:7-9;
Hebrews 7:23-28; Mark 10:46-52
Year C Joel 2:23-32 or Ecclesiasticus 35:12-17
or Jeremiah 14:7-10, 19-22;
2 Timothy 4:6-8, 16-18; Luke 18:9-14

Confession

We come into God's holy presence,
aware of our failings and wrongdoing, saying,
Lord, we are truly sorry and repent of our sins;
forgive us and make us whole.

Our actions are too often motivated
by personal concerns
rather than by the needs of others
and the building of your kingdom.
Lord, we are truly sorry and repent of our sins;
forgive us and make us whole.

Our words are too often formed
by our own opinions and interests
rather than by the feelings of others
and the proclamation of your kingdom.
Lord, we are truly sorry and repent of our sins;
forgive us and make us whole.

Our thoughts are too often dominated
by our personal viewpoint
rather than by the welfare of others
and the truth of your kingdom.
Lord, we are truly sorry and repent of our sins;
forgive us and make us whole.

Our lives are too often directed
by selfish ambition
rather than by serving others in Christ's name
and demonstrating the power of his kingdom.
Lord, we are truly sorry and repent of our sins;
forgive us and make us whole,
fill our mouths with your praises
and make us faithful servants,
for the sake of your Son,
our Saviour Jesus Christ. Amen.

Absolution

Our heavenly Father, by whose grace alone
we are worthy to stand before him,
have mercy on *you*,
forgive all *your* sins,
free *you* from guilt,
and set *you* free to praise and glorify his name,
through Christ our Lord. Amen.

Prayer

We offer thanksgiving and prayers
to our Lord Jesus,
who gave sight to the blind, saying,
Lord, open our eyes to your presence;
help us to walk in your light.

In faith we pray for the Church
in every country and circumstance,
especially . . .
May we and all Christian people
rejoice at your presence in praise and worship,
in fellowship and companionship,
in service and mission.
Lord, open our eyes to your presence;
help us to walk in your light.

In faith we pray for the world's leaders
as they tackle the problems
of famine and poverty,
disaster and crisis, education and health,
especially . . .
May we see your hand at work in the world,
in international affairs, in the community
and in each other.
Lord, open our eyes to your presence;
help us to walk in your light.

In faith we pray for those we know
who are living through times of
illness, depression or uncertainty,
especially . . .
May they know your Spirit
comforting and guiding them
through their trials.
Lord, open our eyes to your presence;
help us to walk in your light.

In faith we pray for those
who have finished their earthly pilgrimage
and now rest in your love,
especially . . .
May their example inspire us to persevere
and continue our walk with you.
Lord, open our eyes to your presence;
help us to walk in your light,
until we rejoice in the eternal day of heaven,
through Jesus Christ our Lord. Amen.

as well as they do but also leaves them silent. Their refusal to recognise Jesus as the promised Messiah demonstrably contradicted the Scriptures they claimed to believe in. (This address outline is similar to the one for the Sunday next before Lent, which celebrates the Transfiguration.)

1) Disfigure a large magazine-sized photo of a well-known personality with moustache, glasses, and so on. As you display it, ask for identification, and point out that the Pharisees were deliberately distorting their image of Jesus so as not to recognise him. Unfortunately for them, too many other people realised who he really was.

2) Play a small section of a tape of someone's voice and see if anyone knows who it is. Sometimes it's the subject matter as much as the qualities of the voice itself which is the giveaway. Jesus certainly had a reputation in Israel, but it was what he taught that showed his authority, not just the way he presented it.

3) Now hold up a large copy of a famous painting and ask who the artist is – often it's obvious just from the subject and style of the painting. We recognise the work even though the person who produced it may well have died many years ago. The Pharisees could have worked out that Jesus was the Christ from what he did as well as what he said, but so determinedly blind were they that they could only think of ways to get rid of him by setting traps. But in answering their silly questions, Jesus demonstrated even more clearly that he was who he claimed to be.

All-age address 1

Jesus was often asked trick questions in the vain hope that he'd say something incriminating. He never did, but that didn't stop the questions coming. Here he's asked about the most important law by a legal 'expert', who should have known better. Jesus' knowledge of the Law is as superior to theirs as is his understanding of the human condition. In response, he throws *them* a question, based on the Law, which not only demonstrates that he knows it

All-age address 2

Most people, if asked, would say they value sight more than any of the other senses. Today we have guide-dogs, braille, and the medical knowledge to prevent at least some blindness, but for Bartimaeus to be unsighted was a life sentence. As with so many others healed by Jesus, he was made whole not just in one area but in every aspect of life. Most important he could live and work normally, no longer feeling the social stigma attached to disability and certain illnesses. For this simple outline you need just two willing volunteers (preferably, though not necessarily, primed in advance) and a blindfold.

1) Tie the blindfold around your first volunteer's eyes, making sure it's effective! Give him an apple (or something similar) and ask him to identify it. A person who can't see has to rely on his other senses to recognise objects.

2) Now ask him what colour it is. Someone blind from birth has no concept of colour – a whole dimension of life is missing.

3) Bring up a friend of the blindfolded volunteer and see if he can be recognised by touch or general shape. Blindness means that parents, spouses and children have to be identified by voice or touch.

4) Turn your volunteer round three times and ask him to find his way to the organ (or wherever is convenient). A blind person can't identify places or distance, and finds his way about either with a trained dog, or by learning to use a white stick.

5) Bartimaeus had an even bigger problem – he couldn't work, and was a social outcast, so his life revolved around begging. No one expected Jesus to bother with him (apart from Bartimaeus himself), so when he responded to the persistent cries for help, some people were surprised, even offended, and tried to dissuade him. But the touch of Jesus' hand transformed Bartimaeus – he could see people, places, objects and colours, and no longer had to endure being marginalised and vulnerable.

Conclude by explaining that Jesus is concerned not just to cure a condition or illness but to transform every part of our lives with his love, so that we can be free to get up and follow him, as Bartimaeus did.

All-age address 3

One of the most besetting of all the human race's failings has to be that of comparing ourselves with each other in the most favourable light. We constantly seek reassurance about our own moral status by trying to denigrate other people's, and while we may focus on typically twenty-first-century issues, Jesus perceptively pinpoints the universality of this condition. In this case it was the Pharisees who indulged in spiritual and moral oneupmanship, and as the parable makes clear, self-righteousness of this kind is the biggest single stumbling-block to membership of God's kingdom. Significantly, the tax collector doesn't dwell mawkishly on his sins and personal inadequacy, but compares himself only with the standards expected of him by God, which he has manifestly failed to attain. This outline aims to pick up on the areas in which we're tempted to compare ourselves with others, and on the areas in which we should try to outdo each other. You need to draw a large tree with ten branches, on which you place or draw five rotten and five juicy red apples.

1) The five rotten apples represent the ways in which we like to think of ourselves as superior to others – education, wealth, personal standards, social standing and popularity, and moral viewpoints (if the picture's large enough write the relevant word on each fruit). Each of these is self-evident, and it's straightforward to think of other examples. Our education can easily tempt us to think of ourselves as more knowledgeable or better-informed; wealth soon convinces us that we're in favour with God; personal standards are an easy way of putting down anyone who's different to us; social standing persuades us that God thinks the same of us as our friends; while on moral viewpoints – well, how many people do we know who admit they might have 'got it wrong'?

2) The five juicy red apples are fruits of the Spirit – love, joy peace, patience and kindness (you could add others if you've time). In God's kingdom no one is superior or inferior to anyone else. Instead our thoughts should be about what we can do to improve the lives of other people. All the time we're thinking about ourselves and whether we're better than someone else, we're preventing our lives from being fruitful. As followers of Jesus we're called to bear fruit for his glory.

BIBLE SUNDAY

The last Sunday after Trinity falls on the last Sunday of October (or 24 October if 31 October is a Sunday and kept as All Saints' Day). The Collect is adapted from the one in the Book of Common Prayer for the second Sunday in Advent, a day often known as 'Bible Sunday', but Common Worship relocates Bible Sunday to tie in with what some denominations call 'Reformation Sunday', and provides a three-year cycle of readings for those churches wishing to keep it. All three Gospel readings deal with God's word and our belief: in Year A Jesus reassures his disciples that his words will never pass away, in Year B he accuses the Jews of refusing to believe that the Scriptures bear witness to him, and in Year C we have Luke's well-known account of Jesus preaching in the synagogue in Nazareth.

Hymns

TRADITIONAL

- *Firmly I believe, and truly (174)*
- *Hail to the Lord's anointed (259)*
- *Hark, the glad sound (265)*
- *Lord, thy word abideth (420)*
- *O for a thousand tongues to sing (485)*
- *O Lord my God (511)*

CONTEMPORARY

- *As the deer pants for the water (45)*
- *God's Spirit is in my heart (231)*
- *I give you all the honour (308)*
- *Make way, make way (438)*
- *Open our eyes, Lord (532)*
- *The kingdom of God (646)*

CHANT

- *Veni, lumen cordium (947)*

CHILDREN'S SONG

- *Have you heard the raindrops (817)*

Readings

Year A   Nehemiah 8:1-4a (5-6) 8-12; Colossians 3:12-17; Matthew 24:30-35

Year B   Isaiah 55:1-11; 2 Timothy 3:14-4:5; John 5:36b-47

Year C   Isaiah 45:22-25; Romans 15:1-6; Luke 4:16-24

Confession

Lord, you have given us your word to guide;
we are sorry for going our own way.
You have given us your word to instruct;
we are sorry for not learning of you.
You have given us your word
to reveal your love and grace;
we are sorry for turning our backs on you.
Have mercy on us,
and forgive all our sins;
open our hearts
to receive your word with gladness,
and make us worthy ambassadors
of your kingdom,
for the sake of our Saviour, Jesus Christ.
Amen.

Absolution

Almighty God, whose word brings life and joy,
have mercy on *you*,
pardon all *your* wrongdoing,
and deliver *you* from the death of sin
into the new life to be found only
in the Living Word, Jesus Christ our Lord.
Amen.

Prayer

We approach the throne of the Lord our God,
bringing our prayers and burdens,
and waiting for him to speak to us.
Lord, we praise you for your word,
and wait on you in faith.

Speak to your Church, Lord,
words of encouragement and challenge,
as it fulfils your great commission
to bring the Gospel to all the world.
Release the gifts of the Spirit in your people,
that teachers and leaders,
evangelists and mission workers,
pastors and carers

may bring your love to those
who do not know you.
Lord, we praise you for your word,
and wait on you in faith.

Speak to those in authority, Lord,
words of wisdom and guidance,
as they confront wickedness and violence,
poverty and starvation,
degradation and exploitation.
Influence their decisions and direction
that they may uphold the justice
and righteousness of your kingdom.
Lord, we praise you for your word,
and wait on you in faith.

Speak to those in distress or despair, Lord,
words of comfort and healing,
that in their suffering they may know
the touch of your hand.
We remember especially . . .
Bring them relief from their pain and distress,
wholeness of body and mind,
and the unfading hope of eternal glory.
Lord, we praise you for your word,
and wait on you in faith.

Speak to those who mourn
the loss of loved ones, Lord,
words of peace,
that in their grief
they may know you beside them.
We remember especially . . .
May we be uplifted by the example
of those who have died in faith,
and follow after them
in the way of truth and light that leads to you.
Lord, we praise you for your word,
and wait on you in faith,
trusting in your mercy and obeying your call,
until we reach our home in heaven,
for Christ's sake. Amen.

All-age address

The passage from Luke 4 is covered by the outline address for the Third Sunday in Epiphany, while the Second Sunday in Advent has two addresses suitable for Bible Sunday. As an alternative, this simple outline uses the concept of a library to illustrate the varied types of literature contained in the Bible, and ways in which we can use it. Do point out that there are unhelpful ways of reading Scripture, such as taking short phrases out of their context or using 'proof texts' to justify personal opinions or behaviour. You could underline the points by putting your chosen books on a small bookrack.

1) Start off by displaying a couple of history books, perhaps a glossy, illustrated coffee-table volume and something that looks a bit more erudite. Ask the congregation why we read about events of the past and people who have died. Several reasons may emerge – e.g. to learn from their examples or mistakes; to remember milestones in the history of a community or nation; to learn about the history and culture of other peoples; to interpret facts about the past for our own times. The Bible contains history for all these reasons, but with one addition above all – to recall the saving acts of God in the history of his people, supremely in the person of his Son Jesus Christ.

2) Next move on to biography, using an example or two. History is made by people, and most of us are fascinated by the lives of the history-makers, whose names live on after their death. We may be inspired by their example and achievements, motivated by their commitment and enthusiasm, or warned by their mistakes. The Bible also focuses on people, but not just biographically. It leaves out some of the small details we like to know (e.g. what Jesus looked like), and concentrates instead on their relationship with God, and the part they played in his plans.

3) We all like a good novel, either for its depiction of characters or its gripping plot – you could ask for some congregational favourites at this point before revealing your own! However, a good novel does more than entertain; it seeks to present a perspective on human life and enable the reader to see a situation in a particular light. The four Gospels and Acts certainly make for good reading, but they describe real people and events rather than using

invented situations. The books of Job and Jonah are good examples of writing aimed specifically at helping the reader understand or come to terms with the problem of suffering.

4) Poetry may seem a more esoteric kind of reading-matter (again tastes may be sampled from the congregation), but there's plenty of it in the Bible. It was a normal way of expressing the whole range of human emotions, and while the Psalms are the most obvious example, the prophets often expressed their message in poetic form too, maybe as an aid to memory. Some of the most profound parts of the Bible are expressed in its poetic sections (Handel made good use of some in his oratorio *Messiah*).

5) Collections of letters written by the famous are also popular, shedding light on their character and feelings. Much of the New Testament is taken up with letters, but while they reveal something about their writers, they were written to some of the earliest churches to be read aloud at meetings; those included in the Bible were considered to be important for all Christians in all generations and cultures.

6) Books are also published to promote and spread the views of their authors – Stephen Hawking's *A Brief History of Time* is a well-known recent example. The prophets weren't afraid of saying what they thought, but they knew this was a message from God for his people. The books in the Bible weren't written to popularise an individual's thoughts, but to ensure that God's word reached those he wanted to hear it.

Conclude by emphasising that the Bible consists of a wide range of books, and we can learn from all of them, not just about a nation's history, nor even just about the words and deeds of a few inspiring people, but most of all about our heavenly Father, who through his written word leads us to his Son Jesus, the living Word.

DEDICATION FESTIVAL

The Dedication Festival is not to be confused with the Patronal Festival. It provides an opportunity once a year to give thanks for the bricks and mortar of the church building and its role in the local community. Churches in newer buildings will be aware of the date of its dedication or consecration to God, and celebrate this festival on or near that date. Most ancient buildings, however, have no records of this, so Common Worship suggests that it is kept either on the first or the last Sunday of October. It would be wrong to become fixated on buildings, and no one disagrees that the Church consists of dedicated people rather than building materials. However, an annual thanksgiving for a 'holy place' also gives the opportunity to review how it might be used for the benefit of the people who worship there, and those who don't. The Gospel readings for Years A and C both concern Jesus' cleansing of the Temple, while Year B's is the conclusion of the Good Shepherd discourse.

Hymns

TRADITIONAL

- *Angel voices ever singing (37)*
- *Christ is made the sure foundation (97)*
- *Christ is our cornerstone (98)*
- *City of God, how broad and far (106)*
- *Jerusalem, my happy home (339)*
- *We love the place, O God (718)*

CONTEMPORARY

- *As we are gathered (47)*
- *For I'm building a people of power (181)*
- *Give me joy in my heart (201)*
- *I will enter his gates (336)*
- *Lord, for the years (409)*
- *We are marching (709)*

CHANT

- *In the Lord I'll be ever thankful (929)*

CHILDREN'S SONG

- *As Jacob with travel was weary one day (775)*

Readings

Year A   1 Kings 8:22-30 or Revelation 21:9-14; Hebrews 12:18-24; Matthew 21:12-16

Year B   Genesis 28:11-18 or Revelation 21:9-14; 1 Peter 2:1-10; John 10:22-29

Year C   1 Chronicles 29:6-19; Ephesians 2:19-22; John 2:13-22

Confession

God, our merciful Father,
you call us to be the Body of Christ
here on earth.
We confess our sins against you
and one another;
sins of word and action, and of failure to act.
We have harboured unjust attitudes;
we have uttered rude, insensitive words;
we have acted selfishly and irresponsibly.
In your mercy pardon all our sins,
help us to celebrate goodness and truth,
and build us together in the love of your Son
Jesus Christ our Lord. Amen.

Absolution

Almighty God, whose mercy never fails,
grant you pardon for all *your* sin,
deliverance from temptation,
and the peace which binds us together in love,
for the sake of his Son,
our Saviour Jesus Christ. Amen.

Prayer

We bring to God our thanksgiving and praise
for his goodness in the past
and offer him our prayers,
our gifts and our service, saying,
Lord, we rejoice in your goodness;
accept the offering of our praise.

We thank you for the blessings
you have showered
on your people over the years:
for faithful ministry, loyal service
and generous provision.
Grant us wisdom to use our resources wisely,
to encourage one another in the life of faith,
and to work together in fulfilling

your great commission to make disciples.
Lord, we rejoice in your goodness;
accept the offering of our praise.

We thank you for the gifts and strength
with which you have equipped your people:
gifts of leadership,
evangelism, teaching and healing.
Grant us discernment to use our abilities
and gifts to build up the whole Church
in faith and unity,
and to bring your care and mercy
to our needy world.
Lord, we rejoice in your goodness;
accept the offering of our praise.

We thank you for the prayers
you have answered,
the times when you have heard
your people's cry,
in times of crisis and anxiety,
of illness and misery,
of anguish and grief.
We name before you now . . .
Grant us compassion to come alongside them
in this time of darkness,
and bring them the light of your presence.
Lord, we rejoice in your goodness;
accept the offering of our praise.

We thank you for those
who have served you faithfully and well,
and now rest in you,
having completed their earthly pilgrimage,
especially . . .
Grant us faith to follow in their footsteps
and finish our journey,
that we may one day share with them
the joys of eternal life.
Lord, we rejoice in your goodness;
**accept the offering of our lives,
for the sake of your Son,
our Saviour Jesus Christ. Amen.**

All-age address

Many Christians, especially church leaders, feel ambivalent about their church buildings. There's good biblical precedent for setting aside a hallowed space, dedicated to the worship of God, but it can seem out of all proportion to the often small number of people using it. Many churches are attractive, even beautiful, yet their maintenance can be costly, absorbing money which might otherwise be used to help the needy. Ancient buildings, in particular, take up an inordinate amount of time which might otherwise be devoted to mission and evangelism. Some will even point out that St Paul and the earliest Church had no buildings set apart for their use – in fact, the world's earliest surviving Christian building (in Syria) is a converted dwelling, dating only from the third century. True, the Church is made up of people rather than bricks and mortar, but buildings do reflect the life of those who use them, and for many regular church-goers their premises feel like a second home. There's good reason to give thanks for a church building, and the celebrations may provide an excellent opportunity to draw in other members of the local community. This outline aims to demonstrate how a church building is just an empty shell unless it's also built up with God's people. It requires some preparation, and the involvement not just of key church officers but also of the whole congregation. You'll need an outline drawing, as large as possible, of a church building (ideally your own), together with a brick-sized piece of paper for as many members of the congregation as you think feasible, including those who hold positions of responsibility.

1) The drawing of the church should be displayed prominently on a wall, an easel, or any other convenient surface. Start by asking what different parts there are to the church, and as you get answers, ask someone connected with each part to come forward and place a 'brick' on the picture on which they write what they do. The organ is represented by the organist, the sanctuary by the chief sacristan, the guttering by the churchwarden and so on. Explain that while the building may be beautiful or functional (rarely both!), it won't be much use if there aren't any people using it. God gives each of us gifts and wants us to use them for the benefit of the whole church. Practical people can use their gift to keep the building in sound and safe condition; artistic people can make it look beautiful; musical people can fill it with God's praise; friendly people

can make it a place of encouragement and fellowship; those with a pastoral gift can make it a place where people feel cared for. This can be developed as much as time allows.

2) Now invite the rest of the congregation to write on their piece of paper what part they think God wants them to play in his building. When this is done, each of them comes and attaches their 'brick' to an appropriate part of the drawing. Finally, when all are seated again, say that while we thank God for our buildings, all Christians are called to be built together so that the church isn't a dead shell but a living fellowship.

ALL SAINTSTIDE TO ADVENT

The Book of Common Prayer ended the season after Trinity on the Sunday before Advent Sunday, known to many from its Collect as 'stir-up Sunday'. The ASB treated the weeks between All Saints' Day and Christmas rather differently, regarding them as the 'nine Sundays before Christmas, with their own distinctive themes. When *The Promise of His Glory* appeared, followed by the Franciscan Daily Office book, *Celebrating Common Prayer*, the weeks before Advent became a season in their own right, called the 'Kingdom Season'. Common Worship takes a step back from turning them into a separate season, but still sees this period as a distinctive time of preparation for Advent, culminating in the festival of Christ the King on the Sunday before Advent. Unlike All Saints' Day, it is not a Principal Feast, but does have a status equal to the Baptism of Christ, and therefore takes precedence over other celebrations. Common Worship assumes that All Saints' Day will be celebrated on the Sunday between 31 October and 6 November. Readings are provided for the Fourth Sunday before Advent, but if this is kept, All Saints' Day must be celebrated on 1 November. Remembrance Sunday is always observed on the second Sunday in November, for obvious historical reasons, though it clearly has greater significance in some communities than in others. If the specific readings provided for it are not used, or are kept for a special civic liturgy, the readings for the Third Sunday before Advent are suitable for the essential themes of the day to be kept (though please note that very occasionally Remembrance Sunday falls on the Second Sunday before Advent).

ALL SAINTS' DAY

All Saints' Day has seen something of a revival in recent years, with an increasing number of churches observing it each year. There is considerable evidence that satanism and occult practices are growing in popularity, and they certainly receive more media attention, but as well as this many Christians are concerned about the way in which Hallowe'en is now celebrated – it takes up almost as much shop space as many of the Christian festivals. Pumpkins, witches on broomsticks wearing black pointed hats, and black cats belong in fairy tales, but the forces of evil in the world are real enough, and should be both recognised and taken seriously. As Christians we believe that Christ has won the ultimate victory over them, but their continued hold over some people and situations adds to the significance of the Church offering an enjoyable and meaningful alternative.

An All Saints service, as many churches have demonstrated, is an excellent antidote to all this, and also helps to keep children away from the unpleasant practice of 'trick or treat'. It's also a great opportunity for a firework party afterwards, when everyone can let their hair down. Our church even decorated a pumpkin with Christian symbols and placed a candle inside – dullness and dreariness aren't part of the Christian tradition! Another reason for observing All Saints' Day is as an effective counter to our increasingly fragmented, individualistic culture, which affects churches as much as it does society. We need to be reminded that God created us for himself and for one another, to live in community. Rather than focusing our attention on evil, it's far better to celebrate all that's good and right, to give thanks for those who share the Christian journey with us, and to remember those whose journeys are now finished, but who lived the life of faith and brought God's love to the world, and to us.

Common Worship assumes that the Sunday between 31 October and 6 November is to be kept as All Saints' Sunday. If an additional service is planned for 1 November itself, alternative readings are provided to cover all three years.

Hymns

TRADITIONAL

- *Blest are the pure in heart (77)*
- *For all the saints (177/178)*
- *Through the night of doubt and sorrow (687)*
- *Thy hand, O God, has guided (689)*
- *Ye holy angels bright (755)*
- *Ye servants of God (756)*

CONTEMPORARY

- *Bind us together (72)*
- *For I'm building a people of power (181)*
- *From the sun's rising (197)*
- *O, heaven is in my heart (499)*
- *O Lord, all the world belongs to you (509)*
- *We'll walk the land (717)*

CHANT

- *Bless the Lord, my soul (923)*

CHILDREN'S SONG

- *O when the saints go marching in (876)*

Readings

Year A   Revelation 7:9-17; 1 John 3:1-3; Matthew 5:1-12

Year B   Isaiah 25:6-9; Revelation 21:1-6a; John 11:32-44

Year C   Daniel 7:1-3,15-18; Ephesians 1:11-23; Luke 6:20-31

For 1 November:

Years A, B and C   Isaiah 56:3-8
Hebrews 12:18-24
Matthew 5:1-12

Confession

We stand before our heavenly King
to give account of what we have done
and acknowledge our sins and failings,
saying,
Lord forgive us,
and fix our eyes on you.

You call us to be members
of your kingdom of light,
yet often we prefer to walk in darkness.

Lord forgive us,
and fix our eyes on you.

You call us to be citizens of heaven,
yet often we prefer to belong
to this passing world.
Lord forgive us,
and fix our eyes on you.

You call us to the vision of your glory,
yet often we see only the things of this earth.
Lord forgive us,
and fix our eyes on you.
In your mercy forgive our sins
and raise us with Christ to the heavenly places
where you dwell for ever. Amen.

Absolution

The Lord of eternity,
whose forgiveness has no limit,
pardon all *your* sins,
cleanse *you* from every kind of wrong
and set *your* minds on the things above,
for the sake of his Son,
Jesus Christ our Lord. Amen.

Prayer

As citizens of God's eternal kingdom,
we come to him
with our prayers and concerns, saying,
Heavenly King,
hear your people's prayer.

We rejoice with all God's saints
in Christ's victory over sin and death;
and pray for those whose lives
are overshadowed
by the consequences of evil . . .
May our lives reflect what is good and right,
and display the joy of our eternal home.
Heavenly King,
hear your people's prayer.

We remember with gratitude
those whose lives and words
awakened our faith and led us to Christ;
and pray for all Christian ministers
and leaders . . .

May we so live and speak
that other people are drawn to your love.
Heavenly King,
hear your people's prayer.

We rejoice that in the face of ill-treatment
and death
your saints have remained steadfast
in faith and witness;
and pray for Christians throughout the world
whose open faith puts them at risk
of persecution . . .
May we be given strength
to follow their example
and courage to declare your truth.
Heavenly King,
hear your people's prayer.

We remember all who have served you
faithfully,
both those whose names are familiar
and those known only to you;
and pray for those who feel discouraged
or despondent in their walk with you . . .
May we serve you without wavering,
for no other reward than hearing you say,
'Well done, good and faithful servant'.
Heavenly King,
hear your people's prayer,
and go with us through our earthly pilgrimage
until we reach at last the joy
of your eternal kingdom,
through your Son, Jesus Christ our Lord.
Amen.

All-age address

All Saints' Day has several interlinking themes
– heaven; those who've become known for
their service to God; encouragement on our
earthly pilgrimage. The common theme is that
our life is a journey towards heaven, our ultimate home, although for all of us there'll be
plenty of obstacles, diversions and detours to
negotiate before we reach our destination. This
address requires some setting up in advance,
though it doesn't have to be complicated –
indeed, it might work better if it isn't! The
concept behind it is to ask two volunteers to
walk blindfold around the church – one without any assistance, one with – and get past a

number of 'obstacles' you've left in their path. (You may prefer to brief someone to put these out just before they're needed, so that no one else falls over them!) The simplest method is to use a few loose chairs with a large label attached to each, strategically placed around the building. If this is very large, the circuit will need to be constructed within a smaller area visible to everyone. Three volunteers are needed, two of whom will be blindfolded. Any number of 'obstacles' can be created, but the following six cover most problems, and won't take too long to overcome.

1) The first barrier is *distraction*. When this has been reached, explain that it's all too easy to be lured away from the journey by something which looks attractive but will take us away from our destination. If we're heading for a particular place by five o'clock, suddenly turning off at four o'clock to do something else will at best delay us, and at worst get us hopelessly lost. This shouldn't be taken as an injunction to avoid enjoyment and pleasure, but as an encouragement not to lose sight of where we're aiming for. The world is full of distractions which take our attention away from God – they may not be wrong in themselves but if they become too important our spiritual journey will be interrupted.

2) The second obstacle is *pressures of life*. Being too busy also hinders our faith journey. Sometimes it's hard to avoid, especially at work or when exams are looming, and in the rush we forget about God, and where we're meant to be going.

3) The third hurdle to clear is *discouragement*. On a long journey the end can seem far away, and one of the temptations on the Christian pilgrimage is to give up. Many things in life can discourage us – such as failure, personal setbacks and financial worries. No one's suggesting they're a good thing or easy to overcome, but the journey doesn't end when we encounter them. God will see us safely past them if we trust him.

4) The fourth obstruction is *crises*. Sometimes things go seriously wrong, perhaps because of what we've done, but more often due to external factors we can't control, such as illness, bereavement, redundancy or breakdown of a relationship. These are often extremely painful, but they still don't signal the end of our journey of faith. We have to keep going, strengthened by God, until the crisis is past and the pilgrimage easier as we move on towards our final goal.

5) The fifth stumbling-block is *opposition*. This is slightly different in that someone or something else is deliberately trying to take us off the journey. The attempt may be direct or it may be very subtle, but we need to recognise it when we come across it, and not be put off. Not many of us like conflict, but while we shouldn't seek it, we have to accept its inevitability in the Christian life.

6) The final obstacle is *doubt*. Unlike the other five, this is something within ourselves, even if it's fuelled by an outside agency. All of us have periods of doubt – on a journey, especially in the dark or in foggy conditions, we might suddenly think, 'Am I really going the right way?' Christians also have times of doubt and uncertainty, but stopping, giving up or trying another route isn't going to help much. God calls us to trust him, even when we're not sure about the next step, and he's promised to bring us safely to our destination in heaven if we trust him.

One volunteer having made it past the obstacles, the other can now do it with a 'sighted' assistant. As they do so, point out that doing it alone was much more difficult. God doesn't want us to make our journey of faith alone, but alongside others who share it. Together we encourage one another and help each other when the obstacles appear. Above all we're with the Lord Jesus, who's made the journey before us and knows all about the barriers we encounter, and with him guiding us we know we'll reach our destination. If time allows, it can be helpful to illustrate some or all of the above points by referring to the lives of the saints and 'great' Christians of the past.

FOURTH SUNDAY BEFORE ADVENT

Sunday between 30 October
and 5 November inclusive

Many churches will use this Sunday to celebrate All Saints, but if you've chosen to keep it on 1 November, the Common Worship lectionary continues on this Sunday with the consecutive Gospel readings, although the four Sundays before Advent don't include an alternative Old Testament lesson. In Year A we come to Matthew's account of the 'Little Apocalypse', Jesus' description of the 'last days'. The Year B reading from Mark is Jesus' answer to the question about the greatest commandment, and in Year C Luke tells of the tax-collector Zaccheus' life-changing encounter with Jesus.

Hymns

TRADITIONAL

- *Alleluia, sing to Jesus (12)*
- *At the name of Jesus (54)*
- *Father, Lord of all creation (163)*
- *O Jesus, I have promised (503)*
- *Thy way, not mine, O Lord (692)*
- *O happy day (498)*

CONTEMPORARY

- *Almighty God, we come to make confession (27)*
- *God of all human history (223)*
- *Lord of all life and power (414)*
- *Love is the only law (430)*
- *The Spirit lives to set us free (666)*
- *Who sees it all (749)*

CHANT

- *Confitemini Domine (925)*

CHILDREN'S SONG

- *Zaccheus was a very little man (919)*

Readings

Year A   Micah 3:5-12; 1 Thessalonians 2:9-13; Matthew 24:1-14

Year B   Deuteronomy 6:1-9; Hebrews 9:11-14; Mark 12:28-34

Year C   Isaiah 1:10-18; 2 Thessalonians 1:1-12; Luke 19:1-10

Confession

Lord Jesus, risen Master,
we come before you burdened with guilt,
weighed down by our sins.
We are ashamed of our wrongdoing,
and long to be set free.
Forgive us all that is past,
and in your mercy take away our heavy load.
Restore and renew our lives, we pray,
and release us from the oppression of sin
into the joy of your salvation,
for your name's sake. Amen.

Absolution

Almighty God, who forgives all
who confess their sins in penitence and faith,
have mercy on *you*,
cleanse *you* from every kind of wrong,
make *you* faithful in following him,
and keep *you* in eternal life,
through his Son, our Saviour Jesus Christ.
Amen.

Prayer

The presence of the risen Jesus
transforms every person and situation.
Confident of his power and love,
we bring him our requests and concerns,
saying: Gracious Lord,
in your mercy hear us.

Risen Lord, transform your Church
by your Spirit.
Take away barriers of suspicion and fear,
fill our hearts with your joy and praise,
and unite us in serving you joyfully.
Bless our ministry of mission and evangelism . . .
Gracious Lord,
in your mercy hear us.

Risen Lord, transform this world by your power.
Give wisdom and courage to world leaders,
encouragement to the downtrodden
and afflicted,

tranquillity to lives wrecked by hostility
and conflict.
Bless all who provide aid and work for peace . . .
Gracious Lord,
in your mercy hear us.

Risen Lord, transform by your love
the lives of those overwhelmed by pain or fear.
Give healing to the sick in body and mind,
comfort and peace to the dying,
and new hope to the weary.
Bless any we know who are suffering . . .
Gracious Lord,
in your mercy hear us.

Risen Lord, transform us by your grace
so that we become more like you.
Touch us with your presence,
restore us by your mercy,
and equip us to serve you faithfully
in whatever task you call us to.
Gracious Lord,
in your mercy hear us,
and answer our prayers
for the sake of your Son,
Jesus Christ our Lord. Amen.

All-age address 1

There have always been wild theories about
the end of the world, especially at the turn of
a century or millennium. Jesus' words, as
recorded by the evangelists, have been applied
to all kinds of world events with absolute
certainty, even by Christians, in the firm belief
that his return in glory is imminent. We can
hardly blame the disciples for their question,
but nowhere does the Bible encourage us to
indulge in eschatological crystal-ball-gazing –
'even the Son of Man does not know the day
or hour'. At the same time, however, Jesus
wanted his followers to be real about the way
things would go, to teach them how to recognise
the 'signs of the times', and to be encouraged
in their discipleship. This outline aims to avoid
speculation and concentrate attention instead
on signs. Four large-scale drawings (or OHP
slides) of road signs are needed, to be displayed
at the appropriate time.

1) The first sign is the one for a slippery road.
   Begin by asking the drivers present if any

of them have ever skidded their car.
Sometimes a road surface can deceive us by
looking secure, or a bend can be sharper
than we think. We need the sign to warn us
that our eyes might be fooled. Jesus told
his disciples that many people would be
deceived by impostors, who would claim to
be him and lead them astray. It's easy to be
taken in by clever talkers, and Christians
need to make sure that what they hear
measures up to the teaching of Jesus.

2) The second sign is for low-flying aircraft.
Point out that the sign isn't to warn of a real
danger – it's unlikely that a plane will land
on the roadway by mistake. But a driver
could be alarmed by the sudden noise of an
aircraft, and possibly cause an accident as a
result. There are plenty of things to alarm
us in the world, such as wars, natural
disasters and poverty. However, they aren't
in themselves signs that the end is about
to happen.

3) The third sign is for roadworks – and for
most drivers that means a frustrating
experience! There's hard work involved in
the Christian life, too, and we can be
tempted to give up, especially when we
encounter difficulties or opposition. Jesus
knew his followers would face plenty of
both, which is why he encouraged them to
'stand firm to the end'.

4) The final sign says 'End', a welcome sight
after miles of cones and contraflow! Jesus
promises that our journey of faith will end
in the joy of heaven, and, before that, all the
peoples of the world will hear the good
news of the kingdom. The journey won't
always be easy, but we know that Jesus will
travel alongside, guiding and protecting us.

All-age address 2

Getting priorities in the right order is a task
everyone can identify with! Jesus' questioner
on this occasion was clearly trying to set a
trap, but he highlights a problem which can be
on one level simply practical or on another
seriously ethical. It may be nothing more

complex than choosing which of two events to attend; it may also involve choosing between two people in a way which is bound to hurt one of them; at worst, for Christians, there may be an impossible moral choice between two courses of action, neither of which would be desirable. Context and conscience will both play their part in deciding how to handle these problems, but this outline aims simply to provide an indication of how we might go about establishing our priorities as Christians. Four large sheets of paper with three 'multiple choice' answers need to be prepared in advance.

1) Ask the younger children which should have the priority: (a) watching a TV programme; (b) playing in the garden; (c) tidying the bedroom. None of these have a moral element, but if parents have asked for tidying up to be done, obeying their request takes priority over other things. This is a simple way to obey Jesus' law of love.

2) Now ask the teenagers for their priority from a choice of: (a) revising for GCSEs; (b) helping parents mow the lawn; (c) keeping a friend company by watching a video with them. This is tougher! All of these are constructive, even if revision is most important in the longer term. Helping around the house is also important, as is being a good friend, and the decision in this case will depend on the immediate context. Jesus' law of love needs to be applied thoughtfully – revision shouldn't be used as an excuse for laziness or unhelpfulness, nor should being a good friend become an excuse for not working or helping.

3) Ask the young parents next which of the following they would regard as top priority: (a) working hard to earn enough money for a nice house or car; (b) spending quality time with the children; (c) enjoying an active social life. Again this is hard, as all three are good in themselves. Work is part of God's created order, as are families and friends. But if work dominates too much, families and friends suffer, while too much socialising affects family life and performance at work. We have to demonstrate the love of Jesus in all those areas.

4) Finally, ask the older members of the congregation for their number one choice out of: (a) making sure they have an adequate pension; (b) providing for their children and grandchildren; (c) making the most of the later years of life while still fit to do so. Again, these are all good in themselves – the question is which should take priority and when. Sensible financial provision, care for the family, and living life to the full all have their place, but not if one excludes the others. Jesus' law of love indicates that we should live in such a way that as many people benefit as possible.

Conclude by saying that the first priority for all Christians is God himself. That doesn't necessarily mean attending lots of meetings at church, but it does mean that God and his kingdom will be at the forefront of the way we use our money and time, and organise our lives.

All-age address 3

Zacchaeus is one of the most memorable characters in the New Testament. Not that we know a great deal about him, but few people demonstrate more effectively the transforming power of Christ. As a tax collector for a hated occupying power he was hardly going to be at the top of many people's party invitation list, but, to make it worse, he used his powers to line his own pocket at the expense of his fellow-countrymen. Most people would have viewed him as 'beyond the pale'. We've no idea what drew Zacchaeus to Jesus, or why he wanted to see him without being seen himself, but the turn of events must have given him a severe shock! Others were less impressed by Jesus giving his time to such a dubious character, but, even in disapproving of his choice of company, they couldn't deny the subsequent change. A few years ago a very popular toy was the Transformer, a seemingly innocuous car which, with a few strategic twists, could be turned into a fearsome robot – barely recognisable as the same lump of plastic! Zacchaeus was still recognisably the same person after Jesus called him out of his tree; he hadn't undergone a personality refit but no one could believe that this fraudulent, exploitative, scheming little man was now so different.

1) Jesus transformed his *sadness*. A box of tissues is a good visual aid here, though it's unlikely that Zacchaeus would ever have been so overtly emotional. Deep down he was miserable and afraid. His wealth had left him with few friends and many enemies – the tree was a useful hiding place as well as a vantage point. But when Jesus stopped and asked him to climb down, he didn't seem to mind who saw him! Jesus' perfect love 'casts out fear'.

2) Jesus dealt with his *guilt*. Because Zacchaeus faced up to his wrongdoing he was set free from guilt and from the inward damage caused by its fearful, furtive secrecy. A symbol of punishment, such as a cane, would reinforce this point, though it would be wise to point out that past rather than present generations of schoolchildren were afraid of this punishment! Once guilt has been brought out into the open and dealt with, it no longer has any power to create fear or harm.

3) Jesus transformed his *lifestyle*. Filofaxes, laptops, credit cards are all good symbols of the controlling factors in life today. Zacchaeus' life was totally dominated by his money-making, but his riches didn't do anything for the quality of his life. By choosing to follow Jesus, his whole life was transformed because these other factors no longer controlled it.

4) Jesus transformed his *relationships*. Friendless, lonely Zacchaeus no longer had to live in fear of the consequences of his behaviour. By putting matters right with those he'd exploited, he removed the major blockage between himself and other people. Only his encounter with Jesus could have achieved such a change. Zacchaeus was still recognisably the same person, but now his life was positive in direction and had a purpose.

Third Sunday before Advent

Sunday between 6 and 12 November inclusive

In most years Remembrance Sunday falls on the Third Sunday before Advent, and most churches will want to focus on the issues that raises. However, readings are provided in Common Worship for those churches where Remembrance doesn't dominate the main service, although they cover the same broad themes. In Year A we read Jesus' parable of the Ten Bridesmaids, for which an outline address is provided, in Year B Mark's account of the start of Jesus' ministry (for which a suitable outline address is found under the Second Sunday of Epiphany, All-age Address 1), and in Year C Jesus answers the Sadducees, who had come to him with a crass question designed to prove their belief that there was no such thing as resurrection. With only very slight adaptation, the outline address for Lent 5 addresses the theme of eternal life.

Hymns

TRADITIONAL

- *Dear Lord and Father of mankind (144)*
- *I know that my Redeemer lives (311)*
- *Jesus calls us: o'er the tumult (347)*
- *Now is eternal life (470)*
- *O God of Bethel (491)*
- *Wake, O wake! with tidings thrilling (703)*

CONTEMPORARY

- *Give me joy in my heart (201)*
- *God is my great desire (218)*
- *I, the Lord of sea and sky (332)*
- *O God, please listen (495)*
- *When God almighty came to earth (733)*
- *Will you come and follow me (752)*

CHANT

- *Wait for the Lord (949)*

CHILDREN'S SONG

- *Clap your hands, all you people (785)*

Readings

Year A   Wisdom of Solomon 6:12-16 or Amos 5:18-24; 1 Thessalonians 4:13-18; Matthew 25:1-13

Year B   Jonah 3:1-5, 10; Hebrews 9:24-28; Mark 1:14-20

Year C   Job 19:23-27a; 2 Thessalonians 2:1-5, 13-17; Luke 20:27-38

Confession

Lord God,
we confess before you and one another
that we have sinned both in doing wrong
and in failing to do what we know is right.
We have disregarded the cry of the poor
and left the needy without justice or hope;
our worship has been
concerned with appearance
rather than obedience.
Have mercy on us,
forgive our hypocrisy and lack of care,
and fill our hearts with a new commitment
to your kingdom of love,
as we see them in Jesus Christ our Lord. Amen.

Absolution

Almighty God, whose promise
is that all who seek him will live,
have mercy on *you*,
forgive all *your* sins of action and neglect,
and fill *you* with his Spirit of justice and love,
that *you* may serve him faithfully
and worship him joyfully
for the sake of his Son,
our Saviour Jesus Christ. Amen.

Prayer

God of glory, we pray for your justice and peace
to rule the Church, the world and our lives,
as we say:
Glorious Lord, may your kingdom come;
your will be done here on earth.

We pray for the world,
filled with injustice and oppression:
for lives diminished by materialism and greed;

for street children and homeless teenagers;
for casualties of violence or conflict;
for those sidelined by society . . .
Bless all peacemakers and bridge-builders,
and guide those who hold the reins of power
to act justly for the good of all.
Glorious Lord, may your kingdom come;
your will be done here on earth.

We pray for the Church,
and for Christians facing threat and persecution,
corruption and wickedness;
whose faith is tested by opposition,
or who are tempted to follow the easy path
that leads to destruction . . .
Bless your people as they proclaim
the good news of Jesus Christ,
and share your hope with a despairing world.
Glorious Lord, may your kingdom come;
your will be done here on earth.

We pray for those we know
in difficult or stressful situations;
without jobs or livelihood;
without home or friends;
without health or strength;
without hope or joy in life . . .
Bless and heal them,
that they may put their trust in you
and know your peace within.
Glorious Lord, may your kingdom come,
your will be done here on earth,
in us and through us,
to bring glory to Jesus Christ our Lord. Amen.

All-age address

Jesus' parable of the ten bridesmaids is one of his best-known, but the challenge of its message is easily diluted by assumptions about its meaning. Matthew incorporates it into Jesus' teaching about the end of the age and precedes it with a parable about a faithful servant, while the conclusion makes it clear that a major part of being ready is 'keeping watch'. The two groups of bridesmaids are contrasted, but the distinction is between the foolish and the wise, the foolish being excluded from the feast because they'd not prepared themselves adequately, rather than by doing anything wrong – it can't have occurred to them that they might miss out. In this context Jesus is warning his hearers not to be complacent or unaware, because his coming will take everyone by surprise. This outline addresses the need for all Christians to be alert and ready.

1) *We must be ready for God's call.* If you have a member of the congregation who works for the emergency services, ask them to wear their uniform or bring in some equipment. Alternatively, use a large drawing or poster. A doctor or nurse must be ready to handle a medical emergency; a firefighter has to jump to action as soon as the call comes. They don't know when they might receive a call, so if they're not alert and fully prepared they can't do their job properly. Christians must be ready to obey God's call whenever it comes.

2) *We must be ready for work.* Any willing employee – a mechanic, a sales representative or a secretary, for example – could help with this by explaining their role and duties, ideally with a demonstration. To perform any task well we need the correct gear, set up to use. The bridesmaids all had the same duties, but five hadn't bargained on a long delay. They'd failed to think ahead so they had no light, and had to go off to buy more oil. Meanwhile, the bridegroom arrived, and the bridesmaids returned too late to be of any use. Prayer, Bible reading and meditation are all ways to make sure our light is still burning when Jesus returns, but they must also be translated into practical Christian service.

3) *We must be ready for what comes next.* Finish by saying that when Jesus returns in glory it will be a great celebration for those who love and serve him. If we spend all our time thinking about this world we won't be ready for the next one! God wants us to think ahead like the five wise bridesmaids, and recognise that this life is only the waiting period until the celebration starts. We don't know when that will happen, so it's up to us to be ready, and not taken by surprise.

REMEMBRANCE SUNDAY

Strictly speaking, Remembrance Sunday doesn't form part of the Christian Year, but it features somewhere in the landscape of the Second Sunday in November for almost every Christian community. It is arguably the most difficult occasion in the year for all-age worship. For the older generation, and for those associated with the armed forces, it is a major event – there are many memories to be awakened, and more than a few prize corns waiting for the unwary to tread on. On the other hand, many of the younger generation feel it is outside their experience and of limited relevance – if pressed, they might argue that it would be better to concentrate our energies on working for future peace than to hark back to past conflicts. The two World Wars are now part of the history syllabus for most children, and few remain alive who had experience of the First World War. However, there have been many conflicts in the intervening years, with major military deployments in Ulster, the Falklands, the Gulf War, the Balkans and Afghanistan, raising issues which many Christians would want to highlight. Strong views may be held about them, but Remembrance Sunday is neither an opportunity to glamorise militarism and conflict, nor a platform from which to deliver a pacifist manifesto. Whatever one's legitimate personal opinions, all-age worship isn't the best arena to air them – those who disagree with you may well also dismiss everything else that's said and done.

Leaving the 'just war' debate for a more amenable occasion, it's best to focus on the root of all conflicts in sinful human nature. We may laugh at children's squabbles, but fail to recognise the childishness of many disputes between adults – and the Church can hardly claim immunity from accusations of engaging in petty conflict. Only the peace of Christ ruling our lives can overcome our natural tendencies, so as well as the primary focus of remembering all who have died as a result of military conflict, Remembrance Sunday is a good time to think about relationships, both interpersonal and international.

Hymns

TRADITIONAL

- *All people that on earth do dwell* (21)
- *Eternal Father, strong to save* (153)
- *Forgive our sins, as we forgive* (180)
- *My soul, there is a country* (464)
- *O God of earth and altar* (492)
- *O God, our help in ages past* (494)

CONTEMPORARY

- *For the healing of the nations* (186)
- *God! As with silent hearts* (210)
- *Lord, unite all nations* (421)
- *Make me a channel of your peace* (437)
- *Peace is flowing like a river* (553)
- *We have a dream* (715)

CHANT

- *Exaudi nos, Domine* (927)

CHILDREN'S SONG

- *I'm black, I'm white, I'm short, I'm tall* (832)

Readings

Year A   Amos 5:18-24; 1 Thessalonians 4:13-18; Matthew 25:1-13

Year B   Jonah 3:1-5, 10; Hebrews 9:24-28; Mark 1:14-20

Year C   Job 19:23-27a; 2 Thessalonians 2:1-5, 13-17; Luke 20:27-38

Confession

We kneel in humility before God our Father,
conscious of our weakness
and confessing our wrongdoing, as we say,
Lord forgive us our sins,
as we forgive others.

We confess that we have wallowed in pride,
instead of mourning our sinfulness.
Lord forgive us our sins,
as we forgive others.

We confess that we have promoted self-interest,
instead of hungering and thirsting for right.
Lord forgive us our sins,
as we forgive others.

We confess that we have harboured resentment,
instead of showing mercy.
Lord forgive us our sins,
as we forgive others.

We confess that we have created dissent,
instead of acting as peacemakers.
Lord forgive us our sins,
as we forgive others.
Make us obedient to you
and worthy to be known as your children,
through our Saviour Jesus Christ. Amen.

Absolution

Almighty God,
who saves completely
those who call on his name,
have mercy on *you*,
forgive all *your* sins and failings
and restore *you* to the joy of his kingdom,
through Jesus Christ our Lord. Amen.

Prayer

We respond to God's invitation
to come into his presence
and bring our prayers and requests, saying,
Lord of Eternity, hear our prayer;
may your peace rule over all.

When we are filled with dismay
at the state of this world;
when hatred and discord have the upper hand;
when nations and peoples
are in conflict and turmoil;
we ask that your peace will overrun this earth,
especially . . .
Lord of Eternity, hear our prayer;
may your peace rule over all.

When we are disturbed by problems
in the community;
when friends urge us to take sides;
when apathy allows wrong to prevail;
we ask that your peace will reside among us,
especially . . .
Lord of Eternity, hear our prayer;
may your peace rule over all.

When we are tempted to live only for this world;
when distractions divert us from your way;
when selfishness blinds us to the needs of others;
we ask that your peace will overrule in our lives,
especially . . .
Lord of Eternity, hear our prayer;
may your peace rule over all.

When we are inclined to promote
our own opinions;
when dissent threatens our fellowship;
when discouragement tempts us to give up;
we ask that your peace
will govern our words and actions,
especially . . .
Lord of Eternity, hear our prayer;
may your peace rule over all.

When we are concerned for those
we know and love;
when friends and loved ones
are unwell or anxious;
when sadness and grief preoccupy our thoughts;
we ask that your peace will comfort
and sustain us, especially . . .
Lord of Eternity, hear our prayer;
may your peace rule over all,
and fill the hearts and minds of all people
until your glory covers the whole world.
Amen.

All-age address

Whatever differences of opinion may exist as
to whether or not warfare can be justified, you're
unlikely to find anyone who will seriously
argue that war or conflict are in themselves
good. Peace, therefore, is an excellent
Remembrance theme, and doesn't undermine
our remembrance of those who've given their
lives to defend their country, or fight against
evil. This address is based on the different
ways in which we use the word 'peace'. It
requires a small amount of preparation, either
by using props or cartoon-style pictures.

1) Sometimes we think of peace simply as an
   absence of noise. You can demonstrate this by
   turning up a portable radio/cassette/CD
   player to full volume, and then reducing it
   again. No one likes their eardrums to be

assaulted for too long, and we all long to escape from excessive noise. We feel better once it's over, and there's a sense of peace and calm again. This is certainly one aspect of God's peace, but there's more to it than acceptable volume levels.

2) Often peace implies an *absence of conflict*. You can stage this by asking two volunteers to conduct a brief mock argument, which they then resolve by shaking hands; or you can play a recording of two people in dispute. (Ensure, however, that any form of physical contact is avoided.) We aren't happy when people are in conflict, physical or verbal, and the world seems a better place when the matter is settled and relationships are restored to normal. This is also an important aspect of God's peace, and his love can overcome all the barriers and arguing points created by people.

3) We also think of peace as an *absence of activity and busyness*. A volunteer lying on a reclining garden chair illustrates this well, and there can't be many people who don't look forward to sitting down and relaxing after a busy day or week. God rested after he'd created the universe, and he wants us to take time out to spend with him, just as Jesus did. Work and activity have their proper place, but they can damage health, relationships and society if not balanced by peace and relaxation. This too is part of God's peace, though not the whole story.

4) The Old Testament word for peace is 'shalom', familiar enough to us from the song, but not necessarily understood. It's not just an absence of something – noise, conflict, busyness – it's a gift from God, *a state of harmony and wholeness*. Jesus died to bring us peace in this sense, so that as we enjoy once again a relationship of love and trust with our heavenly Father, his peace comes into our lives. We know we're loved and forgiven by God, and, whatever may happen around us, nothing can separate us from his love. As a result, our relationships with other people are transformed too, enabling us to be peacemakers, not just by arbitrating in disputes but also by bringing 'shalom' to those around us. If everyone lived in the light of God's peace, the world would be a very different place.

SECOND SUNDAY BEFORE ADVENT

Sunday between 13 and 19 November inclusive

Our journey through each of the Gospels comes to an end next Sunday, on the Festival of Christ the King. For this Sunday, we reach in Year A the famous parable of the Talents, and in Years B and C Jesus' warnings about the future, for which you can use All-age Address outline 1 from the Fourth Sunday before Advent. These readings, along with those for Christ the King, prepare us for the themes of the Advent season, and the start of another Christian Year.

Hymns

TRADITIONAL

- *Be thou my vision (70)*
- *Christ, whose glory fills the skies (105)*
- *Fill thou my life, O Lord my God (171)*
- *Jerusalem the golden (340)*
- *Judge eternal, throned in splendour (372)*
- *The God of Abraham praise (642)*

CONTEMPORARY

- *Heaven shall not wait (272)*
- *Light a candle for thanksgiving (396)*
- *Lord, we thank you for the promise (424)*
- *Shout for joy and sing (596)*
- *Sing to God new songs of worship (603)*
- *You are the King of Glory (762)*

CHANT

- *Within our darkest night (950)*

CHILDREN'S SONG

- *Over the mountains and the sea (875)*

Readings

Year A   Zephaniah 1:7, 12-18;
1 Thessalonians 5:1-11;
Matthew 25:14-30

Year B   Daniel 12:1-3; Hebrews 10:11-14
(15-18), 19-25; Mark 13:1-8

Year C   Malachi 4:1-2a; 2 Thessalonians 3:6-13;
Luke 21:5-19

Confession

We confess to the Lord
the sin that so easily entangles us, saying,
In your great mercy,
Lord, forgive us.

Lord Jesus,
we repent of our faithlessness and doubt,
and ask you to help our unbelief.
In your great mercy,
Lord, forgive us.

Lord Jesus,
we repent of our self-will and pride,
and ask you to deal with our arrogance.
In your great mercy,
Lord, forgive us.

Lord Jesus, we repent of our stubbornness
and refusal to change,
and ask you to heal our insecurity.
In your great mercy,
Lord, forgive us.

Lord Jesus, we repent of all that hinders us
from following you in faith.
In your great mercy,
**Lord, forgive us,
and make us loyal and trustworthy servants
of your kingdom,
through Jesus Christ our Lord. Amen.**

Absolution

Almighty God, who is just and forgiving,
have mercy on *you*,
forgive the wrong *you* have done
and the good *you* have failed to do,
and give *you* strength to serve him
faithfully and boldly
until you see him face to face,
through our Lord and Saviour Jesus Christ.
Amen.

Prayer

We stand in the presence of Christ our Master,
bringing our requests and concerns,
and seeking his help in serving him faithfully.
Lord, receive our prayers,
and increase our faith.

We ask for your help
in being responsible members of your Church.
Give us joy in serving your purposes;
faith to trust your leading;
boldness to take your good news
to those who have not heard it;
courage to persevere
in the face of apathy and discouragement.
Lord, receive our prayers,
and increase our faith.

We ask for your help
in being responsible citizens
of the world and our local community.
Give us strength to uphold your kingdom;
wisdom to act for the good of all people;
confidence to challenge evil and dishonesty.
Lord, receive our prayers,
and increase our faith.

We ask for your help
in showing compassion and care to the needy.
We pray in particular for . . .
Give healing to the sick in body or mind;
peace to the troubled and anxious;
hope to the depressed and despairing.
Lord, receive our prayers,
and increase our faith.

We ask for help to serve you faithfully.
Fill us with your Spirit,
that we may be equipped with your gifts
and protected by the armour of faith.
Lord, receive our prayers,
and increase our faith,
until the day when we hear you say,
'Well done',
and enjoy for ever the presence
of our Saviour, Jesus Christ. Amen.

All-age address

Jesus' parable of the talents may seem like a gift to the British mentality of 'trying one's best', but unfortunately that's not what Jesus was referring to. Nor was he talking about our natural gifts and abilities, though these can, of course, be used for his kingdom. The talent was originally a weight, but over time it had come to mean a year's wages, and Jesus' hearers would certainly have understood him to be implying that the servants had been given considerable responsibility. However, what counts in this parable isn't the amount given to each but what they'd done with it. The religious leaders were again the target because they'd failed to fulfil their responsibilities as guardians of the law. They'd preserved it unchanged, and unspoiled by ordinary people, but, in so doing, had turned Israel from being a faith community into a quagmire of religious and legal red tape. They couldn't handle a relationship with God over which they had no control, so they refused to countenance any changes to the *status quo*. They'd misunderstood totally what God was like and, like the third servant, tried to use this as an excuse. Today's Church would do well to look to itself before condemning that servant! This outline aims to highlight some unhelpful views of God, and then to illustrate how faith demands that we take risks. Preparation involves a trip to the dressing-up box, or some simple drawing.

1) Find a police helmet and truncheon, and dress a volunteer in them (alternatively, show an OHP slide of a very stern-looking police officer). Ask the congregation what comes to mind. Likely answers include getting into trouble, being arrested, or being handcuffed. Point out that many people (including some Christians) see God in the same way, a stern figure who watches our every move, noting down each misdemeanour to use in evidence against us, always on the lookout for faults to incriminate us with.

2) Next find a wig and red cloak, and maybe a gavel, so that someone can be dressed up as a judge (or show a picture of an angry judge wagging his finger). If you ask how people view a judge, you're likely to get answers like being sent to prison, being told off, being condemned. Again, explain that many people see God as an angry judge who can't wait to prove that we've done wrong and punish us. God is certainly our judge, but he longs to set us free rather than imprison, and to forgive instead of condemn.

3) The third dressing-up costume is for Santa Claus (a picture would be a simple alternative). This time the general opinion will be that he's benevolent and kind, turns a blind eye to our faults, and hands out presents to everyone. This is the opposite view of God, seeing him as a kindly uncle figure who makes no demands and showers us with gifts.

4) For the second part of the address you'll need a packet of small seeds and a sample of the plant they will grow into. A small pot of compost is also needed. Take a handful of seed and ask someone to identify it (seed can appear to be dust). The only way to prove whether or not you're telling the truth is to plant them and see what happens. When they've been placed in the pot, leave them for a few seconds, then look again and complain that they're not growing. Eventually the seeds will grow into beautiful plants, but patience and time are needed before this happens. God gives us the seeds of faith, but it's our responsibility to nurture them. If we don't open the packet it will still look intact and beautiful on the outside, but there's no chance of any plants growing. For that to happen we have to open the packet, sow the seeds in suitable soil, and let them grow. It involves a certain amount of risk, but the end result makes it worthwhile. Likewise, if we don't use our faith, take a few risks for God, and give it a chance to grow, our lives will never bear fruit for God's kingdom. If we offer God our faith, however small it may seem, and move forwards trusting his guidance, it will grow like the seed, into something infinitely greater.

CHRIST THE KING

Although some festivals have been given a higher status in Common Worship than they enjoyed previously, the only new one is Christ the King, which always falls on the Sunday before Advent (between 20 and 26 November). After a very long stretch of Ordinary Time, broken only by the autumn festivals of Harvest, All Saints and Remembrance Sunday, the readings for this Sunday not only conclude the consecutive reading of the Gospels; they also lead us directly into the central themes of Advent, in particular that of Christ's kingship. Year A's Gospel from Matthew 25 draws our attention to Jesus the King passing judgement; in Year B we see Jesus himself on trial in John 18; and in Year C Luke shows us the paradox of Jesus the King of kings being crucified as a common criminal, yet exercising his kingship on behalf of a penitent thief. All of these provide a welcome redirection of view before the Christmas themes of his incarnation and nativity take over.

Hymns

TRADITIONAL

- *Crown him with many crowns (137)*
- *O worship the King (551)*
- *Praise, my soul, the King of heaven (565)*
- *Praise to the Lord, the almighty (573)*
- *Rejoice, the Lord is king (580)*
- *The Lord is King! (650)*

CONTEMPORARY

- *Ascribe greatness to our God (42)*
- *Christ triumphant (104)*
- *God is love, his the care (216)*
- *God is our strength and refuge (219)*
- *Majesty, worship his majesty (436)*
- *Praise the Lord (567)*

CHANT

- *Jesus, remember me (931)*

CHILDREN'S SONG

- *He is the King (818)*

Readings

Year A	Ezekiel 34:11-16, 20-24; Ephesians 1:15-23; Matthew 25:31-46
Year B	Daniel 7:9-10, 13-14; Revelation 1:4b-8; John 18:33-37
Year C	Jeremiah 23:1-6; Colossians 1:11-20; Luke 23:33-43

Confession

We kneel before Jesus our King
in sorrow and repentance
as we confess our sins to him, saying,
In your mercy,
forgive us and help us.

We are sorry for giving in to our own desires,
instead of obeying your will.
In your mercy,
forgive us and help us.

We are sorry for listening to the world around,
instead of responding to your voice.
In your mercy,
forgive us and help us.

We are sorry for idolising material things,
instead of worshipping you.
In your mercy,
forgive us and help us.

We are sorry for putting self on the throne,
instead of bowing before you,
the King of kings.
In your mercy,
forgive us and help us,
for your name's sake. Amen.

Absolution

Almighty God, our eternal Lord and King,
have mercy on *you*,
pardon and deliver *you*
from every kind of wrong,
and restore *you* to new life,
in Jesus Christ our Saviour. Amen.

Prayer

As we praise and worship Jesus our King,
we bring him our requests and concerns,
confident that he will hear and answer us
as he knows best, saying,
Lord of eternity,
hear and answer our prayers.

We pray for your Church,
both throughout the world
and in our own community.
Renew us and all Christian people in your love,
unite us by your Spirit,
strengthen us for your service,
and fill our hearts with your joy and peace.
Especially we ask . . .
Lord of eternity,
hear and answer our prayers.

We pray for this world,
with all its needs and sadness.
Bless and guide all who govern the nations,
making laws and decisions
which affect lives everywhere.
Inform their judgements,
inspire them with your wisdom,
and give them courage to pursue the paths
of justice and peace.
Especially we ask . . .
Lord of eternity,
hear and answer our prayers.

We pray for our families and friends,
and those we know
who are going through times of difficulty
and distress.
May they know your comforting presence
in their sadness,
your healing grace in their illness and pain,
and your guiding hand
in their anxiety and uncertainty.
Especially we ask . . .
Lord of eternity,
hear and answer our prayers.

We remember those who have died in faith
and now dwell with you in glory for ever.
May their example challenge us
and their commitment inspire us
to worship and serve you,
our King and Master,
until we join them in eternal praise

around your throne.
Lord of eternity,
**hear and answer our prayers
for the sake of your Son,
Jesus Christ our Lord. Amen.**

All-age address

If the all-age address for Palm Sunday wasn't used then, the same idea could be used today, with appropriate seasonal adaptations. The following is a slightly different approach to the same idea. It could be illustrated very simply with an OHP or flashcards, but if you find bigger illustrations more effective, you could round up a large legal tome, some regal-looking robes and apparatus (a cope and decorated churchwarden's staff can look impressive) and one or two items related to domestic chores, including a shoe-cleaning kit.

1) Ask a few leading questions about what monarchs actually do. One likely answer is that they make rules and punish those who break them. You could point out that our own monarch is ultimately responsible for our laws as head of state, even if she doesn't make them up herself. Produce the volume of legal technicalities, and read out a convoluted sentence if time permits. Then ask how Jesus was different from the average king. God gave us rules to live by and, of course, there are consequences if we fail to keep them, but unlike any other ruler he came to share our life and kept those rules himself. Because we couldn't keep them he died to take on himself the death which we would have experienced otherwise as the consequence of our wrongdoing. His love eliminates all legal gobbledegook and small print – through his death and resurrection we can have eternal life, starting now!

2) Another kingly trait is the royal lifestyle of wealth and privilege. Dress someone up in the regal gear and then point out how Jesus never dressed or behaved in a way which drew attention to himself or flaunted his status. He was so unlike a king that some people refused to see him as anything more than a provincial carpenter's son.

3) A third characteristic of kings is their status and authority – no one is likely to question our own queen, at least to her face! Jesus certainly spoke with great authority and people listened to him gladly, but instead of asserting himself he acted more like a servant. At this point bring out a broom, a duster or some washing-up liquid, and finally the shoe-cleaning kit. If possible, ask a volunteer to clean a pair of shoes (it's wise to provide some protective clothing), and as they do so describe how Jesus washed his disciples' feet, a similarly grubby task in those days and one usually ascribed to the lowest servant.

Jesus was seen as king supremely on the cross, even though he died as a criminal and seemed to be totally defeated. He died to release us from the power of sin and death, to give us new life and to make us one in him. He now lives for ever with his Father in heaven as King over all things, and invites us to share in his kingdom for ever.

HARVEST FESTIVAL

Harvest Festival has always enjoyed considerable popularity beyond the ranks of regular churchgoers. No doubt its themes have a wider general resonance with most people, not least at the start of the twenty-first century because of now almost universal concerns about exploitation and destruction of our environment, and fears over issues such as food safety and scientific research. Even granted that some of this has been given wide publicity by the media, the wider concerns remain, and Harvest Festival continues to draw into church many folk who otherwise attend worship very rarely. Perhaps part of the appeal is also the possibility of using the occasion for charitable giving, traditionally offerings of fresh home-grown produce to be distributed among the elderly and needy. Good though this is in principle, in practice many churches find that perishable foods start to perish before they have time to sort and distribute them, while most residential homes and day-centres tend to plan their menus well in advance. They prefer tinned or packaged products as these are easier to use over a longer period, and also find that other essential disposable items such as soap, razors and toothpaste are rarely considered as Harvest gifts. Many charities also suggest ways of raising money for their cause at Harvest, and some provide suitable liturgical material. Whether you collect goods for local distribution or money for wider use, therefore, prior planning will be of the essence if administrative hassle is to be avoided. Be aware also that the 'Telethon' approach, effective though it is for large-scale fund-raising, has encouraged the attitude that charitable giving consists simply of making a passive financial contribution, without any personal involvement or engagement with the recipients.

Christian giving is about offering our whole selves to God, who has given us everything. He doesn't just want the fruits of our freezers and larders, but looks much more for the fruits of lives dedicated to his service. Harvest is probably the best opportunity of the year to raise awareness of global and third-world issues, to advocate a Christian lifestyle in our present society, and to encourage Christian giving as a regular part of that. However, this should be motivated not by provoking guilt feelings in everyone but by drawing out gratitude and praise.

Alone among the festivals recognised in Common Worship, Harvest has no fixed date, though there is some expectation that it will be celebrated around the first Sunday in October. The celebration of St Francis of Assisi on 4 October falls conveniently with Harvest, both in timing and overall theme. Common Worship provides readings for each year as well as several alternatives, while there are many hymns on the themes of creation and gratitude to God which fit the occasion perfectly.

Hymns

TRADITIONAL

- *All creatures of our God and King (6)*
- *Come, ye thankful people, come (133)*
- *For the beauty of the earth (184)*
- *Let us, with a gladsome mind (392)*
- *To thee, O Lord, our hearts we raise (696)*
- *We plough the fields and scatter (719)*

CONTEMPORARY

- *Dance and sing (139)*
- *For the fruits of his creation (185)*
- *Fill your hearts with joy and gladness (172)*
- *Jesus is Lord! (352)*
- *Now join we to praise the Creator (471)*
- *O give thanks (488)*

CHANT

- *Lord of creation (934)*

CHILDREN'S SONG

- *Think of a world without any flowers (900)*

Readings

Year A Deuteronomy 8:7-18 or Deuteronomy 28:1-14; 2 Corinthians 9:6-15; Luke 12:16-30 or Luke 17:11-19

Year B Joel 2:21-27; 1 Timothy 2:1-7 or 1 Timothy 6:6-10; Matthew 6:25-33

Year C Deuteronomy 26:1-11; Philippians 4:4-9 or Revelation 14:14-18; John 6:25-35

Confession

We confess our sins
to our heavenly Father, saying,
Merciful God,
forgive our sins.

We confess our ingratitude
for all that you have provided us with,
and ask you to pardon our self-reliance.
Merciful God,
forgive our sins.

We confess our thoughtlessness
in ignoring the plight of the starving
and despairing;
and ask you to forgive our selfish attitudes.
Merciful God,
forgive our sins.

We confess our carelessness
in not treating the world as your creation
or acting as good stewards of your gifts;
and ask you to deliver us
from self-centredness.
Merciful God,
forgive our sins.

We confess our unwillingness
to acknowledge you
as the source and giver of all we have;
and ask you to cleanse us from self-will.
Merciful God,
forgive our sins
and fill our hearts with gratitude to you
and concern for the needs of all people,
through Christ our Lord. Amen.

Absolution

God, our Creator and Redeemer,
have mercy on *you*,
forgive *your* sins and failures,
and strengthen *you* to live for his glory,
through Jesus Christ our Lord. Amen.

Prayer

Thanking our Creator God for all his blessings,
we bring him our prayers and requests, saying,
Father, accept our praise,
and receive these prayers.

For the beauty of hills and mountains,
for the richness of forest and farmland,
and for the bustle of town and city,
we thank you, Lord.
Bless all who work
to provide for our needs and enjoyment,
and those who care for this wonderful world,
especially . . .
Father, accept our praise,
and receive these prayers.

For the peace of the river,
the power of the sea,
and the fish that live in them,
we thank you, Lord.
Bless all who work on them
to harness their power and bring us food,
especially . . .
Father, accept our praise,
and receive these prayers.

For the produce of farms and gardens,
for rain and water to sustain growth,
and for all we eat and drink,
we thank you, Lord.
Bless all who live in situations
of drought and starvation,
for whom living is a struggle to survive,
especially . . .
Father, accept our praise,
and receive these prayers.

For health and strength to work in your world,
to husband its resources
and to enjoy all its blessings,
we thank you, Lord.
Bless all who work in caring
for the sick, elderly, handicapped and dying,
especially . . .
Father, accept our praise,
and receive these prayers.

For strength and reassurance in times of crisis,
for healing and courage in times of suffering,
and for hope in times of despair,
we thank you, Lord.
Bless all who are suffering
through illness, infirmity, anxiety or grief,
especially . . .
Father, accept our praise,
and receive these prayers.

May our lips declare your glory
and our lives show forth your love
as we see them revealed
in Jesus Christ our Lord. Amen.

All-age address

This address is focused on the parallel themes of growth and fruitfulness, to emphasise that God doesn't want a once-a-year offering of garden produce so much as a daily offering of the fruits of lives dedicated to serving him. To illustrate it you'll need two plants in pots, one healthy and vigorous, the other sad-looking and weedy. You'll also need two apples or oranges, one shiny and enticing, the other brown and shrivelled.

1) Growth is the primary way of telling whether something is alive or not. Anything that isn't growing is dead! This is patently true of physical things, but it's equally true in the spiritual realm. God wants us to bear fruit for him in our lives, but we can only do that if we're spiritually alive, and connected with him, the source of all life. Plants start to grow from seeds, but they don't always grow well, or even at all. (You could demonstrate this by throwing a few seeds on the floor and asking if they're likely to germinate.) Many seeds do start to grow into plants, but things can easily go wrong. Bring out the poor-looking plant and ask why it hasn't done too well. Answers will probably include not enough water (or too much), the wrong soil or lighting conditions, or being placed in a draught. Explain that God has put the seeds of spiritual life within all of us, but there are many reasons why they don't grow well or bear fruit for him. Maybe we haven't listened to God's word properly, and have been distracted instead by pressures of work and family life, materialism, the media or other people's opinions. Now produce the thriving plant and explain that it's been cared for and kept in the right conditions. God wants us to grow spiritually like this plant, strong in our faith because it's well rooted in the soil of his love.

2) Plants that are growing well should produce a good crop of fruit or a display of colourful flowers – a crisp, tasty apple or firm, juicy orange will make the point clearly. As we live in God and allow him to live in us, our lives will bear fruit as naturally as a tree does in good conditions. But . . . (bring out the dried-up apple or orange) fruit has to be used; otherwise it soon perishes. The fruit of our lives committed to God will be seen as it's used for the benefit of other people and the world.